AF607907

Bringing the Nation Back In

SUNY series, James N. Rosenau series in Global Politics

David C. Earnest, editor

Bringing the Nation Back In

Cosmopolitanism, Nationalism and the Struggle to Define a New Politics

Edited by

MARK LUCCARELLI,
ROSARIO FORLENZA,
and STEVEN COLATRELLA

Published by State University of New York Press, Albany

Printed in the United States of America

For information, contact State University of New York Press, Albany, NY
www.sunypress.edu

Library of Congress Cataloging-in-Publication Data

Names: Luccarelli, Mark, 1952– editor. | Forlenza, Rosario, 1975– editor. | Colatrella, Steven, 1960– editor.
Title: Bringing the nation back in : cosmopolitanism, nationalism, and the struggle to define a new politics / [edited by] Mark Luccarelli, Rosario Forlenza, and Steven Colatrella.
Description: Albany : State University of New York Press, 2020. | Series: SUNY series, James N. Rosenau series in global politics | Includes bibliographical references and index.
Identifiers: LCCN 2019013090 | ISBN 9781438477732 (hardcover : alk. paper) | ISBN 9781438477749 (ebook)
Subjects: LCSH: Cosmopolitanism. | Nationalism. | State, The—Philosophy. | Political culture—Europe. | Political culture—United States. | World politics—1989–
Classification: LCC JZ1308 .B754 2020 | DDC 306.2094—dc23
LC record available at https://lccn.loc.gov/2019013090

10 9 8 7 6 5 4 3 2 1

Contents

Acknowledgments

We would like to thank the Norwegian Research Council for funding the project, Discourses of the Nation and the National, and extend our appreciation to the University of Oslo, School of the Humanities and the Department of Literature, Area Studies and European Languages (ILOS) for further financial and administrative support. Thank you to Professor Karen Gammelgaard, Chair of ILOS and to Professor Ljiljana Saric, who served as head of the project. Special thanks to David Andrew Burke for his editorial work on the manuscript.

Chapter 1

On the Persistence and Difficulties of Political Community

Existential Roots and Pragmatic Outcomes of National Awareness

Mark Luccarelli

Prologue

After many days' journey, [the explorers] came to towns, and cities, and to commonwealths, that were both happily governed and well peopled. Under the equator, and as far on both sides of it as the sun moves, there lay vast deserts that were parched with the perpetual heat of the sun; the soil was withered, all things looked dismally, and all places were either quite uninhabited, or abounded with wild beasts and serpents, and some few men, that were neither less wild nor less cruel than the beasts themselves. But, as they went farther, a new scene opened, all things grew milder, the air less burning, the soil more verdant, and even the beasts were less wild: and, at last, there were nations, towns, and cities that had not only mutual commerce among themselves, and with their neighbors, but traded both by sea and land to very remote countries. (More 12–13)

Before cultural nationalism rooted political community in the inheritances of a folk group, Thomas More looked for *communitas* as an expression of birth and place. Traveling with companions, Raphael, More's fictitious explorer of New Iberia, finds himself amidst a harsh, hostile, and inhumane environment. Suddenly a stretch of countryside appears before his eyes. Here we have a place of mild climate and verdant landscape, a fertile setting for agriculture and a settled life: the foundation of pastoral and of the proto-nation. The natural setting and the reference to landscape provide an important correspondence to nation—for nation, like landscape, speaks simultaneously to pastoral myth and to the inclination to find meaning within the complications of our local existences.

Pastoral has served as vision, a reflection of urban dwellers' poetic quests for the simplicity of the bucolic countryside, for the imaginative power inherent in places of origin. But pastoral's origin is neither fanciful nor imagined. In anthropological terms, *agro-pastoral* may be described as a social-ecological system; the "idyllic" qualities attributed to it by poets might be seen as an expression of its qualities before the intensive exploitation by humans combined with stress inherent in all natural systems reached a "tipping point," undoing ecological balance and causing a "regime shift" (Scheffer). To call forth pastoral is to find the quality of place in the real and imaginative geographies of peoples.

Similarly, nation, from Latin *natio* for birth and by extension a people, is a quality embedded within real communities. When More speaks of towns and cities he is referring to the requisite infrastructure; when he speaks of nations he refers to the people. The people of New Iberia are like all people: born to a place and engaged in a way of life. Their association takes the form of engagement in agriculture and "mutual [i.e., local] commerce," the necessities of settled life and their particularity reflects common birth, and the potential inherent in the commonality of birth and the commonality of place, magnified over time, forms the basis of political community. In New Iberia that community takes the form of a "commonwealth" that perhaps has implications for all nations in the future, but only insofar as their arrangements are suitable to different climes and also worthy of emulation.

Introduction

This book by European and American scholars based in Europe examines the anthropological and political foundations of nation and expressions of nationalism in our time. Our approach might be termed "radical" in the sense that we seek to consider the most contemporary issues in a broad anthropological perspective, considering as in More's fable, the roots of nation.

We begin with a simple question: Why are people still interested in expressions of nation? We have been particularly concerned to identify the existential and affective rationales for this continued attachment. Thus, we look at nation and nationalism in terms of an array of concepts—*genos*, *ethnos*, citizenship, place, and environment—utilizing disciplines of philosophy, history, political science, anthropology, literary/cultural studies, and environmental studies. We suggest that "cultural" and "political" definitions of nationalism can neither be conflated, nor placed in isolation. Furthermore, while expressions of the national vary considerably from one country to the next, what they share is that nation is central to democracy and to the real question of democracy's survival.

Confronting Assumptions

As crude restatements of nationalism began to appear in Western societies in recent years, journalists were surprised and equally dismayed. Witness this response by a British journalist to the use of strong-arm tactics in the conflict between the Spanish state and the Catalan national independence movement: "We are told constantly that the problems of today are global, that economic crisis, climate change, terrorism and migration can be tackled only by supranational action. Yet here we have, once again, people and politicians turning instead to the nation state as the answer to their problems" (Landale).

Landale is right to express disbelief on behalf of much of the public and particularly the well-educated public. On the one hand, the tendency of peoples to resort to their national identities seems to confirm conservative attitudes regarding the endurance of nationalism and the shallowness of European and global identities. On the other hand, the decision by the Spanish government to resort to force suggests the stupidity of resorting to the old nation-state framework.

Those judgments are a response to and a reflection of the major trends we have seen dominating the media sphere in the last decades as the progress of liberal institutionalism—animated by the global human rights movement, the development of stateless NGOs, economic globalization, and cultural globalization particularly in music and film—has called the older identities around nation and locality into question. Ideologically, postcolonialism has been a major force in raising doubts about the legitimacy of nation-states, particularly in the western hemisphere, and the concept of globality on the macro level and gender and ethnic identities on the micro level have provided alternatives to national citizenship. Taken together, these trends and ideas imply a shift in perception and understanding of the world. For many, this turn has been confirmed historically by the end of history thesis that followed in the wake of the collapsing Communist system (Fukuyama). Western publics have been encouraged to see globalism as the realization of Kant's democratic peace, while nationalism must be seen as regressive and reactionary.

Of course, one could point out that there are many more sophisticated ideas that have developed in the fields of history, political science, and international relations that understand that national institutions and national actors remain important; as, for example, that the national reflects one layer among many that constitute globality as a whole. At the same time, the global turn has been interpreted more radically in fields that have been influenced by postmodernism, such as sociology and geography, and particularly in literary and cultural studies. Popularizers in the 1990s (Friedman; Barber) advanced a strong globalization hypothesis that has had a lasting impact on media perceptions of globalization. What matters is not the academic question of whether globalization should be understood through a weak or strong hypothesis (Held and McGrew), but how it has been perceived by audiences and publics. That is difficult to gage, but we can make certain assumptions based on the association of globalization with job loss and large-scale immigration, two of the more important issues that underlie the rise of the nationalist right in Europe and the United States. At the same time, the apparent inability or unwillingness of many politicians to address these issues has given rise to the idea that globalization is akin to a wrecking ball, a force that cannot be contained and is wholly negative in character. This raises the question: What do people attracted to or tolerant of the new nationalism believe is being wrecked?

Commentators have rushed to find explanations. They have pointed out that a growing number of people in the democratic West have felt left out of the economic and political changes of recent decades, that the critical events that preceded and accompanied the Brexit vote and the election of Donald Trump—particularly the great recession of 2008–2009 and the breakdown of the vaunted US economy—convinced insurgents of the declining fortunes of the democratic Western nations. These events have produced grievances, but more importantly they have helped provoke an aura of loss and decline. Arguably then, material insecurity cannot fully explain the reattachment to nation, much less the manner in which people have resorted to raw expressions of nationalism. Beneath doubt and the fear of falling lies the fear of losing one's identity: there is a growing feeling that globalization projects a future of institutions rather than of peoples, of forces rather than established political traditions, of losses rather than gains. The chief loss is that of nation, which for most people in the Western countries also means the loss of democracy. At the moment, appeals to national identity are an attempt to reassert those earlier political choices in response to the overwhelming media attention given to globalization, international social movements, and cosmopolitan opinion. This is a particularly important message in the American context, given both the importance of social movement politics in the United States since the 1960s and the fact that American national identity has been deeply intertwined with democratic liberalism (Hartz), which in recent decades has actively delimited and perhaps even suppressed both national and civic expressions of the public.

Opponents of the current order seek to make space for the reassertion of the political, without necessarily understanding what this implies. The real point is that politics here is a statement for the recovery of *agency* of the commonweal and the empowerment of the majority in the face of a divided public and the overwhelming presence of the technosphere that operates to "disembed" the assumptions of modernity by "a lifting out of social relations from local contexts of interaction," a process that results in the destabilization of the "political, social and cultural unity of modern society" (Marden 6, 9). Government now reconceived as "governance" replaces the supremacy of the legislative process with experts who serve as "repositories of technical knowledge" that operate through closely associated activist networks (7, 11–12). Nationalism appears to offer to "return" agency to the majority—peoples who are becoming aware once again of the collective and inclusive idea of nation. The manifestations differ, ranging from the powerful, but largely defensive nationalisms of the Anglophone countries (noted in the Brexit campaign and Donald Trump's election), to the assertive independence campaigns for Scotland, Catalonia, and Kurdistan—positive nationalisms that express the desire of buried nations to assert their existence and their right to self-determination. For the moment, the world stage is divided between the expression of nationalism (left or right) and proclamations of global cosmopolitanism and progress to a world society. There is also the division between the passions of the populace and the cool deliberations of academics. The task of this volume is to look behind these divisions and dilemmas.

The "Trinity" and the Imbroglio of the Nation-State

The most important foundational justification for international institutionalism and global awareness rests with the standard interpretation of twentieth century history. There can be little doubt about the character of the historical record: two world wars, systematic genocide, and the development of weapons of mass destruction. Considering the fact that the long nineteenth century that preceded the world wars was characterized by nation-building and nationalism, it might seem reasonable to blame nation-states for unleashing a plague of chauvinistic attitudes and policies onto the world. The solution, accordingly, lies with cultivating a transnational governance by institutions and civil society at various levels, as well as encouraging economic interdependence that would make war unlikely in the future. In the first version, as advanced by Woodrow Wilson at Versailles, the integrity of nation-states would be a foundation of the new world order, but after World War II, with the rise of Soviet and American global reach, nation-states became less important. By the time the Cold War ended, nation-states seemed to have become outmoded obstacles to global integration and world peace.

Recently, one scholar has directly challenged this view, arguing that the greatest threat to peace is not nation-states, but real and aspiring empires. Indeed, liberal institutions that form the basis of globalism as an idea actually rest, he tells us, on "national cohesion . . . the bedrock on which a functioning democracy is built." By contrast, confused and competing national identities bred authoritarianism: "no multinational empire has ever been ruled as a democracy. Lacking mutual loyalty, its respective nationalities see one another only as a threat. That was the case in multinational states such as the Soviet Union, Yugoslavia, Syria and Iraq" (Hazony).

Although states perform important and irreplaceable tasks of governance, the conceptualization of the state given prominence in Westphalia Treaty (1648) embodied in the concepts of territorial supremacy and political sovereignty, combined with the nation understood as the essence of a people, created in the nation-state something of a super-organic life force:

> Naked life (the human being), which in antiquity belonged to God and in the classical world was clearly distinct (as *zoe*) from

> political life (*bios*), comes to the fore-front in the management of the state and becomes, so to speak, its earthly foundation. Nation-state means a state that makes nativity or birth [natio] (that is, naked human life) the foundation of its own sovereignty. (Agamben 93)

Agamben points to two problems that follow from this conceptualization. In the first, the unification of the birth of the people (natio) and the rise of the state, is a form of appropriation (i.e., the appropriation of the powers of human biology by the state). The subsidiary problem is the decline of political life, what Arendt calls the *polis*—not the sovereign state, nor the bureaucratic state, but the *ongoing* participatory political life of cities, regions, nations. In its most articulated and dangerous form, the nation-state has cannibalized these political and anthropological processes by literally absorbing the biological lives of the people into its own essence. But by disconnecting human nativity (natio) and other localizing processes from the historical development of the nation-state, Agamben opens a path to the possible reconstruction of the national as a basis for a new politics. Thus, a sharp distinction between national identity and nationalism is fundamental to his thought, somewhat parallel to the distinction between patriotism and nationalism.

Other reactions to nationalism have been more reductive. The most important line of development, which we might term "neo-functionalist Marxism," found its origin in the work of Anthony Giddens's characterization of the nation-state as an engine of modernization. Beneath political rationales and cultural markers of the nation, Giddens found a simple functionalism: national territorial expansion made possible a national market; a national market required and promoted the standardization of culture and both were necessary to modernization and pursuit of economic power of the few. Social forms are an outcome of the quest for modernization within the limits of the technological and political powers that can be mustered against the forces of inertia and reaction. The price that is paid for success is the sacrifice of the old values of an organic order. Functionalism then stands at the origin of the strong globalization hypothesis as well, taking modernization as the determining factor—and again, social values such as loyalty and place become mere obstacles to its achievement (see discussions in Beck; Held; Giddens; Hardt and Negri; Rosenau).

In postmodern theories of nationalism, Giddens's emphasis on modernization and nationalization as the twin processes of capital accumulation, underscores what Anderson identifies as the social project of the rising owner class. Birth (natio) does not belong to people, but rather to the projection of an "imagined community" that served to confound and manipulate captive populations. Accordingly, nations do not really exist prior to their "invention"; nationalism arises by an act of usurpation—absorbing the mythmaking powers once held by the church and royalty (22–23). Consequently, the seizure of power/knowledge takes the form of narratives that "allow the society in which they are told, on the one hand, to define its criteria of competence and, on the other, to evaluate according to those criteria what is performed or can be performed within it" (Lyotard 20). Thus, the so-called national narratives constructed the world through their own categories; their progenitors in the social sciences adapted a methodological nationalism (Beck) that became self-perpetuating and self-justifying, in this view. It remained for scholars in cultural studies to find the hidden rationale for national narratives by harnessing linguistic deconstruction to postcolonial perception. The nation rests on its exclusionary borders, while border crossings contest exclusion and must be valorized (Wiegman and Pease). The bottom line is this: rather than contesting the meaning of nation, postcolonialism has wished to transcend it and to reveal the underside of locality and place as the driver of the modern nation-state. Consequently, we are encouraged to see nations as monsters of rationalization, the building of national identity inherently racist, territory a form of exclusion and its state a means for exclusionary decision-making—propositions that possess some measure of truth, but function to transfer the symbolic powers of biology once possessed by the nation-state to international institutions and global bureaucracies—far removed from the realm of everyday life and the political.

Bringing the Nation Back: A Catalogue of Approaches

Michael Mann criticized the strong globalization hypothesis that the nation-state was disappearing, asserting instead that the power of nation-states was on the rise. An even stronger counterargument was Hirst and Thompson's study *Globalization in Question*, which provided empirical evidence to suggest that "globalization, as conceived by the more extreme globalizers, is largely a myth" (2). These are important works because they inserted realist judgments based on traditional analyses into a highly theoretical field by suggesting that even if a unified global society was emerging, it lacked the political foundations for its completion—a judgment that seems amply confirmed by recent events.

A second critical development also emerged in the 1990s. Michael Billig's 1995 book *Banal Nationalism* is one of the first significant works that sought to reexamine the nation in a cultural context of everyday life—an important contribution to the political anthropology of the nation. Billig redefined the origins of political in everyday life, identifying four major components of national identity formation and retention that seem to him to persist in everyday life: ways of behaving (habits), practices for "talking" about nationhood, means of being "situated" in a homeland, and methods for retaining beliefs about national identity. "Nationhood," he tells us, is empirically verifiable in populations and is experientially real; it is "still being reproduced: it can still call for ultimate sacrifices; and, daily, its symbols and assumptions are flagged" (8–9).

Billig's work was empirically circumscribed, but in proving the existence of national feelings in an age assumed by many scholars to have moved to a new global identity, he provided a great service and pointed the way to the current debate over the origins of nationalism. Modernists such as Hans Kohn, Elie Kodourie, Ernest Gellner, Benedict Anderson, and Eric Hobsbawm, among others, understand national identity as a consequence of alienation produced by modernization. Traditionalists (sometimes called "perennialists") see national identity as ubiquitous and recurrent throughout history (Jensen 11–14). Jensen traces awareness of nationhood to widely perceived perceptions about national character in the Middle Ages and shows its development in the early modern period well before industrialization and the formation of the modern state. She shows that in contrast to ancient notions about character formation as a consequence of physical geography, in the seventeenth century Hume understood the origin of national character in being "subject to the same government" (9). National identity formation was thus both political and existential: the peoples of Europe were evolving new ways of talking about their identities as a result of the growth of trade and changes in political forms.

Understanding populations' interactions with their areal and social environs supports the traditionalist position in regard to national identity. Awareness of commonalities of birth can be seen as an outcome of the human condition. In consequence, a much broader and complex understanding of nation is possible: a definition that bridges the lifeworld and avoids stigmatizing national feelings, but this explanation also leaves us bereft of an explanation for the historical origin and political impact of the nation—and in particular the development of the modern nation-state.

A useful starting point to mediate the traditionalist position on the origin and persistence of national consciousness and the development of the modern state may be found in the work of Anthony Smith. He is a traditionalist in that he understands the importance of premodern identities based on myths and memories, but he is keen to explain the role of nationalism in the context of the rise of the modern nation-state. For example, he argues that aristocratic "ethnies" (ethnic identity groups) were able to encourage, when possible, or impose, when necessary, a deeper and wider national identity on subject peoples ("The Origins" 148).[1] In the task of explaining the rise of the nation-state, Smith is instrumentalist and determinist in his approach: history is used to explain the present—which is not an unimportant task considering the persistence of social and political patterns in the present, but this leaves out the possibility that new sociocultural formations may be in the process of developing. Nation building and the formation of nation-states for Smith can be said to be "organic" (i.e., not manipulated and multidimensional). There is the civic dimension as societies become urban and more complex; there is the process of elite-directed "cultural regulation" backed up by the creation of a "strong and stable administrative apparatus" ("The Origins" 148). But behind these modern developments lies the deep-seated "territorial nation" that itself develops in conjunction with ethnic formation (*Ethnic Origins* 134–40). Smith was undoubtedly driven by a wish to counter modernist and postmodernist theories of nationalism as a whimsical invention for self-interested purposes, an idea based on what one reviewer referred to as the fad of social constructivism (Neuberger). Smith points out that without territorial markers, peoples are merely "populations bounded in political space" (*Ethnic Origins* 2).

In the present context of this book and ongoing political developments, Smith's synthesis may be less interesting than its identification of the components and processes of nationalism. One such component is national sentiment. Azar Gat defines nationalism as "solidarity with one's people and one's state" (32) and finds it throughout history. It was there in the city-state and among different peoples who formed the ethnic cores of empires. In the Middle Ages, it took the form of tribal kingdoms north of the Alps. It is central to the political: all national cores are "rooted in primordial human sentiments of kin-culture, affinity, solidarity and mutual cooperation" (31). Most of humanity inherits a community and arguably all of us are subject to the wish for these larger identifications, but these apparent truisms beg the question of how these formulations can be made relevant to our crowded and fragile world. What processes and creative formulations are emerging?

National Politics in the United States: The Threat of Negation

After Donald Trump's surprising and narrow election victory, the United States was plunged into a crisis of legitimacy even worse than that which followed George W. Bush's contested election victory in 2000. Not only had Mr. Trump run a very divisive electoral campaign, for the first time since the arrival of the global age a candidate openly challenged the assumptions of a post-national, open-border, multicultural conception of society. Under the circumstances, perhaps one should not be surprised that various demonstrations against the Trump presidency ensued, but there is one very personal act of defiance that I would like to consider in some detail.

On July 4, 2017, a young, otherwise anonymous American woman from Philadelphia by the name of Emily Lance posted a video on Facebook depicting herself with an attached artificial device designed to direct her urine stream; in this case she directed it all over an American flag that had been draped over a toilet. She captioned her video: "F*** your nationalism. F*** your country. F*** your stupid f****** flag" ("Emily Lance Threatened after Urinating on the US Flag on 4 July"). Later, in response to the ensuing outrage from various quarters, as well as threats by right-wing extremists, she raged on: "Freedom (of speech/expression) means that I'm entitled to do and say as I please, EVEN if you don't like it—and no your feelings don't count; that's your own problem. . . . What don't you people understand? You're celebrating freedom while damning me for doing the same. You can't have it both ways. FREEDOM OR NONE" ("Women Pees on American flag, Now All of America Is Pissed Off").

At the present in a country bitterly divided over the election, her act might be excused as intemperate but without significant consequence. Alternately, one could very well categorize her performance as an act of sexually inflected civil disobedience that, like Thoreau's refusal to pay the poll tax, asserts the priority of a higher moral law. In the process, their actions might be said to begin what Victor Turner calls a "social drama"—a means of playing out and resolving social conflict (23–59). But unfortunately, unlike indigenous cultures on which Turner based his observations, we lack the capacity to carry social dramas to symbolic resolution. We are much more likely to see public urination on the national symbol in ideological terms and forget its social and personal psychological dimensions.

The ideological misreading of Lance's act is by no means limited to the right. Indeed, it begins with the antagonist herself, in her own assertions.

Her thinking is very much in line with the recent turn from liberalism that once served as a set of principles for national governance, to liberalism as an ideology of national negation. Significantly, while Lance expressed herself in the familiar political language of liberty—Patrick Henry's well-worn dictum comes to mind—the act's referent had little to do with engaging the social or political order, even in a revolutionary sense. Henry wished for political revolution and the creation of a new state. Lance's act refers only to the negation, one could well say; the degradation of America and the assertion of (her)self: an act of narcissism. One is reminded that in his thinking about the "totality" of the social world, Hegel posited his theory that the zeitgeist moves forward through the repudiation of current ideas and assumptions, but that during a period of transition, the dialectic depends on the perpetuation of these oppositions before a new synthesis emerges. In the case of Lance and the American left, the fixation on negation has rendered the alternative, presumably a borderless world of the multitudes (Hardt and Negri), invisible. In the left politics of symbol, negation means we need not ask the question of where the alternatives lie.

Recently, Nancy Fraser has argued that while the fundamental driver of world politics today is neoliberal financialization and globalization, neoliberalism's symbols and temperament derive from the left: "In its U.S. form, progressive neoliberalism is an alliance of mainstream currents of new social movements (feminism, anti-racism, multiculturalism, and LGBTQ rights), on the one side, and high-end 'symbolic' and service-based business sectors (Wall Street, Silicon Valley, and Hollywood), on the other" (Fraser). In effect, Fraser has restated the thesis first lanced by Christopher Lasch in his 1995 book *The Revolt of the Elites and the Betrayal of Democracy*. The question raised by these critiques is systematic to liberalism as the predominant ideological formation in the United States for the past one hundred and fifty years.

When it rose to a position of prominence in the twentieth century, liberalism rested on balancing rights-based discourses with the interest and concerns of the majority. American liberalism is deeply rooted in the Declaration of Independence, the Bill of Rights, and the long-standing practice of open immigration, to mention a few instances. This is problematic in the sense that political integrity and integration is difficult in an ideology, and to some extent a legal Constitutional system, which asserts the absolute right of dissent and self-fulfillment. Consequently, the extent to which an American political community has existed for itself, has depended on liberalism's engagement with a republican ethos of the commonweal—as, for example, in the progressive era of the early twentieth century.[2] American liberalism, as defined in its "classic" era by FDR's New Deal, built on those developments in civic orientation and democratic pragmatism and combined them with state planning and regulation. The result was a number of important political and economic reforms *and* a spirit of national community, which made possible national survival during the Great Depression and World War II.

If Nancy Fraser is correct, progressive neoliberalism (or the "progressive" liberals) has moved us precisely the opposite direction. It has become the symbolic force behind the technostructure; it provides the content by which "cognitive capitalism" broadcasts itself to the entire world. Ironically operating in the name of liberal social theory—of the capacity to self-identify and generate social movements based in subjective self-identification—has meant that contemporary liberalism has lost the necessary dimension of critical realism and has misunderstood the content of globalization. In contrast to the historical precedence of the state assuming the biological powers of the people (as observed by Agamben), we now face the prospect of an authoritarian state identifying a power abstract from and above the people. This is a different authoritarianism from that which the left fears; it is an authoritarianism consonant with the ideology of technological supremacy, a putative universal culture, and the triumph of bureaucracy (*The Myth of the Machine*; *The Bureaucratization of the World*).

Back to the Future

Nation in the broad anthropological sense remains a central component of the political. The resurgence of communities provides the basis for pursuing common interests and developing effective responses to the existential threats we face. The gravest threat experienced by populations across the globe is the one to their sense of collective identity and value in a world that seems to be defined by and for global elites. In effect, we live in an era in which the foundations of the political are threatened. States endure, but the political and cultural linkages to the state are threatened.[3] For a segment of academic opinion, this is not problematic. As globalists, they are projecting a world of universals—human rights, environmentalism, and technological modernization—organized around a gaggle of private but somehow "global" institutions (NGOs) governed by an international financial architecture as theorized and monitored by institutions such as the IMF and backed by a cartel of states operating in the "global interest." Such a political formation lacks a future, partly because it lacks a mechanism for overseeing how fairly benefits are being distributed. That is another matter of pressing importance. In this volume, the question concerns a related but distinct matter: Is the future of global modernization really a return to an authoritarian past? In projecting global governance and cosmopolitan values, are we lining up against the peoples of the world, against the localizations of culture and politics, and against the (potentially) creative processes of historical development? Do we threaten to collapse democratic societies and usher in an age of unrestrained technocracy?

Summary of Chapters

Reassertions of the national are conventionally seen as a revival of hard politics hatched by "irresponsible" "populist" and "nationalist" elements—euphemisms for uneducated, xenophobic people. In this volume we have presented a balanced view that accounts both for the base and higher motivations of people in search of nation. The argument considers historical and practical uses of natio within specific contexts.

The backdrop for the articles in part 1 is the rise of international institutionalism and globalism in various forms and phases. These trends specifically affected academic discourses in the humanities and three of the four chapters in this section pertain to literary and cultural studies. Collectively, the essays point to the persistence of national identity and suggest that disappointments with globalism and cosmopolitanism are not limited to right populism but are expressed in the experience of writers, environmental reformers, theorists of international relations, politics, and civics. Taken together, these chapters are groping toward a new politics of culture that reestablishes the link between people and places. For some, these linkages are observed as limits; for others, they are advocated as key to address political questions. In the latter case, nation may be seen to promote commonalities of identity, engagements with fellowship, and experience of place/landscape.

In chapter 2, Steven Colatrella takes a wide berth, offering both a critique of the liberal international order and a revision of the history of the American left from its current postcolonialist orbit, calling into question assumptions about the relation of social justice on the one hand and internationalism and globalism on the other. Applying—but also critically appraising Hannah Arendt on the crisis of rights theory—Colatrella argues that today's universalist doctrine of human rights is vague, abstract, and unenforceable. In reality, human rights today depend on the efforts of nongovernmental organizations that lack the power to legislate. Having one's own country, by contrast, has the potential of making rights real and enforceable. A country of one's own is measured by participation in the public sphere. For Colatrella, the struggles for social justice by subaltern classes and minority groups has had the effect of widening the public sphere and, in the process, creating the nation.

Chapters 3 and 4 both argue that the preconditions of national identity and statehood in the political and cultural landscape show us the limitations of a politics based on cosmopolitanism and globalism. In chapter 3, Ole Sneltvedt applies Hannah Arendt's concept of the "world of common things" to critically examine the epistemological foundations of "methodological cosmopolitanism," which misses the importance of materiality and of locality in the creation of polity. The physical world of things provides Sneltvedt's foundation for his claims that American polity is materialized in landscape and composed of layers derived from both early republican and national periods.

In chapter 4, Werner Bigell takes aim at global environmentalism for its failure to account for the cultural character of landscape. Tracing eco-globalism to its beginnings in American nature and ecological writing, he argues that its initial concerns and solid footing have been displaced by vague and unrealizable "solidarities" with animals and plants. The evolving field of the environmental humanities is an example of misplaced communitarianism, according to Bigell—we should rather direct our quest to reestablish a commons to the intersection of public space and the cultural landscape, as in noted Finnish and Russian examples and in utopian literature.

The articles in part 2, "Contextualizing the National: Constraints and Possibilities," remind us of the continued threat posed by the attempt to found and sustain polities on the basis of a narrow sense of biological or ethnic origin. If nation is essentially a matter of ethnos to the exclusion of civic ends, we risk repeating errors of the past. Expressed positively, a larger view of politics founded on the concerns of civil society and ongoing cultural concerns—the search for identity and meaning—can be beneficial and is arguably necessary to free societies. At the same time, we learn that the national can be easily submerged in a fragmented social world filled with competing signs and narratives. There are two fundamental questions raised. First, how does the nation (the sense of belonging, of community, of home) survive in a world where its value is so sharply contested? Where is it embedded and how does it persist? Second, from what perspective should we read the interaction between culture, politics, and the state—from a position of hermeneutical suspicion or political engagement?

In chapter 5, Venla Oikkonen examines popular interest in national origin. The article follows conflicting claims around the discovery in 1991 of Ötzi, a fifty-three-hundred-year-old mummy. Interestingly and somehow appropriately, the mummy was found in the Alps right on the rather indistinct border between Italy and Austria. She describes the ensuing scramble to claim the body as "Austrian" or "Italian" and the attempt in the media sphere to lay claim to genetics as a means of verifying national origin. Oikkonen, noting the differences between evolutionary and political time frames, not only shows that national populations are not creations of human evolution and that genetic research is not very useful in verifying national origin stories, but also that there is a widespread willingness on the part of national publics to make *zoe* (biology) the foundation of *bios* (civil society and the state). Thus, as Oikkonen notes, while the contemporary science of genetics has not supported research in the origin of nationalities in Europe, it has served as an occasion for furthering public misunderstanding and simplification of national origin.

In chapter 6, Bruce Barnhart picks up the thread of the critique of biological and ethnic essentialism discussed in Oikkonen's chapter. He argues that biological conceptions of nation may be used to discipline the civil society, such as in the case of US immigration restrictions in the 1920s traced to belief in an Anglo-Saxon ethnic superiority. Applying Hannah Arendt's critique of totalitarianism to a reading of two novels, including *The Great Gatsby*, Barnhart reflects what has become received postmodernist understanding: nations are social constructions of modernity, which carry on the colonial project by constructing migrants and minorities as "others." In this sense, the piece reflects social constructivism and postcolonialism, two of the most important developments in the turn to a hermeneutics of suspicion. At the same time, Barnhart pushes this theory into an interesting direction by linking nationalism to capitalism as an implicit condition of national development manifest in "national time." In Barnhart's account, the authoritarian themes of Fordist American capitalism (i.e., regularity, control, and hyper-development) are consonant with the quest for ethnic uniformity and the suppression of minority voices.

One interesting context for revisiting the national character, even in light of its often disappointing and even oppressive character, is taken up in chapter 7. Here the anthropological need of human beings to find a sense of belonging takes some surprising twists and turns in the life of an exiled Italian writer. Sergio Sabbatini narrates the story of a self-exiled Italian writer, Luigi Di Ruscio (1930–2011), who left Italy in the 1950s to take a production line job in Norway—a country presumably more in line with his socialist inclinations. Sabbatini explains that the writer's subsequent reassertion of his Italian national identity is subject to the complications of the contested meaning of being Italian. We learn that standard (American) tale of the migrant writer struggling to adapt to his new home while remaining true to his origin simply fails to explain the layers of identification and practice with which Di Ruscio struggled. Furthermore, in the European context, bilingualism and binationalism (Italian and Norwegian) takes the form of multiple linguistic/literary commitments on the part of Di Ruscio, including: engagement with formal literary Italian, the fluidity and expressiveness of his regional dialectic, the exercise of everyday Norwegian, as well as the perpetuation of political "language" of international socialism in a capitalist world. Linguistic multiplicity, ideological strife, and familial and social estrangement were the background to his conflicted commitments. But what stands out in the context of this volume is Di Ruscio's ironic repossession of the idealized Italian national literary language—despite his discomfort with its elitism, formalism, and suppressive qualities—as the most important basis for his wish to recover a sense of national belonging.

In chapter 8, Stefano Adamo furthers the recontextualization of the nation by considering its potential for civic re-formation. In Adamo's account, nation is not so much an object of thought or emotion, as a product of social interaction and human memory. He traces the definition and the redefinition of Italian national feeling in the last half a century from a heroic-political stance in the 1970s to apathy and finally to the rise of an emotive pathos at the turn of the century. National awareness requires self-consciousness, which in this case arises through the process of addressing its problems. The circumstances are the persistence of poverty in Italy and the cultural hangover created by the glamour, grandeur, and individualist ethos associated with Hollywood in general and the American Mafia film in particular. In his reading of two Italian Mafia films released in 2000, *Placido Rizzotto* and *One Hundred Steps*, Adamo reveals Italian moviemakers as having undertaken a limited but not insignificant national project: the films are at least partly didactic in character. Furthermore, by shifting the pathos of the typical gangster film from repulsion to compassion (for the victims), the Italian films have engaged in creating symbols for reconstruction of the foundation of an ethical society, contributing to nation as a civic project.

If this book could be read as constructing an opposition between reassertions of nation and skepticism toward that project, the conclusion by Rosario Forlenza addresses that opposition by employing political anthropology. He argues that any political project for recovering the nation must be rooted in reconstruction and recovery. Nation is a form of the familiar and has historically played a positive role in combatting the ever-present threat posed by the growing development of an abstract, cold, legalistic, and ultimately dangerous view of the world.

Notes

1. Smith distinguishes between lateral and vertical strategies for the development of latent national identifies and the formation of states. The two processes are linked. In one case, it is managed through a bureaucratic regulation and in the other, through the articulation of a cultural ideal resting on learning and vision.
2. Alternately with a socialist ethos, but this has been largely absent.
3. Argument from globalization discourse on the rise of global states.

Works Cited

Agamben, Giorgio. "Beyond Human Rights." *International Institute for Nonviolent Action*, novact.org/wp-content/uploads/2012/09/Beyond-Human-Rights-by-Giorgio-Agamben.pdf.

Anderson, Benedict. *Imagined Communities: Reflections on the Rise and Spread of Nationalism*. Verso, 2006.

Bailyn, Bernard. *The Ideological Origins of the American Revolution*. Harvard University Press, 1968.

Barber, Benjamin. *Jihad vs. McWorld: How Globalism and Tribalism Are Reshaping the World*. Crown, 1995.

Baron, Hans. *The Crisis of the Early Italian Renaissance: Civic Humanism and Republican Liberty in an Age of Classicism and Tyranny*. Princeton University Press, 1955.

Beck, Ulrich. "The Cosmopolitan Perspective: Sociology of the Second Age Modernity." *British Journal of Sociology*, vol. 51, no. 1, March 2000, pp. 79–105.

Bellah, Robert. "Civil Religion in America." *Journal of the American Academy of the Arts and Sciences,* vol. 96, no. 1, Winter 1967, pp. 1–21.

Berry, Wendell. *The Unsettling of America*. Sierra Club Books, 1977.

Billig, Michael. *Banal Nationalism*. Sage Publications, 1995.

Buell, Lawrence. *The Environmental Imagination: Thoreau, Nature Writing, and the Formation of American Culture*. Harvard UP, 1996.

Connor, Walker. "The Timelessness of Nations." *Nations and Nationalism*, vol. 10, no. 1, 2004, pp. 35–48.

BBC News. "Emily Lance threatened after urinating on the US flag on 4 July." *BBC.com,* 6 July, 2017, www.bbc.com/news/world-us-canada-40518395.

Fox News. "Women pees on American flag, now all of America is pissed off." *The New York Post*, 5 July, 2017.

Fraser, Nancy. "The End of Progressive Neoliberalism." *Dissent*, 2 January, 2017.

Friedman, Thomas. *The Lexus and the Olive Tree*. Anchor Books, 1999.

Fukuyama, Francis. "The End of History?" *The National Interest*, no. 16, Summer 1989, pp. 3–18.

Gat, Azar, "Premodern Nations, National Identities, National Sentiments, and National Solidarities." *The Roots of Nationalism: National Identity Formation in Early Modern Europe, 1600–1815*, edited by Lotte Jensen, Amsterdam UP, 2016, pp. 3–46.

Giddens, Anthony. *The Consequences of Modernity*. Polity Press, 1990.

Hardt, Michael, and Antonio Negri. *Empire*. Harvard UP, 2000.

Hazony, Yoram. "The Liberty of Nations." *The Wall Street Journal*, 8 September, 2018, www.wsj.com/articles/the-liberty-of-nations-1535120837?mod=e2tw&page=1&pos=1. Accessed 9 September, 2018. Excerpt from *The Virtue of Nationalism*. Basic Books, 2018.

Hartz, Louis. *The Liberal Tradition in America*. Harcourt, Brace & World, 1955.

Heise, Ursala. *Sense of Place and Sense of Planet: The Environmental Imagination of the Global*. Oxford UP, 2008.

Held, David. "Law of States, Law of Peoples." *Legal Theory*, vol. 8, 2002, pp. 1–44.

Held, David, and Andrew McGrew. "The Great Globalization Debate: An Introduction." *The Global Transformations Reader*, edited by David Held and Andrew McGrew, 2nd ed., Polity Press, 2003.

Hirst, Paul, and Grahame Thompson. *Globalization in Question: The International Economy and the Possibilities of Governance*. 2nd ed., Polity Press, 1996.

Jensen, Lotte. Introduction. *The Roots of Nationalism: National Identity Formation in Early Modern Europe, 1600–1815*, edited by Lotte Jensen. Amsterdam UP, 2016, pp. 9–27.

Jacoby, Henry. *The Bureaucratization of the World*. U of California P, 1973.

Kesting, Stefan. "Countervailing, Conditioned and Contingent: The Power Theory of John Kenneth Galbraith." *The Journal of Post Keynesian Economics*, vol. 28, no. 1, Autumn 2005, pp. 3–23.

Landale, James. "EU Looks Away as Catalan Crisis Unfolds." *BBC.com,* www.bbc.com/news/world-europe-41464712. Accessed 2 October, 2017.

Lasch, Christopher. *The Revolt of the Elites and the Betrayal of Democracy*. W. W. Norton, 1995.

Lefebvre, Henri. *The Production of Space*. Translated by Nicholson-Smith, Wiley-Blackwell, 1991.

Lowi, Theodore. "The Public Philosophy: Interest Group Liberalism." *American Political Science Review*, vol. 61, no. 1, March 1967, pp. 5–24.

Luccarelli, Mark. *The End of Urbanism and the Greening of Public Space*. White Horse, 2016.

Lyotard, Jean-Francois. *The Postmodern Condition: A Report on Knowledge*. Translated by G. Bennington and B. Massumi, Manchester UP, 1984.

Mann, Michael. "Has Globalization Ended the Rise and Rise of the Nation-State?" *Review of International Political Economy*, vol. 4, no. 3, "The Direction of Contemporary Capitalism," Autumn, 1997, pp. 472–96.

Marden, Peter. *The Decline of Politics: Governance, Globalization and the Public Sphere*. Ashgate, 2003.

Marx, Leo. *The Machine in the Garden: Technology and the Pastoral Ideal in America*. Oxford UP, 1964.

More, Thomas. *Utopia*. 1516. *History-World.Org*, history-world.org/Utopia_T.pdf.

Mumford, Lewis. *The Culture of Cities*. Harcourt Brace, 1938.

———. *The Myth of the Machine: The Pentagon of Power*. Harcourt Brace, 1970.

Neuberger, Benyamin. Review of *Nationalism: Theory, Ideology, History*, by Anthony D. Smith. *Nations and Nationalism*, vol. 9, no. 3, 2003, pp. 455–56.

Purcell, Edward A. *The Crisis of Democratic Theory: Scientific Naturalism and the Problem of Value*. U of Kentucky P, 2014.

Putnam, R. D. "Bowling Alone: America's Declining Social Capital." *Journal of Democracy*, vol. 6, no. 1, Winter 1995, pp. 65–78.

Rosenau, James N. "Governance in a New Global Order." *Governing Globalization: Power, Authority and Global Governance*, edited by David Held and Anthony McGrew. Polity Press, 2002.

Schlesinger, Arthur M., Jr. *The Age of Jackson*. Little, Brown, 1945.

Scheffer, Marten. *Critical Transitions in Nature and Society*. Princeton UP, 2009.

Smith, Anthony. *The Ethnic Origins of Nations*. Basil Blackwell, 1986.

———. "The Origins of Nations." *Nationalism*, edited by John Hutchinson and Anthony D. Smith, Oxford UP, 1994, pp. 147–54.

Tosh, John. *The Pursuit of History*. 6th ed., Routledge, 2015.

Turner, Victor W. *Dramas, Fields, and Metaphors: Symbolic Action in Human Society*. Cornell UP, 1974.

White, Theodore. *The Making of the President 1960*. Jonathan Cape, 1962.

Wiegman, Robyn and Donald E. Pease. *The Futures of American Studies*. Duke UP, 2002.

Woods, Ngaire. "The European Disunion: How the Continent Lost Its Way." *Foreign Affairs*, vol. 95, no. 1, January/February 2016, www.foreignaffairs.com/reviews/2015-12-14/european-disunion.

Part I

Reassertions of the National

Chapter 2

Solidarity or Human Rights?

National Sovereignty and Citizenship in the Twenty-First Century[1]

Steven Colatrella

Seek Ye First the Political Kingdom.

—Kwame Nkrumah

If slaves will make good soldiers, our whole theory of slavery is wrong.

—Confederate Brigadier General Howell Cobb

It's not wrong to expect justice. It's not wrong to expect freedom. It's not wrong to expect equality. If Patrick Henry and all of the Founding Fathers of this country were willing to lay down their lives to get what you are enjoying today, then it's time for you to realize that a large, ever-increasing number of Black people in this country are willing to die for what we know is due us by birth. The white man is being given a favor, when you give him a chance today to solve a problem that stems from a crime that he committed himself . . . What you need to realize, you from India, you from Iraq, you from Egypt, and you from right here in America, and we who are enslaved—that a crime has been committed against the Negro. Some of you from over there, you knew we were over here and never come over here to help us, and

> now when we stand up and are ready to help ourselves, don't come with your criticism. Help us.
>
> —Malcolm X (Perry 55)

Freedom as Self-Determination

Recently, I rewatched *Braveheart*, the Mel Gibson movie about the medieval Scottish struggle for independence from England led by the commoner William Wallace. Played by Gibson himself, Wallace's last word in the movie before he is beheaded (apparently historically accurate) is "freedom." And indeed, *freedom* is the word used to inspire his followers throughout the movie. What is striking to us today, watching the 1995 movie, is that freedom means independence for Scotland. At no point is freedom described or treated as individual choice, nor even an end to feudal relations of obligation, even when the local Scottish lords are shown betraying the larger cause of winning Scottish independence. "What will you do without freedom?" Gibson's character asks his followers just before a crucial battle. Freedom, it would seem, is not seen here as an individual attribute, nor as a specific status, and not even as a lack of external limits or restraints. It is instead understood as a combination of home and citizenship; of having "a country of our own," mediated through the experiences of landscape and familiarity with the land, community, family, and membership in clans, together with political independence and self-government.

That almost no one talks like this anymore may merely reflect the sense that the anti-colonial project of winning independence for the former colonial world—of Africa, Asia, the Caribbean, and the Middle East—has been completed for some time (though recently Kurds, Catalans, and others have revived such expression). Or this change in expression may be an element of the intellectual hegemony of public choice theory, neoclassical economics, and neoliberalism in a globalized world. Closely allied to the aforementioned intellectual schools of neoliberal doctrine are two other trends: The reduction of democratic thought to procedure, and the retreat from concern with government, including or especially self-government, to the problematics of governance. In this hyper-neoliberal context, I think it is worthwhile to note that *Braveheart* was made before the second Clinton term, merely a year after NAFTA came into effect and before globalization was expressed as an inevitable destiny for all nations and peoples (such as in Clinton's 1996 campaign slogan of "a bridge to the twenty-first century" and Thomas Friedman's 1999 book *The Lexus and the Olive Tree*, to name just two touchstones on the path of "inevitability"). When we realize that the most important normative inroad into national sovereignty as the operative principle of the United Nations came only in 2006 with UN Security Council Resolution 1674 on the Responsibility to Protect, and that more than a decade has passed since that revolutionary innovation in world governance, we reflect that 1996 suddenly seems long ago.

The Responsibility to Protect (R2P in UN-speak) establishes the duty of the world community, as embodied in the UN Security Council, to intervene militarily to protect civilian lives in cases where the national state fails to protect its citizens from, or is itself the perpetrator of genocide, war crimes, ethnic cleansing, or crimes against humanity. The resolution also explicitly condemns other atrocities not yet specifically listed as sufficient cause for military intervention by the international community, including forced displacement, torture, recruitment of child soldiers, sexual violence, human trafficking, and denial of humanitarian aid. In short, the R2P is the most advanced institutionalization of the doctrine of human rights, as distinct from civic membership, citizenship rights, or civil rights. It explicitly devalorizes national sovereignty as a standard or principle of international relations, putting human rights ahead of it as a value. Unfortunately, R2P has become a central pillar of modern day imperialism—that is, of humanitarian military intervention—and this has happened through the undermining of the idea of popular and national self-determination.

I will argue here that the anti-colonial movements of the post–World War II world and analogous movements, such as the struggles of African Americans for full citizenship, extended the tradition of classical republicanism not only geographically, but conceptually through a fuller exploration of international solidarity. Such solidarity, based on self-determination, can present an alternative to the unhappy choice of being exposed to oppression by forces in one's country (by government or by other sources) and to the present-day regime of human rights doctrine backed up by humanitarian interventions, which often results merely in the creation of yet more refugees and more abuses of people.

The idea that freedom means having one's own country was still attractive, at least to movie audiences in 1995; but today, by international law and by intellectual fashion, the attraction to nation has been replaced by individual choice theory and by human rights. The results of this trend are not hard to find. According to the UN High Commission for Refugees, "an unprecedented 65.6 million people were uprooted from their homes by conflict and persecution at the end of 2016" (UNHCR 2017). That's almost 1 percent of the entire world population now living as de jure or de facto refugees. Various estimates of the number of slaves in the world range from twenty-one million ("Slavery-Today") to thirty million ("This Map Shows") to forty-six million ("46 Million People Living as Slaves"). A horrifying record of one thousand annual deaths by desperate people trying to cross the Mediterranean from Africa to Europe was reached already by April 2017 ("Refugee Death Toll Passes 1,000"), with 8,300 saved from drowning by that date, and 37,000 asylum seekers arriving in Italy alone, as part of a refugee/migration crisis that is already years in the making.

Whatever human rights as a doctrine, a practice, and an increasingly institutionalized principle of international law is supposed to accomplish, it is clearly not working. In fact, human rights is most likely making things worse, and contributing to the likelihood of people facing atrocities and being oppressed, despite the many principled and idealistic people—often working tirelessly and thanklessly to provide succor, protection, and hospitality to the enslaved, the trafficked, the uprooted, the oppressed, and the refugee—and despite the otherwise admirable acts of some governments to welcome and protect refugees.

Hannah Arendt and Rights of Home and Citizenship

In the aftermath of World War II, the world faced a mass refugee crisis without precedent, one analogous to today's global crisis. Ethnic minorities in many European countries, millions of Germans, Poles, and others, fled from countries that their families had lived in for generations. Jews left Europe for Palestine and Palestinians, in turn, were uprooted. Millions fleeing in the wake of the independence of India and Pakistan crossed the borders from one to the other new nation, with untold loss of life. In many cases, a dual problem arose. First, the refugees no longer had anywhere to go, except to other territorial states. As Arendt writes:

> What is unprecedented is not the loss of a home but the impossibility of finding a new one. Suddenly, there was no place on earth where migrants could go without the severest restrictions, no country where they would be assimilated, no territory where they could found a new community of their own. This, moreover, had next to nothing to do with any material problems of

> overpopulation: it was a problem not of space but of political organization. Nobody had been aware that mankind, for so long a time considered under the image of a family of nations, had reached the stage where whoever was thrown out of one of these tightly organized closed communities found himself thrown out of the family of nations altogether. (Arendt 294)

The second problem was that they could not be repatriated anywhere, nor return home. Those without any citizenship could not be repatriated to a country they did not have, and many others had no state willing to accept them.

Hannah Arendt faced the situation with a lack of sentimentality, with courage and intellectual honesty of a kind lacking for the most part today, when we face a similar situation of uprooted millions, and when the mechanisms we have developed for protecting people from harm or oppression are failing. In *The Origins of Totalitarianism*, the chapter entitled "The Decline of the Nation-State and the End of the Rights of Man" is an unblinking examination of the crisis for what it was: a failure of the very concept of human rights, and one that is almost certainly inherent in the concept of human rights itself.

To begin with, human rights are in principle independent of territory, jurisdiction, and place. They are universal in that sense, but also in the sense of applying to everyone, even if the definition of who is included in "everyone" has changed under historical circumstances. In this sense, the two possible understandings of citizenship rights are either that they are less inclusive than human rights, being dependent on government, where human rights are inalienable and apply directly to the individual regardless of any group membership, or else that local citizenship rights are merely translations of the universal human rights recognized by all into the local language and conditions. The latter interpretation is analogous to the gold standard era's conception of national money, by which in each currency was merely the local name for gold in that territory and jurisdictional area. But as Arendt argued, the crisis at the end of the World War II demonstrated that all of these conceptions were in error, for the concept of human rights has, at its core, a fundamental flaw:

> The Rights of Man, after all, had been defined as "inalienable" because they were supposed to be independent of all governments; but it turned out that the moment that human beings lacked

> their own government and had to fall back on their minimum rights, no authority was left to protect them and no institution was willing to guarantee them. (Arendt 291–92)

But the issue of enforcement, and lack of enforceability of human rights, only scratches the surface of the problem.

Human rights as a concept suffers from deeper problems, one of which is that in its universality it is abstract, in the Hegelian sense of being an empty container (Taylor 113; Winfield 103–05). Such rights are, in fact, not at all universal precisely because there is no universal consensus in the real world about whether human rights exist, and if so, which ones:

> The Rights of Man, supposedly inalienable, proved to be unenforceable—even in countries whose constitutions were based upon them—whenever people appeared who were no longer citizens of any sovereign state. To this fact, disturbing enough in itself, one must add the confusion created by the many recent attempts to frame a new bill of human rights, which have demonstrated that no one seems able to define with any assurance what these general human rights, as distinguished from the rights of citizens, really are. Although everyone seems to agree that the plight of these people consists in their loss of the Rights of Man, no one seems to know which rights they lost when they lost these human rights. (Arendt 293)

If no concrete distinction between the rights of citizens and human rights can be delineated, then rather than the former being the local name of the latter, the roles are at best reversed. Human rights become the rights of citizens as available and enforceable to some degree, based on international agreements between national political communities made up of citizens. They therefore define a more limited, not a more expansive sphere. At worst, human rights are but a will-o'-the-wisp, never to be found in reality, even if individuals accept them subjectively. Instead, what *has* concretely been denied refugees and oppressed and abused persons in general is first and foremost not a set of rights, but the very freedom that William Wallace—and, for that matter, every anti-colonialist activist—has fought for and for which many have died: namely, their own political communities:

> The calamity of the rightless is not that they are deprived of life, liberty, and the pursuit of happiness, or of equality before

> the law and freedom of opinion—formulas which were designed to solve problems *within* given communities—but that they no longer belonged to any community whatsoever. Their plight is not that they are not equal before the law, but that no law exists for them; not that they are oppressed but that nobody wants even to oppress them. (Arendt 295–96)

The current debate over refugees and other migrants and asylum seekers roiling Europe and the United States needs to be set in this context if we are to move to any longer-term solutions. Succor is not a solution; it is merely succor. And those providing it—doing the saving and provision of aid—do so of their free will, not as part of any obligation owed due to any experience in common, any mutual solidarity or struggle, any commitment made, oath sworn, law to be enforced. And this lack of enforceability, be it moral, normative, legal, or political, makes all the difference:

> But neither physical safety—being fed by some state or private welfare agency—nor freedom of opinion changes in the least their fundamental situation of rightlessness. The prolongation of their lives is due to charity and not to right, for no law exists which could force the nations to feed them; their freedom of movement, if they have it at all, gives them no right to residence which even the jailed criminal enjoys as a matter of course; and their freedom of opinion is a fool's freedom, for nothing they think matters anyhow. (Arendt 296)

Thus, the concept of freedom as having one's own country, an inherently and indisputably collective form of freedom, not an individual conception, is so important, and is so even to individuals as such, and not only to groups. Home without political citizenship is tragic or is nonexistent. Political membership may not be a sufficient cause of a sense of belonging to community or in a geographic territory or place, but it is a necessary one, and all of the "identity" in the world cannot act as a magnetic field strong enough to keep one there if one does not have a passport giving one a right to remain, and/or a political force, governmental or otherwise, powerful enough to protect that right. Such is the condition of refugees. Certainly the goodwill and action of thousands of enlightened and principled people around the world to save, protect, welcome, and aid refugees and migrants and other asylum seekers is heroic and to be honored; yet we must recognize that this action can save lives, but it cannot address—let alone find a solution to—the causes of people being forced to leave their homes or to face a future without citizenship or community membership in a real, political sense. Arendt continues, regarding this very issue:

> The fundamental deprivation of human rights is manifested first and above all in the deprivation of a place in the world which makes opinions significant and actions effective. Something much more fundamental than freedom and justice, which are rights of citizens, is at stake when belonging to the community into which one is born is no longer a matter of course and not belonging no longer a matter of choice. . . . We became aware of the existence of a right to have rights (and that means to live in a framework where one is judged by one's actions and opinions) and a right to belong to some kind of organized community, only when millions of people emerged who had lost and could not regain these rights because of the new global political situation. (Arendt 296–97)

Meaning in this sense is not primarily the result of cultural or ethnic, or even phenomenological factors, nor is it the consequence of a sense of feeling of belonging to a place or landscape, nor ethnic identity, nor cultural or anthropological variables, but rather it is the result of participation in, and the process of being judged by, the public sphere. Even the free movement of persons, which is a right of EU citizens, primarily takes the form of movement from poorer to richer countries to do work that has less status and lower pay than the average in one's new land of residence, with the hierarchy of international power and wealth remaining in place (Wallerstein; Arrighi).

The exceptions are mainly those for whom the removal of national borders really means an opportunity and seem at least to be a form of freedom: namely, the professional-managerial class or strata that is best placed to take advantage of opportunities embedded in the greater class inequality that has proven to be a ubiquitous outcome of processes of globalization everywhere (McDermott 151–59). The skilled worker, the professional, the college graduate from Country A finds again and again that their status is not recognized on an equal basis and does not have the same meaning in Country B. Women college graduates from Romania, Bulgaria, or Albania work cleaning houses in Italy or work as home health care workers because they cannot work as nurses, technicians, air traffic controllers—their chosen professions in their countries of origin. Lawyers from Egypt or Kenya drive taxis in New York. This is not just ethnic or racial discrimination though it may be verbally expressed as such. It is instead a manifestation of the reality that Arendt shows us: what makes a person that person is a series of achieved statuses (and some ascribed statuses) that have meaning only in the country where they were achieved (Tilly 79–95). Action, accomplishments, statuses, social honor (in Weber's sense), class relations, and sense of public shame or scandal, all of these have meaning only in the country in which the actions took place or the statuses were assigned or achieved. Even the very money in people's pockets and wallets and bank accounts does not have the same meaning outside the territory of one's political belonging, as the existence of exchange rates testifies. In short, meaningful action can only happen in a public sphere and membership in a political community is a necessary, if not sufficient condition in some cases, for such action.

Of course, immigrants who are not citizens in a country in a narrow legal sense can certainly engage in meaningful action in their country of residence, as Federico Olivieri notes, calling such activity by immigrants "acts of citizenship" (Olivieri 221). There is no substitute for citizenship, even if only in a moral-normative sense. The condition of being outside, whether as a slave or a refugee, has been important to the struggle of expanding and strengthening citizenship. The role of the African American in the long struggle to create the democratic public sphere in the United States (Wilentz) must be acknowledged. The function of the disenfranchised—from the working class to women and slaves, in the United States, Britain, and elsewhere, has been central to shaping modern democracy ("Nothing Exceptional"; "Collective Housekeeping and the Revenge of the Oikos").

The person who can engage in meaningful action and speech, then, is one with characteristics that are both part of, constitutive of, and the result of the public sphere of a given political community. These characteristics may even be cultural, ethnic, linguistic, traditional, and social in nature but, as we will see below, these elements are at most aspects of the political community, not alternatives to it, and certainly not sufficient conditions for the construction of a sphere of meaningful action and speech, though they may be necessary conditions thereof. The larger point here, however, is that people are not mere "human beings." That is, they are not just human bodies that can have full human meaning, status, and presence in a practical way if bereft of all characteristics that define them as citizens as members of political communities. There are no generic humans. There are no people without characteristics that define them as part of some political community, and even those, like Palestinians, who technically are not part of a recognized political community, are nevertheless primarily defined politically as part of their actual communities. For, any meaningful action or speech by a Palestinian is inevitably defined as part of the political struggle to create a Palestinian political community in a formal, institutional sense, and so, as an act of citizenship in Olivieri's sense. We shall return to such meaningful action before the fact of establishing the political community sought (with full citizenship and with the desired institutions and conditions) in our discussion of Malcolm X and the anti-colonial expansion of classical republican theory and practice. But the point is, there can be no abstract human being, nor can human rights exist on an abstract plane outside of territory, place, community, status, institutions, and citizenship. Again, Arendt weighs in:

> These facts and reflections offer what seems an ironical, bitter, and belated confirmation of the famous arguments with which Edmund Burke opposed the French Revolution's Declaration of the Rights of Man. They appear to buttress his assertion that human rights were an "abstraction," . . . Not only did loss of national rights in all instances entail the loss of human rights; the restoration of human rights, as the recent example of the State of Israel proves, has been achieved so far only through the restoration of the establishment of national rights. The conception of human rights, based upon the assumed existence of a human being as such, broke down at the very moment when those who professed to believe in it were for the first time confronted with people who had indeed lost all other qualities and specific relationships—except that they were still human. The world found nothing sacred in the abstract nakedness of being human. (Arendt 299)

But as her mournful citing of Burke indicates, here Arendt's liberalism prevents her from proceeding any further than the merciless critique of universal abstraction. For an alternative to both Burke and neoliberalism, we must look elsewhere.

The Political Community

In the concluding essay in this volume, Rosario Forlenza reminds us of the importance of home, both materially and conceptually, in human and social life. I do not disagree about the centrality of the experience of home, but based upon Arendt's analysis and warning, I argue that it is home *qua* citizenship that counts—home as membership in a political community, in a place—the community and context in which one's actions are meaningful, in which speech is relevant, be it agreed with or opposed by fellow citizens. Arendt treats home and citizenship as the most important experiences and the basis for any social standing:

> The first loss which the rightless suffered was the loss of their homes, and this meant the loss of the entire social texture into which they were born and in which they established for themselves a distinct place in the world. . . . What is unprecedented is not the loss of a home but the impossibility of finding a new one. Suddenly, there was no place on earth where migrants could go without the severest restrictions, no country where they could be assimilated, no territory where they could found a new community of their own. (Arendt 293)

For Aristotle, famously, a political community is sui generis, consisting of an association whose purpose is to achieve "the good life." A trade alliance, a military alliance, ethnic belonging, common language, extended kinship ties—none of these, nor even a combination of several of these, constitute a political community. Nor can intermarriage among different communities create a polis, nor common laws among people living at a distance. For "the end of the state is not mere life; it is rather a good quality of life" (Aristotle 118–19). It is only in such a context that injustice can be identified, and justice imagined, and hopefully realized (Plato 59), and only in such a political community can speech have meaning, can actions be meaningful, can one be judged by one's fellow citizens or have one's own criticisms of the latter be taken seriously. Kant's first principle for Perpetual Peace was that all states must become political communities, an association for the good life; even a monarchy must behave as it were a republic (Tomba 50). With due respect to the important experiences of one's territory, landscape, family, and other elements of home, these, too, like the elements whose limits are demonstrated by Aristotle, remain at most preconditions, some necessary, some only secondary and derivative conditions for constituting home and belonging. In the end, it is citizenship in the full sense, membership in a political association whose end is the good life, which makes home a realizable possibility. Surely association to achieve the good life, so long as it maintains and protects the necessary preconditions to achieving self-government in the first place, is superior as a vision and a practice, to the lowest common denominator conception of rights as mere limits on state action, or as appertaining to individuals as such.

The second loss, according to Arendt, was the loss of government protection, one of the basic elements of citizenship, a necessary but not sufficient precondition as discussed above. That loss, stemming from the original loss of one's own government's protection, led to a loss of any guarantee of protection from other governments. Home, in this sense, involves security, a sense of belonging, which is very concrete, and at times a matter of life and death. The conclusion is clear: "The fundamental deprivation of human rights is manifested first and above all in the deprivation of a place in the world, which makes opinions significant and actions effective" (Arendt 296). But this condition is the result of the confluence of three forces, one of which is a structural element of the very doctrine of human rights. For if one issue is the capacity of local governments to deny human rights or citizenship rights to their own populations (*Homo Sacer*; *State of Exception*; "Nothing Exceptional"), a second is the political organization of the world into a society of national states ("The Anarchical Society"), and the third follows from the first and second, a fundamental problem of the very concept of human rights itself *qua* human rights:

> From the beginning the paradox involved in the declaration of inalienable human rights was that it reckoned with an "abstract" human being who seemed to exist nowhere, for even savages lived in some kind of a social order. . . . the Rights of Man, after all, had been defined as "inalienable" because they were supposed to be independent of all governments; but it turned out that the moment human beings lacked their own government and had to fall back upon their minimum rights, no authority was left to protect them and no institution was willing to guarantee them. (Arendt 291–92)

When one is seen by others to be only a human being, without any of the social, political or cultural characteristics that make one fully human, the result may be compassion and charity but it may also be just as likely be seen as an invitation to further abuse. "Bare life," as Arendt and Agamben term it, cannot be the basis for human dignity.

For human rights still require states to enforce them, just not the same state that is repressing or violating them. But the enforcement of rights by external states or by "the international community" means war. Immanuel Kant warned that peace could not come from forcing a single state that refused to accept even a positive value or policy of the world community to get in line, since that is not peace but war (Kant). Machiavelli warned that republics need a plurality of republics, able to criticize each other, encourage each other to best practices, engage in competition. When all republics fall under a single central power—even a collective one—we find an empire, not a republic. A condition in which the world community was unanimous and forced a recalcitrant state into accepting policies it and its citizens had not approved would be analogous to empire, to that world polity that Arendt likewise warned would not result in a stronger enforcement of rights, but in the greatest threat to them, and one without external recourse for redress (Arendt 298).

Nor are these abstract problems. Mark Mazower has painstakingly shown that the entire conception of international law has always been based on the "standard of civilization" in which certain states were within such a standard, and so legitimized to enforce their conception of international law, while other peoples and states and communities were outside of it, and so vulnerable to having the will of others imposed upon them (Mazower 70). In short, colonialism, neocolonialism, and the current regime of human rights are closely linked, and it is no accident that the countries that find themselves targets of humanitarian interventions under the "responsibility to protect" are ones that are not within the current updated version of the standard of civilization—that is to say, not allies of the United States and often opposed to neoliberalism. Thus, even in shifting from the older national government's responsibility to its own citizens to a conception that the international community has a responsibility to protect human rights, we find that we have merely changed which fox is guarding the chickens.

Human Rights and Global Citizenship

As a legalistic concept, human rights require a political authority to define what they are legally. One of the most widely cited works on human rights, Jack Donnelly's *Universal Human Rights in Theory and Practice* fails from the start on this point with its key analogy: human rights, like property rights, are a preexisting condition. This notion has already been dismantled by Arendt as shown above. By contrast, international relations theorists recognize that human rights must be granted and recognized by global institutions, but the lack of a central international authority makes this very difficult. The realist school of international relations (Morgenthau; Waltz) sees anarchy reigning in a state of nature in world politics, making the protection of human rights well nigh impossible. The so-called English School of International Relations sees an international society as precarious, in which norms, though real, are enforced by national states that see adherence to such norms as advantageous for maintaining the international society and in the interest of the individual states in question (Bull). These theories are united in that they see international organizations as instruments for carrying out what has already been agreed to by national states. Neither position posits a global polity as existing, and many theorists in each camp would see such a polity as undesirable.

Others are less pessimistic. Constructivists view human rights as a discourse that has achieved a certain degree of autonomy from institutional settings, though the geopolitical limits on the discourse remain (Risse; Ropp and Sikkinke 16). Some political theorists seek to found human rights solely on the narrow basis of historical liberal theory, with all the baggage that this involves—from class privilege and economic doctrine to the policies of existing international organizations such as the IMF and WTO, and with the historical affiliation with Anglo-American hegemonies intact (Charvet and Nay). Samuel Moyn's demonstration of the Christian roots of human rights merely shifts the instrument of human rights formation from political constitutionalism to Christian ethos. In both cases, however, the Western origin of the rights concept belies its alleged universality. Donnelly's influential work engages in intellectual gymnastics to find a plausible basis for universal human rights. But even this work admits that despite all, people must live in determined polities or they would find themselves in a Hobbesian state of nature, and that in the end states have human rights responsibilities only to their own citizens and territorial residents (Donnelly 30–32).

Clearly, only global citizenship could address all of these difficulties, and there has been considerable work done on developing that idea. Robert Paehlke seeks the basis for global citizenship in the movements to limit corporate depravity and U.S. militarism worldwide, hoping ironically that the opposition to the current global governance regime will provide that same regime with a stronger basis for legitimacy (Paehlk 15, 200–02). Andrew

Moravcsik instead argues that democratic republican governments have often accepted the limitations on sovereignty imposed by international human rights regimes when the gains in reducing domestic political uncertainty—the risk of having a domestic opposition reverse preferred policies—outweigh that compromise (Moravcsik 217–52). Efforts at conceptualizing a "global democracy" are perpetually challenged by the lack of any global, or even international, or even European demos or people (Held 220). Aristotle's criteria continue to matter in the twenty-first century. It seems difficult to avoid the conclusion that even under the most global of human rights regimes, rights remain inextricably tied to domestic politics and national governments. If there is a role for civil society and popular social movements, their impact must be primarily at the national level, and be differentiated in that impact in different countries and political communities. To be effective beyond national boundaries, they must act in concrete ways in solidarity with brother and sister movements and struggles or with efforts to bring about analogous gains to those already won or being fought for in each other's national political communities. This means that the struggles, acts of solidarity, and discourses of movements from the pre-globalization era, especially from the immediately preceding era of anti-colonial and analogous movements, are surprisingly relevant to addressing our problems today.

The Political Kingdom and Expanding Republican Virtue

The crux of the problem is that if rights are universal but must be enforced by national states, how do we address the needs of those whose own governments are the cause of violations of rights? Clearly, the system of national sovereignty on which the UN was based after the war left this issue in the hands of national governments, with little redress unless people were able to flee *and* provided there was a country willing to welcome them. But the "duty to protect" recognized by the UN Security Council has led to an attempt to establish a mechanism to address the problem Arendt so courageously faced. Now, if one's government abuses one's own human rights, the UN Security Council will authorize a military attack on that country, or failing that, in some cases, the United States and its allies or NATO will invade or attack that country. This solution is clearly as bad as or worse than the problem it addresses. First, because war leads to new and greater abuses; second, because it does not always accomplish its goals; third, because such a system enhances the power of the most powerful national states at the cost of the weaker ones, which means that abuses of power are more, not less, likely internationally; and fourth, because the abuses by governments or private sector actors favored by the U.S. government and its allies as in Thailand, Bahrain, Turkey, Saudi Arabia, Yemen, Israel/Palestine are excused.

If universal rights are counterproductive, if letting one's own government be the fox guarding the chickens is unacceptable and inviting the wolf in to redress such abuses is worse, where are we to look for an answer to the problem Arendt addressed? My answer is to look to advance the ideas most recently expressed in the anti-colonial movements and the struggles for full equality. As Exhibit A, I offer Malcolm X, a counterpoint to the dead end offered by Arendt's inability to transcend liberal theory. For one thing, Malcolm X always made clear in his speeches that rights are collective and that they are the result of struggle—of historical, collective struggle. To protect individual rights in the sense of John Stuart Mill is not necessary, because no one is repressed for being an individual but rather for being a member of a group, community, organization, or because of their ethnicity, or because of their being part of the political opposition and so on. And not just any group membership—the current fashion for noting how people have many identities in a postmodern world (Nussbaum and Sen; Sen) is swatted down by Malcolm X: We are not oppressed because we are Methodists or Baptists, he would say, or because we are in the Rotary Club or the Elks. Not all lives matter in the same way ("Message to the Grassroots" 4).

Malcolm X stands in here for a wide range of actors, experiences, theories, ideas, movements, organizations, and parties. Nevertheless, I think Malcolm X's approach is consistent with those of Gandhi (47), Martin Luther King Jr., Ho Chi Minh (De Caro 48, 56–59), Kwame Nkrumah, Amilcar Cabral, and many others; the basis of the movements led by all of these leaders was the idea that people must fight for full citizenship and for self-determination, and that very willingness to struggle and to risk one's life in the process demonstrated fitness for self-government. And coming from these very sources—the formerly colonial or enslaved world—this theory and practice of citizenship expands traditional classical republicanism beyond any Eurocentric limitations, as the women's movement expanded it beyond its traditional gender limitations. I find in Malcolm X's and the anti-colonialist approach to these issues a different perspective that opens up possibilities unavailable in Arendt's disillusioned liberal universalism, in the US–backed neoliberal regime globally, and in the postwar order based more narrowly on state sovereignty.

Rights are not at the center of this analysis. Instead, as Malcolm X continued to repeat throughout his political career, "freedom, justice and equality" are not rights, but goals (Malcolm X Quotes). Rights are at most a means to those ends. Rights in this perspective are *not* inalienable, nor universal. We didn't land at Plymouth Rock, to paraphrase another famous Malcolm X line, Plymouth Rock landed on us. Rights are rather historical accomplishments, won through hard struggle and defended by hard struggle, as suggested by the struggle waged by oppressed groups for citizenship rights discussed earlier. For African Americans in theory, universal human rights have never been lacking, but rights as Americans—that is, freedom, justice, and equality as Americans were the real issue ("The Black Revolution" 108). Robin Blackburn recently made the same point about slavery. The potential personhood of slaves was not really controversial, as manumitted slaves even in slave states were legally free persons. What was denied was that they were Americans and could be citizens (Blackburn, 190, 402, 420, 478). Only those willing to struggle for their rights are deserving of them, because only those who struggle for their rights can (1) be recognized by other communities as deserving of them, and so as human beings in a full sense (here we are back to the Aristotelian categories of citizen) and (2) obligate other such communities, organizations, movements, and their own and other governments to come to their aid and to protect or advance such rights as they fight for (Malcolm X "Twenty Million Black People").

For Malcolm X and for Martin Luther King Jr., to demonstrate struggle was very important. To paraphrase Malcolm X: We must show that we are ready to die for your rights in order to have them recognized, by those who would deny them to us, and by those who are obligated to come to your aid as allies ("Not Just an American Problem"). The two leaders differed only in where they prioritized the search for allies. For King, it was entirely within the American national community, as Northern whites and Southern whites of good conscience were obligated to come to the aid of people who showed a willingness to die for equality "You must say, somehow, 'I don't have much money—I don't have much education—I may not be able to read or write—but I have the capacity to die,'" King said ("Sermon"). Malcolm X argued that if blacks in the United States fought for dignity and equality, other countries and governments had an obligation to help, just as Americans had an obligation to protest their government's role in the oppression or exploitation of people around the world ("Not Just an American Problem" 158–59).

In what appears to be a paradox, Malcolm X famously argued that blacks should seek human rights, not civil rights. But this was a strategic choice, not a philosophical one:

> Civil Rights are within the jurisdiction of the government. . . . But "human rights" is part of the charter of the United Nations. All the nations that signed the charter of the UN came up with the Declaration of Human Rights and anyone who classifies his grievances under the label of "human rights" violations, those grievances can then be brought into the United Nations and be discussed by people all over the world. For as long as you call it "civil rights" your only allies can be the people in the next community, many of whom are responsible for your grievance. ("Not Just an American Problem")

Human rights are a good organizing tool, but they can only be realized through civil rights, which by definition are particular to places and times. Coming to international agreement represents an act of solidarity that can create international dimension to national struggles (Baum 58, 72).

The protests against the war in Vietnam in the United States and around the world, the international anti-apartheid movement, and the sanctuary movement with regard to Central American refugees from the wars in Nicaragua and El Salvador in the 1980s (distinct from much of today's defense of refugees in acknowledging the political relationships involved) all stand as appropriate models and examples of solidarity. Solidarity is a political form that avoids leaving the foxes guarding the chickens, both nationally and internationally, and which relies on membership or the possibility of belonging to a community in solidarity with a community in struggle. It is a relation between equals. Today's world is all but bereft of solidarity in this sense; solidarity is replaced by humanitarian succor or intervention. Where were Europeans when the EU and IMF were privatizing and impoverishing the Greek people ("The Greeks")? Where have citizens of the Global North been while the IMF and global finance imposes neoliberalism on the poor of the world (resulting in much of the migration in recent decades)? Where were the professionals and elites of rich countries as factories closed and whole cities, like Detroit, imploded? Where are the antiwar movements? These are all negative examples demonstrating the effects of the hegemony of a hyper-individualized, globalized neoliberal conception of human rights, where instead there should stand a more geographically and socially inclusive conception of the citizen. Nowhere in the world are individuals oppressed as individuals, for being this or that named individual. Always people are oppressed or abused as members of a community, party, movement, religion, ethnicity, nation, gender, or other group that is for some reason confronted with a hostile state, majority population, party in power, or private-sector actor whose profits or status depend on such abuse. How have we forgotten this clear fact? How have we reduced human dignity to "bare life" and then sought to base dignity on that very social and political nakedness? How have we sold our inheritances for a mess of pottage?

Note

1. My thanks to Mark Luccarelli, Rosario Forlenza, Werner Bigell, and Jonathan Feldman for their critical comments, which led to important improvements in this piece. They are in no way responsible for the theses or arguments herein.

Works Cited

Agamben, Giorgio. *Homo Sacer: Sovereign Power and Bare Life*. Stanford UP, 1998.

———. *State of Exception*. U of Chicago Press, 2005.

Arendt, Hannah. *The Origins of Totalitarianism*. Harcourt, 1968.

Aristotle. *The Politics of Aristotle*. Edited and translated by Ernest Barker, Oxford UP, 1979.

Arrighi, Giovanni. *The Long Twentieth Century*. Verso, 1994.

Baum, Gregory. *Truth Beyond Relativism: Karl Mannheim's Sociology of Knowledge*. Marquette UP, 1977.

Blackburn, Robin. *The American Crucible: Slavery, Emancipation, and Human Rights*. Verso, 2013.

Bull, Hedley. *The Anarchical Society*. Columbia UP, 1977.

Charvet, John, and Elisa Kaczynska Nay. *The Liberal Project and Human Rights: Theory and Practice of a New World Order*. Cambridge UP, 2008.

Colatrella, Steven. "The Greeks are Fighting for Us All." *London Progressive Journal*, 5 March, 2010.

———. "Nothing Exceptional: Against Agamben." *Journal for Critical Education Studies*, vol. 9, no. 1, 2011.

———. "Collective Housekeeping and the Revenge of the Oikos: Against Hannah Arendt on Democracy, Work and the Welfare State." *International Critical Thought*, vol. 3, no. 4, 2013.

De Caro, Peter. *Rhetoric of Revolt: Ho Chi Minh's Discourse for Revolution*. Praeger, 2003.

Donnelly, Jack. *Universal Human Rights in Theory and Practice*. 3rd ed., Cornell UP, 2013.

"46 Million People Living as Slaves, Latest Global Index Reveals." *The Guardian*, www.theguardian.com/global-development/2016/jun/01/46-million-people-living-as-slaves-latest-global-index-reveals-russell-crowe.

Gandhi, Mohandas K. *Indian Home Rule, or Hind Swaraj*. Navajivan Publishing House, 1938.

Held, David. *Democracy and the Global Order: From the Modern State to Cosmopolitan Governance*. Stanford UP, 1995.

Kant, Immanuel. "Perpetual Peace: A Philosophical Sketch." *Kant: Political Writings*. Cambridge UP, 1989.

King, Martin Luther, Jr. "Sermon at Montgomery Church," April 1963.

Malcolm X. "The Ballot or the Bullet." *Malcolm X Speaks*, edited by George Breitman, Grove Press, 1965.

———. "The Black Revolution." *Two Speeches by Malcolm X*. Pathfinder Press, 1965.

———. "Speech to the Grassroots." *Malcolm X Speaks*, edited by George Breitman, Grove Press, 1965.

———. "Twenty Million Black People in a Political, Economic, and Mental Prison (23 January, 1963)." *Malcolm X: The Last Speeches*, edited by Bruce Perry, Pathfinder Press, 1989.

———. "Not Just an American Problem, but a World Problem." *Malcolm X: The Last Speeches*, edited by Bruce Perry, Pathfinder, 1989.

"Malcolm X Quotes." www.malcolm-x.org/quotes.htm.

Mazower, Mark. *Governing the World: The History of an Idea, 1815 to the Present*. Penguin, 2012.

McDermott, John. "A Mass Constituency for Globalization." *Rethinking Marxism*, vol. 20, no. 1, Jan. 2008, pp. 151–59.

Moracscik, Andrew. "The Origins of Human Rights Regimes: Democratic Delegation in Postwar Europe." *International Organization*, vol. 54, no. 2, Spring 2000, pp. 217–52.

Morgenthau, Hans. *Politics among Nations*. McGraw-Hill, 2005.

Moyn, Samuel. *Christian Human Rights*. U of Pennsylvania P, 2015.

Nussbaum, Martha, and Amartya Sen. *The Quality of Life*. Oxford UP, 1993.

Olivieri, Federico. "Acts of Citizenship against Neoliberalism: The New Cycle of Migrant Struggles in Italy." *Multicultural Challenges and Sustainable Democracy in Europe and East Asia*, edited by Nam Kook Kim, Palgrave, 2014.

"Our Model for Freedom: Slavery Today." *Free The Slaves*, www.freetheslaves.net/about-slavery/slavery-today/.

Paehlke, Robert C. *Hegemony and Global Citizenship: Transnational Governance for the 21st Century*. Palgrave MacMillan, 2014.

Perry, Bruce, editor. *Malcom X: The Last Speeches.* Pathfinder Press, 1989.

Plato. *The Republic: The Complete and Unabridged Jowett Translation.* Vintage, 1991.

"Refugee Death Toll Passes 1,000 in Record 2017 as Charities Attacked for Conducting Mediterranean Rescues." *The Independent*, www.independent.co.uk/news/world/europe/refugee-crisis-migrants-asylum-seekers-mediterranean-see-libya-italy-ngos-smugglers-accusations-a7696976.html.

Risse, Thomas, and Kathryn Sikkink. Introduction. "The Socialization of International Human Rights Norms into Domestic Practices." *The Power of Human Rights International Norms and Domestic Change*, edited by Thomas Risse, Stephen C. Ropp, and Kathryn Sikkink, Cambridge UP, 1999.

Sen, Amartya. *Identity and Violence.* Norton, 2006.

Taylor, Charles. *Hegel.* Cambridge UP, 1975.

"This Map Shows Where the World's 30 Million Slaves Live. There are 60,000 in the US." *The Washington Post*, www.washingtonpost.com/news/worldviews/wp/2013/10/17/this-map-shows-where-the-worlds-30-million-slaves-live-there-are-60000-in-the-u-s/?utm_term=.c4b4729fddf9.

Tilly, Charles. "Transplanted Networks." *Immigration Reconsidered: History, Sociology, and Politics*, edited by Virginia Yans-McLaughlin, Oxford UP, 1990.

Tomba, Max. *La vera politica. Kant e Benjamin: La possibilità della giustizia.* Quodlibet, 2006.

United Nations High Commission on Refugees (UNHCR). "Forced Displacement Worldwide at Its Highest in Decades," www.unhcr.org/news/stories/2017/6/5941561f4/forced-displacement-worldwide-its-highest-decades.html.

Wallerstein, Immanual. *The Modern World System.* Academic Press, 1974.

Waltz, Kenneth. *The Theory of International Politics.* McGraw-Hill, 1979.

Wilentz, Sean. *The Rise of American Democracy.* W. W. Norton, 2005.

Winfield, Richard Dien. "The Types of Universals and the Forms of Judgment." *Hegel's Theory of the Subject*, edited by David Gray Carlson, Palgrave, 2005.

Chapter 3

The Political Landscape and the Nation-State

Arendtian Commons and the American Revolution

Ole Sneltvedt

Introduction

Consider for a moment this hypothetical, but not altogether unrealistic, scenario: Due to a foreign invasion, hunger crisis, or epidemic disease, you are forced to leave your current nation-state together with your fellow citizens. For some reason, no other nation-state is willing to accommodate you and as an emergency measure the UN decides, in collaboration with the Danish government, to create a settlement on Greenland. Your government is given the resources to build a giant city that will accommodate all its citizens; rights to natural resources that will reestablish a sustainable economy; and its own sovereign territory. Laws, universities, newspapers, language, and the population are kept the same. Is anything in such a hypothetical scenario changed or lost?

According to well-established theories of nation and state, the answer is no. There is still an *imagined community*, a national reflexive identity created and sustained in discourse (Anderson 6). There is still "a human community that (successfully) claims the monopoly of the legitimate use of physical force within a given territory" (Weber 77). What has changed is merely the geographical position—the location—of the nation-state.

In this chapter, I will argue that the answer to the question above is actually yes—something is changed and some things are lost. I do not intend to revise these established theories regarding the nation or the state, but rather to develop a theory and give historical examples, which will enable us to see political communities as comprised of more than just people and their communication. My hypothesis is that this latter reduction of the polity into a discursive community and a system of socially constructed institutions misses the fact that polities also consist of *common public things*, which together establish a political landscape comprised of interlocking spaces in which public speech and action literally *take place*. Subsequently, the spatiality and materiality of political communities should not be seen as the absolute sovereign space of territory, but rather as relational space in-between common things.

I explore this hypothesis by first considering established theories of the nation, the state, and territory in relation to subsequent arguments regarding the *cosmopolitan condition* and transnational public spheres. I further develop J. B. Jackson's notion of the political landscape in relation to Hannah Arendt's concept of the *world of common things* and the formation of a *common sense of reality*. And finally, I look briefly at a historical example of the latter in the prerevolutionary political landscape that would aid the formation of the United States of America.

The Cosmopolitan Condition and the Transnational Public Sphere?

Roughly a decade ago, Ulrich Beck argued that researchers failed to understand "the *Cosmopolitan Condition*" and the process of globalization, because they had become "captured by zombie categories," which held them "prisoners of methodological nationalism" (287). In other words, they failed to see society, territory, and political organization beyond the frame of the nation-state (287). This critique was made possible by a number of similar arguments against the modern nation-state, its territory, and the wider relationship to society and the public sphere.

Territory, according to John Agnew, could no longer be seen as a "container" because social, economic, and political life could no longer be "ontologically contained within the territorial boundaries of states" ("The Territorial Trap" 77). This methodological assumption could be seen as a "territorial trap," what Saskia Sassen later defined as "the analytical flattening of territory into a single meaning . . . national-state territory" (22). Territory should rather be seen, according to Joe Painter, not as "an irreducible foundation of state power, let alone the expression of a biological imperative," but rather an "*effect* . . . the outcome of networked socio-technical practices," which makes territory a "laborious work in progress" (1093–94).

Similarly, the nation, according to Benedict Anderson's famous definition, should not be seen as something naturally given or what Pierre van den Berghe defined as a "politically conscious ethny" (61). Rather, the nation, following Ernest Renan's early definition, should be seen as an "imagined political community—and imagined as both inherently limited and sovereign" (Anderson 6). Subsequently, the nation has been further tied to the notion that it arises out of a discursive formation, which in turn creates "nationalist self-understandings" (Calhoun 4). That, in turn, further enables national identity to trickle "quietly and continuously into reality" and become a "framework of the world as we know it" (Anderson 36; Özkirimli 216).

The modern state, in Max Weber's definition, could be seen as "a human community that (successfully) claims the monopoly of the legitimate use of physical force within a given territory" (77). "Human community" in this sense refers not to the population, which is implicit, but rather to the "politically organized, coercive, administrative and symbolic apparatus" and its governance of both population and territory (Jessop 26). In "Transnationalizing the Public Sphere," Nancy Fraser argued that the nation-state no longer sustained such a sovereign territory, a stable population, control over its economy, its own communications infrastructure, an exclusive national language, or its national literature supporting its social imaginary (15–18). Similar to Beck, she saw Jürgen Habermas's public sphere theory as "implicitly informed by a Westphalian political imaginary," which as a consequence needed reformation in relation to a new global reality (Fraser 8). Subsequently, a gap appeared in public sphere theory. Public opinion, "considered efficacious if and only if it is mobilized as a political force to hold public power accountable," could no longer rely on the coercive, administrative, and symbolic apparatus of the state (Fraser 22). This occurred not only as a consequence of the state being territorially, economically, and socially permeated by a global network of intergovernmental policies, trade, and communication but also due to the rise of what Beck referred to as "global risks" (287).

Habermas, not unlike John Dewey, saw the public as determined by the "all-affected principle," involving the notion that those affected by political decisions—or, as in Dewey's case, externalities of the market—should gain access to the public and the formation of public opinion (Fraser 21; Dewey 15). With the advent of global warming, global financial panics, the threat of global nuclear catastrophes, and global terrorism, a global public should emerge as such issues affected all, and we should create transnational institutions that would "possess the power to solve transnational problems" (Fraser 23).

According to Beck, these global risks had made "reality itself" cosmopolitan ("The Cosmopolitan Condition" 287). Unlike Hannah Arendt's analysis of *The Human Condition* and Jean-Francois Lyotard's *Postmodern Condition*, it was now time to "discover, map and understand the *Cosmopolitan Condition*" (287). For Beck, people were no longer tied to Arendt's activities of labor, work, and action—to bodily necessities, things and public speech and action—nor did they possess Lyotard's postmodern skepticism towards metanarratives. In a globalized world "reality itself" had become cosmopolitan and this new reality of global risk and networks; global flow of commodities, people and capital; and global communication, required a new metanarrative of globalism and a new methodological cosmopolitanism (Beck 287).

Beck and Fraser's positions make use of three interwoven arguments. First, it is assumed that the nation has been incorrectly defined as a reified concept, leading to the methodological assumption that "humanity is naturally divided into a limited number of nations" (Beck 287). Second, this view is refuted by way of the arguments that the nation, state, and territory are socially constructed through language and involve nothing but people and discourse. This in turn opens up the possibility of reconstructing the political community toward the global level and opens up a space for the cosmopolitan metanarrative of an undivided humanity.

Now, a decade later, there seem to be several ways of critiquing Beck's argument for methodological cosmopolitanism. Globalization has not led to a cosmopolitan condition, but rather renewed discourses of national identity, as well as attempts—as in the case of Brexit—to regain the territorial and economic sovereignty of the state. The failure to predict and come to terms with such phenomena might indicate that we are still being held prisoners, only this time by methodological cosmopolitanism.

A similar critique can be directed toward Fraser's argument for transnationalizing the public sphere. Today, it is not only the case that transnational public opinion does not have an addressee in the form of "transnational public powers" (Fraser 23). Rather, it seems that despite the rapid increase in both quantity and speed of global communication, there is no formation of a global public opinion but a relatively stable plurality of not only conflicting but also mutually exclusive arguments.

The purpose of this paper is not to pursue further a critique of methodological cosmopolitanism or the notion of transnational public spheres. Rather, I direct my attention toward the notion that seeing nations, states, and territories as socially constructed and sustained through discourse involves the implicit assumption that political communities contain only two elements: people and communication. This enables the argument that, together with capital and commodities, members of the discursive community of the nation-state are swept away from their national islands into the streams of the global network (*Cosmopolitan Vision* 80). This view, by favoring movement over stability, discourse over action, and people over things, eclipses the fact that political communities contain more than the two elements above. Nation-states, as one type of political community, also involve two additional elements, action and things, which are related to situatedness and stability.

This primacy of communication appears not only in political theory, but also in its underlying metaphors. In considering a transition *From Realpolitik to Dingpolitik or How to Make Things Public*, Bruno Latour argued that "political philosophy has often been the victim of a strong object-avoidance tendency" (15). Discussing the much-addressed frontispiece of Thomas Hobbes's *Leviathan* and Ambrogio Lorenzetti's famous *Allegory of Good and Bad Government,* he makes the observation that they contain not merely people and their communication, but "clothes, a huge sword, immense castles, large cultivated fields, crowns, ships" and an array of buildings, walls, and cultivated landscapes (16–17). Arguably, the same applies to other metaphors of political communities. In Plato's famous example of the *Ship of State*, which illustrates the troubled relationship between the people and the philosopher, the senate and the plebs, the ship, the sea and the wind serves as a mere stage for the unfolding action (Plato Book VI).

In these metaphors the social relationships and struggles for power are made intelligible against a particular context, which is taken for granted. The same arguably applies to theories of nation and state, as well as territory. The discourse of imagined communities, the governance by states or non-state actors, and the constant upkeep of territory take place somewhere and against something. Political communities, of which the nation-state is one type, thus involve more than imagined communities, more than state institutions; they also involve a third layer, a political landscape in which action literally takes place. Places do not easily liquidize and enter global flows. Rather, as Agnew noted, they "form nodes around which human activities circulate" (*Place and Politics* 28). In the following section I will argue that the *cosmopolitan condition* does not transcend Arendt's *human condition*: our "web of human relationships" still relies on a "world of things" (*The Human Condition* 183, 52).

The (Pre)Political Landscape

For J. B. Jackson, landscape could be defined as:

> A space on the surface of the earth . . . with a degree of permanence, with its own distinct character, either topographical or cultural, and above all a space shared by a group of people . . . a composition of man-made or man modified spaces to serve as infrastructure or background for our collective existence . . . which underscores not only our identity and presence, but also our history. (5–8)

In *Discovering the Vernacular Landscape,* Jackson tried to differentiate the different layers of the American landscape. As he discovered the vernacular layer, he found it necessary to juxtapose it against another layer, which could be defined as political. On one side, the *vernacular landscape* is characterized by "mobility and change . . . its spaces are usually small, irregular in shape, subject to rapid change in use" (151). On the other side, the *political landscape* appears in-between "those structures designed to impose or preserve a unity and order of the land" (150). In this latter case, the political landscape is seen as a composition of boundary-creating things of relative temporal and spatial stability, "walls and boundaries and monuments and highways and public places," as well as hydroelectric dams, airports, and power transmission lines (21, 150).

Jackson saw such political objects and the resulting political landscape as a "more or less rigid network of boundaries," stretching across America. These permanent boundaries, made visible by way of durable things, function as stabilizers for social relationships making "residents out of the homeless, neighbors out of strangers, strangers out of enemies." But these also serve as "reminders of long-range, collective purposes, of goals and objectives and principles" (49, 15, 152). As boundaries they do not demarcate uniform regions of homogeneity, but rather appear as a "loose fitting envelope, a way of giving a visible, corporeal identity to a temple, a city, a state" (34). For Jackson, the political landscape provided its citizens with visible stability and order. The epistemological, spatial, and temporal stability of its arrangement of objects lent a sense of history, represented law, distinguished between private and public, and reminded members of society of their rights and obligations as citizens.

Jackson's notion of the political landscape could be seen in conjunction with Carl Schmitt's argument regarding the internal division of land: its manifestation in "fences, enclosures, boundaries, walls, houses and other constructs"; its relation to the *nomos*; and its spatialization as an "immediate form in which political and social order of a people becomes spatially visible" (Schmitt 42). Here instead, I will attempt to step beyond the notion of the boundary into Hannah Arendt's concept of the *world* and its political implications.

In one of her earliest works, Arendt addressed the question of what *we are doing* by dividing *The Human Condition* into the three fundamental physical and visible activities of *labor*, *work*, and *action*. In her latest, and unfinished work, she explored *The Life of the Mind* and those private and invisible activities of *thinking*, *willing*, and *judging*. But, in addition to these two complementary accounts of fundamental human activities, she also indirectly explored a third question throughout her writing: namely, *where we are* and what difference it makes on both our public and private activities.

This question revolves around the connection between *common world* and *common sense* and appears across her works, but perhaps most notably in the two works above, as well as her essays *Introduction into Politics* and *The Crisis in Culture*, which further tie into her theorizing on *things* and the public realm (see discussion in Debarbieux; Frampton; Brown; Canovan; Honig). In the most general terms, Arendt's *world* can be seen as something:

> We enter into when we are born and what we leave behind when we die. It transcends our lifespan into past and future alike; it was there before we came and will outlast our brief sojourn in it. It is what we have in common not only with those who live with us, but also with those who were here before and with those who come after us. (*The Human Condition* 55)

The world gains this independence from humans by being comprised of things in the sense that "to live together in the world means essentially that a world of things is between those who have it in common as a table is located between those who sit around it" (52). People depend on such things to constitute a "world that solidly appears as the location" in which their lives play out among other actors who "acknowledge and recognize its existence" (*Life of the Mind* 22).

Subsequently, understanding the relationship between common sense and the common world hinges on further grasping the important role of common public things in Arendt's political theory. As a third type of commons, those things that belong to the public realm form a center in political communities by establishing temporally and spatially stable foundations against the otherwise cyclical nature of our bodily necessities and the fleeting political phenomenon of public speech and action. Taking *The Human Condition* as a natural starting point, we find three realms with corresponding activities and outcomes. The *private realm* involves the activity of *labor*, which results in those *necessities* needed to sustain life in its biological sense. The *public realm* is constructed out of those *things*, which is the result of the activity *work*. The public realm can be seen as the aggregate of what is not private, and therefore visible and accessible to all. The public realm, in turn, maintains the potentiality of the activity of *public speech and action*, which in turn constitutes the "space of appearance," the fleeting intersubjective realm of interaction in which people can experience *political freedom* and that at the same time holds the potential of *political power* through collective action (*The Human Condition* 136–40, 197–98). It is important to note that the activity of work is not considered as one type of public action but rather "prepolitical," in the same sense as building a theater and a stage is not part of the play but its precondition (195).

In this chapter, I hone in on the overlap between the two latter activities and realms. In other words, How does the *world of things* precondition and influence the latter *space of appearance*? Do certain arrangements of things constitute a world better "fit for action and speech" (173)?

The key to understanding Arendt's concept of world is to understand the notion of the *thing* as fabricated out of nature through the activity of work, resulting in meaningful, temporally durable, and spatially "*inter-esting*" (or binding) human artifice. *Things* come in two types: those that are useful and those that are useless. The first applies to those "use objects," instruments and tools used to fabricate other things. The second refers to objects distinguished by their "uselessness," primarily works of art (*The Human Condition* 142, 167). *Things* then are not limited to those useful objects such as chairs and tables and roads, but also include objects that reify public speech and action by transforming them from fleeting sounds and events into the "the written page, or the printed book, into paintings or sculpture, into all sorts of records, documents, and monuments" (95). Here it should be noted that Arendt applies the notion of reification not negatively as "the apprehension of the products of human activity *as if* they were something other than human products," as defined by Peter L. Berger and Thomas Luckmann, but rather positively as the transformation of speech, action, and imagination into tangible public things (106).

Temporally, and unlike the *necessities* emerging from the activity of labor, things escape the "biological cycle" of nature and "have an independence of their own." A necessity such as bread has little durability as it spoils within a few days. Shoes, on the other hand, "do not spoil if you do not wear them." Due to this inherent durability, they provide a temporal stability relative to the lives of humans as they endure beyond individual lifespans, but also provide a persistent appearance against the "eternal movement" of nature (*The Human Condition* 136–40). The aggregate of things becomes a "world in the proper sense of the word only when the totality of fabricated things is so organized that it can resist the consuming life processes of the people dwelling in it, and thus outlasts them" (*Between Past and Future* 211).

It could, of course, be argued that things such as shoes, monuments, bridges, roads, and buildings do, in fact, wither away. This usually happens, however, at speeds slower than the span of a human life. Another argument could be that things such as plastic bags, soda cans, and discarded computers are increasingly surrounding us. Being surrounded by what is commonly referred to as "trash" does not disqualify the theory, because to refer back to Arendt's table metaphor, there is another important qualifier: we cannot expect that an "ugly table" will "fulfill the same function as a handsome one" (*The Human Condition* 173).

Spatially, and unlike the fleeting space of appearance and ephemeral necessities, things function as common interests as they reflect "the word's most literal significance . . . *inter-est*," to be between (*The Human Condition* 182). Things, by occupying a position in-between people, "relate and bind them together"; they "relate and separate men at the same time" and prevent them from "falling over each other, so to speak" (182, 52). To have something in common means quite literally to share access to a public world of things; to make use of and engage with common things such as parks, roads, bridges, or public squares. By interacting with things, "men, their ever-changing nature notwithstanding, can retrieve their sameness, that is, their identity, by being related to the same chair and the same table" (137).

Our interaction with temporally and spatially stable common things in turn "gives rise to the familiarity of the world," and subsequently leads to a way of life, to particular "customs and habits" (*The Human Condition* 94). This not only implies particular ways of engaging and using things, but also provides the material for public speech and action. In other words, the latter activity is not only related to people's need to disclose themselves as "distinct and unique persons," but can also be concerned with an external "objective reality" (182–83).

Our concern with this external reality is, however, inexhaustible as it cannot be fully perceived by a single individual. As a consequence, the world "appears in the mode of it-seems-to-me," always from a particular vantage point. If one remains completely isolated, this could lead to some sort of Cartesian doubt, but since we are thrown into a world already filled with people and things, we can gain some kind of certainty by taking into account the accounts of others (*Life of the Mind* 46, *The Human Condition* 58). This common search for the meaning of things is limited, however, by the fact that "nothing we see or hear or touch can be expressed in words that equal what is given to the senses" (*Life of the Mind* 8).

This gap is intersubjectively negotiated through the use of metaphors and language (*Life of the Mind* 105). But, for metaphors to function they need to draw upon some common material, a common world. Arendt resolves this paradox by introducing the notion of *common sense*, which involves a

> three-fold commonness: the five senses, utterly different from each other, have the same object in common; members of the same species have the same context in common that endows every single object with its particular meaning; and all other sense-endowed beings, though perceiving this object from utterly different perspectives, agree on its identity. Out of this . . . arises the *sensation* of reality. (*Life of the Mind* 50)

This "sensation of reality" or *common sense* emerges when we form our individual and particular vantage points by directing attention toward a common object or event (*Life of the Mind* 52). As when playing soccer, we keep our eyes on the ball and take for granted that there are goals and grass, rules and spectators. This "*context* in which single objects appear as well as to the context in which we ourselves as appearances exist among other appearing creatures . . . never appears entirely; it is elusive" (51). Despite the elusiveness of the context and the multifaceted things, we still have a *sense of reality* shared among those who find themselves in the same context.

Our common sense of reality is intrinsically tied to a common world, and our common world is comprised of common things.

"Common" does not imply that these things are produced in common, but rather that they are experienced against a common context. The meaning of both things and context is negotiated through language and metaphor, and language and metaphor have no meaning apart from the common world. As John Searle has put it, "a public language presupposes a public world . . . a socially constructed reality presupposes a nonsocially constructed reality" (*The Construction of Social Reality* 191). Nations and states and presidencies and money might well be socially constructed through discourse, but they are constructed against a world of things and our common sense of reality. The "web of human relationships" (*The Human Condition* 183), which has the potentiality of constituting the intersubjective *space of appearance,* takes place within a *world of things*, that common world that makes communication intelligible and imagination possible (*Life of the Mind* 38, 86).

The game of soccer provides a fitting example for understanding Arendt's theory. On one side, it is comprised of various rules such as a ball crossing a certain line between two posts equaling a goal (one point). Or, if the ball rolls over a different line, someone has to throw the ball with their hands, something that in all other cases would result in a free kick for the opposing team. On the other side, soccer involves a whole array of *things*, which, unlike the players, do not move around, such as goalposts, the field, white lines, and nets. The rules of the game only make sense in conjunction with such things. A third element in soccer is people—divided into players and referees. The players, on their respective teams, are occupied with the collective task of getting the ball over a white line in-between the goalposts at the short end of the field, without committing any fouls. Most players are also occupied with a more individual task, namely to distinguish themselves as especially competent players by dribbling the ball, making spectacular banana shots, impressive scissor kicks, etc., which do not always align with the collective task of scoring goals. The referees are occupied with enforcing the rules, by way of whistles, flags, and cards of various colors. These three elements—the rules, the things, and the people—constitute the game itself. If you take out one element, you no longer have the same game. Simply kicking a ball in a park is not equal to the game of soccer; kicking a ball over any white line is not equal to scoring a goal, and showing your co-workers a red card does not mean they must leave the office.

A world fit for human speech and action—a well-functioning political landscape—can be seen as equivalent to a good soccer field. It is comprised of things that are temporally and spatially stable enough to sustain a common sense of reality, on top of which, quite literally, political discourse takes place. If we see the political phenomenon of public speech and action as the game of politics, where the goal is to experience political freedom, we should assume that this game also involves players, fields, and rules. This game is, of course, immensely more complicated than soccer, or any other game, and hence we should expect its playing field to be immensely complex.

In her book *On Revolution,* Arendt argued that the American Revolution constituted an event where all the elements of the political game came together. In the townships and meeting halls of the thirteen colonies, British colonists had found conditions especially fit for the ancient political game of public speech and action (*On Revolution* 238). In fact, they found this experience so intriguing that when interrupted by King George III, who insisted on playing the game of imperialism, they decided "to bring the new American experience and the new American concept of power out into the open" (166). Unlike the French revolutionaries who possessed only the rules of the game, "ideas and principles untested by reality," the American players went in search of "models and precedents" to formalize a game already set in motion (120, 198, 166).

Unfortunately, in attempting to codify the game, they got distracted and forgot about the field. Under the "enormous weight of the Constitution . . . this greatest achievement of the American people," they failed "to incorporate the townships and the town-hall meetings, the original springs of all political activity in the country" (*On Revolution* 242). Arendt followed Lewis Mumford's assertion that as this extraordinary relationship between common things and unimagined communities failed to extend westward, it resulted in a situation where "the abstract political system of democracy lacked concrete organs" (Mumford 332). What was once, in Ralph Waldo Emerson's words, "the school of the people, the game which everyone of them learns to play," now lacked a playing field (quoted in Mumford 332).

The Founding Fathers had forgotten to provide a description of their political landscape as a "spatially limited . . . tangible reality," in which the game of political freedom took place (*On Revolution* 279). When it came to redrawing the white lines in the grass after the Revolution there were only vague memories of that immensely complex field, which had enabled the revolutionary spirit. In the Land Ordinance of 1785, Congress decided to rationalize the political landscape and subsequently Americans would gradually find themselves attempting to play soccer on a baseball field.

In the section that follows I will attempt to look closer at this argument, but also to see it in relation to two similar claims: First, Kenneth

Robert Olwig's argument that "prior to its independence, the United States was thus already a 'country' " (43), and, second, Edmund S. Morgan's claim that "our nation was the child, not the father, of the revolution" (101). Olwig made a connection between landscape and the *country* as a larger political unit and saw the American political landscape as consisting of a "country of countries" (49, 176). Morgan admitted to the fact that although America had no imagined national community prior to the revolution, it had a certain "self-consciousness; a pride in things American" (101). As, in Agnew's term a "territorial coalition of places," this American world of common things gradually developed into a separate realm in opposition to the British imperial network (*Place and Politics* 40). It developed a political boundary, not as homogenous area, but rather a "loose fitting envelope, a way of giving a visible, corporal identity to a temple, a city," or in this case, a country (Jackson 33). Not unlike the relationship between the *chôra*, the *agora*, and the *polis* of Plato's normative *Laws* and Aristotle's descriptive *Politics*, the political landscape of the American Revolution was comprised of a series of places (*topoi*) in which the political communities (*polis)* of men (*andres*) emerged within surrounding country (*chôra)* (Elden 48; Casey 353).

While Arendt and Mumford's arguments relate to the notion that political communities are bound and influenced by their political landscapes, the two subsequent arguments of Olwig and Morgan convey the idea that there is causality between the imagined community of the nation, the institutional framework of the state, and the political landscape we might refer to as the country of the political community.

As far as these three elements are intertwined, it might also lead to a revision of Ernest Renan's answer to "What is a Nation?" Perhaps we should willfully misread his claim that "the essence of a nation is that all individuals have many things in common." In other words, a nation might refer to some approximation of an imagined "spiritual principle," but a principle, which intrinsically appears within a "house that one has built and that one has handed down": lest of course, as Arendt points out, "the succeeding generations change its identity beyond recognition" (Renan 11, 19; *The Human Condition* 198).

The Political Landscape of the American Revolution

Looking back at the American Revolution, John Adams pondered how "the people of thirteen colonies, all distinct, unconnected, and independent of each other . . . had acted in concert" as if "thirteen clocks had struck as one" and considered this event as "surely interesting to humanity to investigate and perpetuate to posterity" (Adams). Histories of the American Revolution have been written from multiple perspectives, seeing it as a political revolution with social consequences, as inspired by Machiavelli's republicanism, or as a social revolution with political consequence inspired by the ideas of Locke's liberalism (Young and Nobles). Historical accounts naturally focus on public speech and action, their reification into records and documents, but to a lesser degree on the landscape in which such action took place. There seems to be no reason to deny the importance of British taxation, the actions of the Founding Fathers, socioeconomic equality, natural rights, or militias in the complex series of events of the Revolution. But neither is there reason to deny the importance of those large or, in James Deetz's words, *Small Things Forgotten*, which made up the context, the political landscape in which such events took place (Deetz).

The public speech and action of the Revolution played out on the Boston waterfront, inside taverns of New York City, and outside the Pennsylvania State House, and such urban places certainly played a major role in making the Revolution possible (Carp). But, in a country in which barely 8 percent of the population lived in cities, the Revolution cannot be reduced to an urban phenomenon (Minty 100). For this reason, I will turn my attention to the political landscape outside the Atlantic cities. This is not intended as a comprehensive study, but rather an attempt to provide sufficient evidence to support Arendt and Mumford's argument—that the very political landscape that gave birth to the revolutionary spirit was eclipsed by the Revolution itself. Two elements stand out in this former landscape: On one side, the importance and possibility of private property. On the other side, the important but relatively limited array of common public things.

Unlike the areas of eastern North America dominated by the French and the Spanish empires, the British parts did not reflect any consistent geopolitical framework. The Spanish colonizers ordered the land in accordance with the Laws of the Indies, establishing a capital town and "designating the position of the plaza, church, and municipal building," which served as the center of authority of the surrounding countryside (Meinig 236). The French areas likewise developed into a simple arrangement of districts and regions, with local government, but administered by the governor-general in Quebec with strong connections back to France (232). The British areas, on the contrary, did not reflect such territorial or political hierarchy. As Edmund S. Morgan described it:

> The government of Great Britain had not been designed to cover half the globe. . . . Administration of the colonies was left to the King, who turned it over to his Secretary of State for the Southern Department. . . . The Secretary left it pretty much to the Board of Trade and Plantations. . . . The Board of Trade told the Secretary what to do; he told the royal governors; the governors told the colonists; and the colonists did what they pleased. (10–11)

This relative weakness of centralized political control also became evident in the spatial and territorial organization of the area. Unlike the Spanish and French, the British had no consistent program for dividing up the land (Meinig 236). As a result, each colony created their own arrangements loosely inspired by English units such as counties, hundreds, shires, and boroughs (237). A dominant arrangement became the township denoting the political organization of a few settlements into a "federation of towns," sharing a common responsibility for local roads, schools, and public buildings (Meining 237; Mumford 330). Unlike the major coastal cities, the rural towns and townships were not closely tied to the Atlantic world and imperial networks of trade (Luccarelli 11; Meinig 318). Towns and villages spread out across the land similar to "cells of an organism" and constituted units that were largely economically and politically independent (Price 333; Mumford 332).

This organic spatiality was also reflected in the distribution of property. There was no consistent method for dividing up private property and public commons. If anything, the only consistent principle was that no consistent principle was applied. Sometimes land was ordered according to *metes and bounds*, letting the claimant draw up his own property as seen fit. Other times, close to large rivers and main roads, land was distributed as *long lots*, giving each resident access to the road or riverbank. On some occasions, regularized surveys were undertaken, mainly visible in the grids of major cities such as New Haven, Philadelphia, and Savannah (Meinig 240–43). However, no pattern was consistently applied across whole colonies or areas. This resulted in the most common pattern being a combination, an "adaptive order," in which all patterns were applied simultaneously. This, according to D. W. Meinig, reflected not only the "English genius for adaptation, for endless tinkering with both forms and substances," but also "the absence in the English empire of a centralized imperial program, with prescribed ways of planting and governing" (243).

This irregular division of private property meant that common land often occupied areas left over after private plots were divided (Price 67). In the compact settlements of New England, common lands were used as communal grazing fields, as well as areas set apart for a common school building and meetinghouse. The public was defined not so much in opposition to, but as negative to the private. The common was in turn defined not by way of collective ownership, but by common access to what was left over. The compact settlements of New England would soon give way to a more dispersed landscape of family farms but maintained the idea that roads, schools, taverns, and meetinghouses of the larger township were a common concern (Price 48; Mumford 332). Dispersion was balanced and kept together by a network of local roads, trails, and waterways—horizontally extended commons to and from the vertical commons of the meetinghouse, schoolhouse, and tavern.

Responding to the lack of external threat, absence of feudalism and spatial abundance, settlements spread out into a sparse political landscape containing few, but important common public things. The extensive relational space that emerged in-between such things constituted a *chôra* around a multitude of micro-*poleis*. The common experience of this political landscape made political freedom seem like common sense.

Behind its largest cities, connected to the Atlantic network of trade, the large majority of what would later become Americans were dispersed over wide areas of land in farms, villages, and townships connected by apt but nonetheless rough roads and waterways with few bridges or ferries. During the War of Independence, loyalist sentiment was mainly limited to the cities on the coast connected to the imperial network (Meinig 317). The political landscape of the townships proved unsuited for the movement of large numbers of British troops and "conditions greatly favored guerilla activity" (383). But, more importantly, it contained a population with private properties and means of subsistence that at the same time was well trained in self-government and political organization (Minty 105). The settlers of the New World had a *common world of things* and a *common sense of reality* before they developed an institutional framework of governance and before engaging in the self-conscious narration of their national identity.

In the century following the Revolution, the political landscape would substantially change and gradually move away from irregularity and adaptability. When it came to organizing the political landscape of new Western territories, Thomas Jefferson found himself on one side well aware of the political power of the New England township, which resonated with his own vision of the agrarian republic. But Jefferson was also fascinated with decimal arithmetic and "Enlightenment abstraction" (Rashid 616; Stilgoe 103). By ordering the land into a system of grids, Jefferson sought the development of regularized townships—hundreds—with similar local political functions spread across the remaining two-thirds of the new American continent.

Jefferson's own revisions of the ordinance, prior to those of Congress, shows his own discord between the relational and organic space of the original colonies and his fascination with geometry and ideal order of the Western territories. His first draft made use of natural boundaries, but in succeeding drafts there was increased emphasis on abstract longitude and latitude (Jefferson 600–13). His final draft in March of 1784 proved unpopular with Congress, was later revised, and a compromise was eventually reached later that year. Jefferson's vision was that portions of land could be bought and platted to accommodate new townships to later be filled with virtuous citizen-farmers. However, this connection between civic virtue and the township pattern would fail to extend westward into the Northwest Territory, where the irregularity of the original townships and their local politics would give way to the regularity of the grid, gradually making space for the centralized governance of the federal government and later the global market (Price 342).

The grid system made it possible to pay national debt by selling surveyed land to speculators and railroads, and gradually new *things* controlled by the federal government or corporations would replace the common things that made up the early political landscape (Nye 23; Price 343). As Albert Gallatin's *Report on Roads and Canals* was gradually realized in the federal building of lighthouses, turnpikes, and canals, these things were no longer locally controlled (Stilgoe 119). Together with bridges and railroads, they constituted a new political landscape more suited to replication and remote control, but also one that marked the "new strength of nationalism over localism, the new power of new government" (Stilgoe 111, 133). As John R. Stilgoe has argued, like the "scepter and roland . . . in ancient and medieval times," these new things of "gigantic scale and permanently fixed to the ground . . . objectified established legal government" (111). Together with national parks, the public works programs of the New Deal, the federal highway system, and the industrial city, a new political landscape arose on a national scale and with it a new framework of governance related to a federal center and a global market. The addition of a new national layer in the political landscape did not fully eclipse the local layer but established a material and spatial representation of the abstract ideas of the market, the absolute space of the state, and to some extent the imagined community of the nation.

Conclusion

By introducing a theory of the political or pre-political landscape as the tangible reality of common public things appearing in-between the institutional framework of the state and the imagined community of the nation, I have argued that this layer of the polity is the indispensable condition of the latter two. In other words, public speech and action are not only influenced by, but also dependent on, a world of common things, which serves as the necessary backdrop for people and their communication.

This brief exploration of the prerevolutionary American political landscape suggests two things. First, that the formation of a reflexive communal identity hinges on a common sense of reality emerging out of the experience of common public things. In other words, political communities cannot be separated from the spatiality and materiality in which public speech and action are rendered intelligible and communities are imagined. Second, it implies that the spatiality and materiality of the political landscape are subject to change and that radical changes lead to changes in the identity of the political community. In other words, changing, replacing, or constructing a new set of common things changes the way we publicly speak and act.

These common things on both the local and national level, and their resulting relational spaces, do not easily liquidize and flow into the flow of global networks. Subsequently, they provide a counterweight to the proposal that we currently live in a cosmopolitan condition. This is not intended as a denial of the emergence of global risks, but rather an argument for the fact that unlike communication, action necessarily takes place somewhere. We are bound to and embedded in an environment of our own making, which acts back on us by remaining spatially separating, temporally durable, and meaningful. This world of things creates a series of external landmarks from which the members of political communities get their bearings. The reification of the public speech and action of the past provides the material for imagining a common future, which leaves the possibility open for a shared identity, without submitting to a single vantage point, and the possibility of forming an *us* without the opposition of *the other*.

Works Cited

Adams, John. "Letter to Hezekiah Niles 13 February 1818." *The Works of John Adams, Second President of the United States: with a Life of the Author, Notes and Illustrations, by his Grandson Charles Francis Adams.* Little, Brown, 1856, www.oll.libertyfund.org/titles/2127.

Agnew, John. *Place and Politics: The Geographical Mediation of State and Society.* Routledge, 2015.

———. "The Territorial Trap: The Geographical Assumptions of International Relations Theory." *Review of International Political Economy*, vol. 1, no. 1, 1994, pp. 53–80, www.jstor.org/stable/4177090.

Anderson, Benedict. *Imagined Communities: Reflections on the Origin and Spread of Nationalism.* Verso, 2016.

Arendt, Hannah. *Between Past and Future: Eight Exercises in Political Thought.* Penguin, 1977.

———. "Introduction into Politics." *The Promise of Politics*, edited by Jerome Kohn, Schocken Books, 2005.

———. *The Human Condition.* 2nd ed., U of Chicago P, 1998.

———. *The Life of the Mind.* Harcourt, 1981.

———. *On Revolution.* Faber & Faber, 2016.

Beck, Ulrich. *The Cosmopolitan Vision.* Polity, 2006.

———. "The Cosmopolitan Condition: Why Methodological Nationalism Fails." *Theory, Culture & Society*, vol. 24, no. 7–8, 1 Dec. 2007, pp. 286–90.

van den Berghe, Pierre L. *The Ethnic Phenomenon.* Praeger, 1981.

Berger, Peter L., and Thomas Luckmann. *The Social Construction of Reality: A Treatise in the Sociology of Knowledge.* Penguin, 1991.

Brown, Bill. *Other Things.* U of Chicago P, 2015.

Canovan, Margaret. "Politics as Culture: Hannah Arendt and the Public Realm." *Hannah Arendt: Critical Essays*, edited by Lewis P. Hinchman, Sandra K. Hinchman, State U of New York P, 1994.

Calhoun, Craig. *Nationalism.* Open UP, 1997.

Casey, Edward S. *The Fate of Place.* U of California P, 1997.

Carp, Benjamin L. *Rebels Rising: Cities and the American Revolution.* Oxford UP, 2007.

Debarbieux, Bernard. "Hannah Arendt's Spatial Thinking: An Introduction." *Territory, Politics, Governance*, vol. 5, no. 4, 27 Sept. 2016, pp. 351–67. *Taylor & Francis*, doi:10.1080/21622671.2016.1234407.

Deetz, James. *In Small Things Forgotten: The Archaeology of Early American Life.* Anchor Books, 1977.

Dewey, John. *The Public and Its Problems.* Ohio UP, 1991.

Elden, Stuart. *The Birth of Territory.* U of Chicago P, 2013.

Frampton, Kenneth. "The Status of Man and the Status of His Objects: A Reading of *The Human Condition*." *Hannah Arendt: The Recovery of the Public World*, edited by Melvyn A. Hill, St. Martin's, 1979.

Fraser, Nancy. "Transnationalizing the Public Sphere: On the Legitimacy and Efficacy of Public Opinion in a Post-Westphalian World." *Theory, Culture & Society* 2007, vol. 24, no. 4, 2007, pp. 7–30. *Sage Journals*, doi:10.1177/0263276407080090.

Honig, Bonnie. *Public Things: Democracy in Disrepair*. Fordham UP, 2017.

Jackson, John Brinckerhoff. *Discovering the Vernacular Landscape*. Yale UP, 1984.

Jessop, Bob. *The State: Past, Present, Future*. Polity, 2016.

Jefferson, Thomas. "Bounds of a Proposed Northwest Colony." *The Papers of Thomas Jefferson*, edited by Julian P. Boyd, vol. 6, Princeton UP, 1952.

Latour, Bruno. "From Realpolitik to Dingpolitik or How to Make Things Public." *Making Things Public: Atmospheres of Democracy*, edited by Bruno Latour and Peter Weibel, The MIT P, 2005, pp. 12–38.

Luccarelli, Mark. *The Eclipse of Urbanism and the Greening of Public Space: Image Making and the Search for a Commons in the United States, 1682–1865*. White Horse Press, 2016.

Lyotard, Jean-Francois. *The Postmodern Condition: A Report on Knowledge*. Manchester UP, 1984.

Meinig, D. W. *The Shaping of America: A Geographical Perspective on 500 Years of History*. Yale UP, 1986.

Minty, C. F. "'Of One Hart and One Mind': Local Institutions and Allegiance during the American Revolution." *Early American Studies: An Interdisciplinary Journal*, vol. 15 no. 1, 2017, pp. 99–132. *Project Muse*, doi:10.1353/eam.2017.0003.

Morgan, Edmund S. *The Birth of The Republic, 1763–89*. U of Chicago P, 1956.

Mumford, Lewis. *The City in History: Its Origins, Its Transformations, and Its Prospects*. Harcourt, Brace & World, 1961.

Nye, David E. *America as Second Creation: Technology and Narratives of New Beginnings*. The MIT P, 2003.

Olwig, Kenneth Robert. *Landscape, Nature, and the Body Politic: From Britain's Renaissance to America's New World*. U of Wisconsin P, 2002.

Özkirimli, Umut. *Theories of Nationalism: A Critical Introduction*. Macmillan, 2010.

Painter, Joe. "Rethinking Territory." *Antipode*, vol. 42, no. 5, Nov. 2010, pp. 1090–118. *Wiley Online*, doi:10.1111/j.1467-8330.2010.00795.x.

Plato. *The Republic of Plato*. A. L. Burt Company, 1902.

Price, Edward T. *Dividing the Land: Early American Beginnings of Our Private Property Mosaic*. U of Chicago P, 1995.

Rashid, Mahbub. "The Plan Is the Program: Thomas Jefferson's Plan for the Rectilinear Survey of 1784." 84th ACSA Annual Meeting and Technology Conference Proceedings, edited by Judith Kinnard and Kenneth Schwartz, 1996.

Renan, Ernest. "What Is a Nation?" *Nation and Narration*, edited by Homi K. Bhabha, Routledge, 1994.

Sassen, Saskia. "When Territory Deborders Territoriality." *Territory, Politics, Governance*, vol. 1, no. 1, May 2013, pp. 21–45, *Taylor and Francis*, doi:10.1080/21622671.2013.769895.

Schmitt, Carl. *The* Nomos *of the Earth: In the International Law of the* Jus Publicum Europaeum. Telos Press Publishing, 2006.

Searle, John R. *The Construction of Social Reality*. Penguin, 1995.

Stilgoe, John R. *Common Landscape of America 1580 to 1845*. Yale UP, 1982.

Weber, Max. "Politics as a Vocation." *Max Weber: Essays in Sociology*, edited by H. Gerth and C. Wright Mills, Oxford UP, 1946, pp. 77–128.

Young, Alfred F., and Gregory H. Nobles. *Whose American Revolution Was It? Historians Interpret the Founding*. New York UP, 2011.

Chapter 4

The Nation in the Universal Language of Eco-globalism

Werner Bigell

In the environmental discourse, the nation is often seen as being irrelevant or problematic, and there are good reasons for a critique of the nation. Many environmental problems are the result of industrialization, and the most successful principle of economic organization of industrialization is capitalism, driven by the growth imperative. Under the industrial stage of capitalism, the main principle of social organization was the nation-state, which allowed unified political control over a larger territory, technological and economic standardization, the creation of a modern infrastructure, and the effective projection of control to secure raw materials and markets, resulting in colonialism. The socialist alternative to capitalism promised to harness the forces of industrial capitalism and to create an economy based not on growth but on human needs, favoring planning over competition. In accordance with this model, increasing cooperation and coordination in the spirit of internationalist solidarity should lead to a gradual withering of the nation. Socialism lost the Cold War, but contemporary global capitalism has more than exceeded socialism's post-national tendencies. In many quarters the nation-state is now understood, at best, as a leftover from a territorial age that fulfills a subordinate function in the global world order, and at worst as a stumbling block for the free flow of goods, human resources, capital, and raw materials. The progressive left, encompassing a major part of the environmental movement—while opposed to the environmental consequences of globalization—has largely adopted this globalist framework, sometimes infused with a local sense of place as seen in the portmanteau term *glocal* or in the motto "think globally, act locally." Abandoned by both global elites and the globalist left, accused of enabling environmental destruction and of egotistical particularism, the nation-state appears to be irrelevant for environmental thought. The aim of this article is to challenge this view.

The first challenge is to question the common rejection of the idea of the nation by the globalist left, which has switched from internationalism to transnationalism. The Old Left, or state socialism, was internationalist but not globalist. It saw the nation not only as an organizational principle but as a powerful and popular imaginary, potentially compatible with the interests of the working class. For the Old Left, the obsolescence of the nation meant that it would wither away in a distant future, not that it needed to be opposed. The second challenge is to present the nation as a future-oriented cultural, political, and environmental imaginary, exemplified by Ernest Callenbach's novel *Ecotopia Emerging* (1981), the "prequel" to his novel *Ecotopia* (1975). The conceptual challenge that Ecotopia presents to contemporary environmentalism lies in its depiction of the quality of national territoriality, both in the sense of a shared culture originating in its birth through separation from the United States and in its pragmatic orientation that effectively sees the building of a sovereign state as the prerequisite for democratic participation and environmental transformation. This participation also encompasses the collective governance and use of the environment as a commons. Only this national meso-level is capable of combining political sovereignty with a cultural imaginary.

Nation-states are constituted by their borders, and borders are a reminder that nations are based on particulars, not universals, and while nation-states can be transformed, they also present geographical limits to transformation. Callenbach's *Ecotopia*, for instance, derives from and responds to the American experience, but while it has inspired environmentalists in other countries, it is not a universal blueprint for political action and organization. An emerging ideological divide is that between globalism, with its universal notions such as human rights on the one hand, and particularism based on collective but not universal interests on the other. Globalism and particularism create different collective frames of communication that determine how we speak and think about the environment; semantic divergences can create a situation where we use the same words but with divergent semantic properties.

Environmental problems are often framed in a universal language with the aim to promote global environmentality; examples are Roderick Frazier Nash's book *The Rights of Nature* and Ursula Heise's book *Sense of Place and Sense of Planet.* Other terms, such as *sustainability*, see their narrow scientific meaning extended into a wide global sense. An example is the Sustainable Development Goals of the United Nations. The problem with this wider or global approach is that it downplays class distinctions, overrides existing political structures and imaginaries, and results in inadvertent "discursive colonialism," as will be exemplified in my reading of Gary Snyder's poem "Mother Earth: Her Whales." A structural problem is that environmental problems are often global, while the political tools to solve them are in the hands of particular states. An ideological divide emerges between transnationalist globalism, which understands states as mere implementers of global plans (such as the Sustainable Development Goals) and internationalist particularism, which is based on culturally and geographically determined nation-states bundling regional and local particularities into sufficiently powerful political agents. Environmentality, substantive participation in the governance of the environment, and shared cultural imaginaries can only be realized in a particularist model.

In environmentalism there has been a long tradition of reverence for the local. Ursula Heise traces this tradition to Heidegger and phenomenology, and it was brought into environmentalism by Arne Naess's Deep Ecology; a current expression is *bioregionalism* (Heise 34). While Deep Ecology and bioregionalism took up elements of science with a predominantly local focus, science also created a global frame for understanding environmental phenomena, and the global view was popularized by James Lovelock's Gaia hypothesis; a current manifestation of the global scientific frame is the concept of the Anthropocene. The language of global framing often draws on science, law, or economy. Both the local and global approaches are functional, based on the biosphere, atmosphere, geosphere, and hydrosphere and their interactions. The resulting functional areas cut across national territories and have little use for thinking in national terms. The greater scientific precision of the functional approaches is also their conceptual limitation, since they downplay historical, sociocultural, and political developments that have been largely the story of states and peoples.

In her book with the programmatic title, *Sense of Place and Sense of Planet: The Environmental Imagination of the Global*, Ursula Heise presents a new version of this globalist strain of environmentalism that nonetheless suffers from avoidance of the national meso-level. Heise's work also reflects an ideological orientation that fails to consider the merits of nationalism.[1] But this absence is unfortunate, since the nation-state is capable of creating a regime of environmentality in the form of administration[2] and also legitimizing it through shared imaginaries, mythologies, and practices that draw on its past. In addition, an exclusion of the meso-level weakens the understanding of the transformative processes of nature where the transforming forces are not humanity in general (as in the debates on climate change) but specific, territorially bound cultural and political units, with different historically and geographically determined conceptions of nature and specific patterns of resource use.

The Nation and the Left

Today, appeals to the nation are often seen as conservative or reactionary—the nation-state is merely as a passing stage on the way to global governance while on the other hand global vision is seen as the progressive trademark. David Harvey claims that: "In the contemporary world the nation-states mostly carved out over the last hundred years maintain a privileged position even though they make no necessary politico-ecological sense" (204). However, since the globalist turn of capitalism in the 1990s, Harvey's position finds itself in collusion with a neoliberal attack on state regulation by global economic actors. To reevaluate the national frame, it is useful to look at the debate of the "national question" during the Second International, in the wake of the October Revolution. According to E. J. Hobsbawm, this debate is underestimated (2).

The premise of the debate is Marx and Engels's insight that the nation is a stage of historical development (Hobsbawm 41; "Critical Remarks on the National Question"), not a mystical essence. The debate was necessary, as the nation had tremendous appeal for the masses and could not be ignored despite the idea that it would wither in later stages of global capitalism (Hobsbawm 43, 124). Writing well before the Russian Revolution, Lenin welcomed the projected global turn as a future ideal, not mistaking it for the concrete historical situation. Therefore, even while he insisted on the primacy of the class perspective, he understood the importance of the nation, expressed politically as the right to self-determination, and consequently he supported the secessions of Poland, Norway, and Ireland ("The Right of Nations"). For Lenin, the litmus test for acceptable nationalism was equality between nation-states and the equal democratic rights of nationalities inside one territory, an ideal that he saw realized in Switzerland ("Critical Remarks"). The globalist left today appears to be caught in the eschatological part of Marxist thought, ignoring the Leninist lesson of adapting politics to concrete historical situations. Complementary to Lenin's understanding of the nation as a political category, linked to a specific historical situation and expressed as sovereignty, is the definition of the nation in cultural terms. Again, in 1913, before the Bolsheviks came to power, Joseph Stalin presented his definition of the nation, which is "well known among historians" (Hobsbawm 2): "A nation is a historically constituted, stable community of people, formed on the basis of a common language, territory, economic life, and psychological make-up manifested in a common culture" (cited in Baudet 61). Stalin further pointed out that the national character is dynamic, it "is not a thing that is fixed once and for all, but is modified by changes in the conditions of life" ("Marxism and the National Question").[3]

Lenin and Stalin exemplify two understandings of nationality—Lenin's is based on political sovereignty and Stalin's on culture. While Stalin's cultural approach could be seen to complement Lenin's idea of political sovereignty, this is not necessarily the case the other way around: cultural sovereignty could override its political counterpart. This is what happened in the Soviet Union, where a predominantly cultural approach to nationality went along with forced relocations of national groups and the dilution of national majorities in the Soviet republics and territories for the sake of political control. Today, the idea of cultural sovereignty dominates the discourse of political globalism, which considering historical precedent, should be reason for concern. The idea that the political sovereignty of nations is obsolete leads to the delegitimization of political structures that have the potential to compete with global capitalism. The lesson here is that sovereignty is a prerequisite for political decision-making, and an understanding of nationality as culture cannot create this mandate.

The key point is that a nation is not "a synonym for state, religion, ethnicity, or lifestyle" but "denote[s] a political loyalty stemming from an experienced collective identity [and is] of a sociological rather than a legal, credal, or ethnic nature" (Baudet 60). The nation in this sense is not inherently exclusive, but "a shared national identity [can] in fact bridge the differences in a diverse and cosmopolitan society" (214). The nation is an imagined community, insofar as it contributes to territorial integrity (62), and as long as it implies "a loyalty towards the way of life in that territory," including "a sense of care for both the human and the natural environment" (223). Nations are defined by social interaction in the public sphere they create.

Elements of the public sphere are a common language, a patrimony in the form of heritage, and the rule of law (229–31). Environmentality can be seen as another aspect of the public sphere, created through political debate regarding the use of resources and the application of conservation measures, as well as through shared mythologies and patterns of using nature.

Citizenship in the widest sense could be defined as structured participation in a larger political entity, in a society or state. Charles Tilly distinguishes between two types of citizenship. One is individualistic and is based on achieving a set of rights; this definition can be seen as a political formalization of the identity discourse. The other definition is relational—Tilly paraphrases Seymour Martin Lipset thus: "Those people who are included in a given state's circle of full political participation" (Tilly 8). Participation and involvement can vary, as Tilly explains: "Citizenship can then range from thin to thick: *thin* where it entails few transactions, rights, and obligations; *thick* where it occupies a significant share of all transactions, rights and obligations sustained by state agents and people living under their jurisdiction" (8). A useful scale to grade participation is Sherry R. Arnstein's "ladder of citizen participation," which has been an influential model (217). Participation here is graded from nonparticipation (manipulation, therapy), to degrees of tokenism (informing, consultation, placation), to degrees of citizen power (partnership, delegated power, citizen control) (217). While meaningful participation in society through the state is a cornerstone of citizenship, the mutual obligations entailed should also include a relation to the environment. Such a relation, encompassing both social and natural values, is coded in the concept of landscape.

While its aesthetic cultural dimension is well known, Kenneth Olwig presents another landscape perspective, distinguishing between a static, aesthetic, and space-oriented or "spatial" perspective on the one hand and a place-oriented or "platial" dynamic one that includes human activity on the other. In the platial view, landscape is marked by transformation, and much of this transformation is based on work. Transformation through work can be informal and symbolic, such as in the community gardens in German cities, or it can be regulated through national law, such as with German allotment gardens or Russian dachas, and supplement the agriculture contributing to national sustenance.[4] Whereas the former socialist states saw their raison d'être in transformation through work, environmentalism tends to be skeptical; the problem here is that the justified pointing at ecological consequences interferes with the communality generated through work. Transformations cannot exclusively be evaluated in terms of their ecological effects. Transformations need to be guided by goals, and these goals are the collective goals for an imagined future, which draw upon shared traditions and values. Rather than following the postmodernist path of rejecting both tradition and Utopia, environmentalism could present particular narratives and their transformational potential, with a basis in the geographical conditions of the territory and its past transformations, history, and myths.

From a socialist perspective, life means struggle and transformation through work. This struggle is multifaceted: creating a society means to tame and transform the forces of nature. From an environmental perspective, this position is easily dismissed as being as destructive as early capitalist industrialization. But what are the alternatives? The easiest alternative is to greenwash capitalism with symbolic policies and new technologies that maintain growth and individualistic patterns of consumption, such as the promotion of electric cars. An ultimately unviable but popular alternative among environmentalists, is to project a universal Edenic future, where nature determines limits, and where both human relations and the human relation to nature are marked by reason and harmony—where all living beings, ecosystems, and eventually the planet have equal rights. One has to be wary of such a non-anthropocentric environmentalism, as it glosses over cultural differences and does not answer the question of governmentality. A third alternative is to update the socialist nation-state centered alternative and infuse it with ecological awareness.

Struggles arise through the perception of limits, and the experience of common limits is an important dimension of citizenship. In its most tangible form, a territory is limited by political boundaries; furthermore, it is limited by geography, climate, the presence or absence of resources, and by its geopolitical position. Participation, transformation, and the awareness of limits are elements of citizenship, and when they are shared by citizens in a territory, a demos is created. It is not impossible that one day a global demos will exist, but the current undermining of citizenship through both consumerist atomization and the mirage of a global order weakens effective political instruments and the affective glue of societies, relational structures, and narratives.

The Dismissal of the National Frame in the Environmental Humanities

The indexes of some standard works in the environmental humanities, Lawrence Buell's *Environmental Imagination*, Cheryl Glotfelty and Harold Fromm's *Ecocriticism Reader*, William Cronon's *Uncommon Ground*, and

Roderick Frazier Nash's *Wilderness and the American Mind* show zero results for *nation* or its derivations (except for terms such as *national parks*).[5] Kate Soper's *What Is Nature?* mentions the nation but treats it as verboten territory: "Romantic conceptions of 'nature' as wholesome salvation from cultural decadence and racial degeneration were crucial to the construction of Nazi ideology, and an aesthetic of 'nature' as source of purity and authentic self-identification has been a component of all forms of racism, tribalism, and nationalism" (32). Soper further explains that "the idea of the nation as tribe or family, whose members are linked by the blood-tie, is manifestly an attempt to create a piece of 'nature' " and that "[b]y means of nationalist bonding—the ideology of the tribe—the attempt is made to secure and legitimate a conventional order of civil power by projecting it back to a primordial state of nature" (110). But defining the nation with blood-ties is reductive and calling nationalism "the ideology of the tribe" is historically incorrect, as the nation is at least in part a product of modern capitalism. Further, this take on the "conventional order of civil power" obscures the fact that the democratic institutions of civil societies rely on this power.

In American literary criticism, the nation was abandoned in a trajectory that transformed American nature writing into global environmental literature. The poet and dedicated environmentalist, Gary Snyder (born 1930) reflects this trend from nature writing as national expression to global environmental literature: "We all know that the 'post–Cold War' era has suddenly and rudely ended, and we have entered a period in which global relations are defined by new nationalisms, religious fundamentalism, developed world hubris, stepped-up environmental damage everywhere, and expanding problems of health and poverty" ("Ecology" 2). As a solution, Snyder suggests: "Why not try the bioregional approach and declare the boundaries between the United States and Mexico, the United States and Canada, null and void" (cited in Heise 43). This is a statement that reflects and represents the economic reality of free trade. NAFTA and its successor, USMCA, have torn down the economic aspects of those boundaries, betraying the similarity between the global capitalist and global environmentalist discourses. Apart from the limitations of taking a functionalist approach to nature, activity at the regional level as advocated by Snyder lacks political force and therefore cannot replace the national level. The local and the regional have become a kind of refuge from the world, an irony considering Slavoj Žižek's observation that all localisms require large-scale organization: "I always try to enumerate how many things have to *function* at a state level so that they could do their so-called 'local self-management or communal organization' " (76, emphasis Žižek).

Global vs. National Framing

A global framing of the environment interferes with emotional attachment to nature in the form of myth. Simon Schama shows that those myths create national landscapes:

> It is clear that inherited landscape myths and memories share two common characteristics: their surprising endurance through the centuries and the power to shape institutions that we still live with. National identity, to take just the most obvious example, would lose much of its ferocious enchantment without the mystique of a particular landscape tradition: its topography mapped, elaborated, and enriched as a homeland. (15)

Cultural geography explores the link between territorial identity, physical landscape, and landscape perception. Christopher Ely, for example, analyzes the Russian attitude to landscape in the nineteenth century: "Only after the need to develop a well-defined sense of national identity became a pressing cultural concern did Russia finally break with the dominance of European landscape aesthetics in order to create alternative aesthetic values capable of embracing the unique appearance of the native land" (5). Maunu Häyrynen makes a similar case for Finland: "Finnish landscape imagery, gradually established during the nineteenth century and becoming a standard during the twentieth, has been a key element in conditioning the Finnish community to perceive the national territory, along with its boundaries, internal divisions, and social differences, as an organic and rational whole" (486). Häyrynen presents this landscape imagery as a dynamic "theory of seeing" where "the national landscape imagery permeates the everyday life of the Finnish society, shaping the very environment it claims to represent" (486). Häyrynen is aware of the risks of a national frame—that it celebrates what it should analyze—but he argues that one can "study the evolution of national representational systems, provided that it is done in a critical and historically context-sensitive way" (486).

Landscape identity is grounded in differentiation to other environments or patterns of landscape perception, as Sverker Sörlin argues: "It is a process of differentiating one area from another, establishing communities of affection and memory, the processes by which people can feel belonging to a place, a nation" (276). Here, Sörlin too swiftly equates local communities of affection (marked by face-to-face contact) and the nation (marked by institutionalized societal relations), but it can be argued that nations are extrapolations of a local sense of belonging. Ironically, as Olwig shows, nation building often eliminated local institutions not fitting into the emerging national frame (643). This loss could be labeled as a variant of the tragedy of the commons by damaging local relations to the environment. However, this does not delegitimize the formation of a national identity, in particular since new national myths are the only remaining tie of the growing urban populations to the older cultural landscape and thus to the environment.

While many environmental problems are global, it is fallacious to assume that their solution is inherently global as well. There is an incongruence between the scale of environmental problems and administrative means to solve them, illustrated by Raymond Williams:

> It is no use simply saying to South Wales miners that all around them is an ecological disaster. They already know. They live in it. They have lived in it for generations. They carry it with them in their lungs. . . . But you cannot just say to people who have committed their lives and their communities to certain kinds of production that this has all got to be changed. You can't just say: come out of the harmful industries, come out of the dangerous industries, let us do something better. Everything will have to be done by negotiation, by equitable negotiation, and it will have to be taken steadily along the way. (cited in Harvey 40–41)

Only a national government can effectively be responsible for negotiations about the economic restructuring of an entire region.

An example for invoking different scales in the form of international coordination and national execution is the European Landscape Convention (ELC). The ELC states its general aim as "consolidation of the European identity," but leaves implementation to the national level and even suggests delegation to the regional levels: "Where local and regional authorities have the necessary competence, protection, management and planning of landscapes will be more effective if responsibility for their implementation is entrusted—within the constitutional framework legislatively laid down at national level—to the authorities closest to the communities concerned" (Council of Europe). The ELC has a realistic multilevel approach to landscape management: its international level speaks a universal language, but political power, including deciding how to delegate power to regional levels remains with the nation-state.

Environmentalism finds itself in a situation where it draws on the mechanisms of globalization that it opposes. How to deal with this problem? One can, like Harvey, aim at a transnationalist remaking of political structures: "Organizations, institutions, doctrines, programs, formalized structures and the like simply have to be created" (433) but this seems an unrealistic path, unlike the internationalist European Landscape Convention model. As Western hegemony is fading, universalist environmentalism is increasingly perceived as a tool to maintain that hegemony against an emerging multipolar world order.

Contesting the Language of Eco-globalism: The Meaning of Solidarity

The 1970s saw the beginning of the environmental movement and in the United States nature writing evolved into environmental literature. Looking at environmental literature, with its activist agenda, is useful because it exemplifies abstract political ideas and thus plays an important role in the formation of a political imaginary. One of the most influential writers at that time was Ernest Callenbach, whose 1975 novel *Ecotopia* imagines the secession of Washington, Oregon, and northern California from the United States, forming a new nation. While Callenbach today is seldom mentioned in environmental literary studies, the poems and essays of Gary Snyder, informed by Buddhism, anti-anthropocentrism, and bio-regionalism, form the core of environmental literature today. Callenbach and Snyder respectively represent an internationalist and a transnationalist strain of environmental literature. In his poem "Mother Earth: Her Whales," Snyder challenges Western ethics:

> Brazil says 'sovereign use of Natural Resources'
> Thirty thousand kinds of unknown plants.
> The living and actual people of the jungle
> sold and tortured—
>
> And a robot in a suit who peddles a delusion called 'Brazil'
> can speak for them?
> [. . .]
> *Solidarity*. The People.
> Standing Tree People!

> Flying Bird People!
> Swimming Sea People!
> Four-legged, two-legged, people! ("Turtle Island" 47–48, emphasis Snyder)

The answer to Snyder's rhetorical question is that the American Gary Snyder speaks for them from a universal and post-national ground. But what could replace the flawed nation, the "delusion called 'Brazil' "? In his essay "Four Changes" he envisions a "type of world tribal council" ("Turtle Island" 100) and claims that "we are the first human beings in history to have so much of man's culture and previous experience available to our study, and being free enough of the weight of traditional cultures to seek out a larger identity" (102). This vision short-circuits the local community level to the global level. Snyder's appeals are untainted by historical, social, and political struggles. However, the moral attack on the "robot in a suit" inadvertently aligns itself with the neoliberal attack on national control of resources and economic regulation.

Both neoliberalism and global environmentalism use a functionalist language that is free of particular meaning, but that can be appropriated, as Harvey explains: "[W]ords like 'nature' and 'environment' convey a commonality and universality of concern that can all too easily be captured by particularist politics" (Harvey 118). It is known that neoliberalism naturalizes its ideology with newspeak terms such as "slim state," justifying its attack on social institutions. Snyder's line "Thirty thousand kinds of unknown plants" appeals to scientific reason, following the same ideological traverse of undermining the state or "robot in a suit." The mechanism for this ideological hijacking is that scientific or legal terms are used metaphorically in a political or ethical context, leading to a false sense of objectivity. The anti-anthropocentrism that is a key element for Snyder's stripe of environmentalism is a legal concept applied in an ethical discourse. Gaia is a medical idea, applied metaphorically to the planet. When Snyder, in the introductory note to *Turtle Island*, writes that the "land, the planet itself, is also a living being—at another pace" it should be clear that the planet is not living in any scientific sense of the word, and that taking the metaphor literally and demanding rights for the planet is an ideological operation, not supported by scientific evidence or a legal tradition. Baudet discusses the problem of metaphorical use in environmental discourse:

> Most advocates of all these universal "rights" speak in metaphors rather than in factual terms. They mistake the wish for the reality.

> What is often meant . . . is not "rights" in any juridical sense but "humanitarian principles," "Christian values" or "natural law" *that ought to be installed as rights.*
>
> The same goes for the great number of other "rights" that are currently advocated—for instance "animal rights" and the "rights of the environment." For the defenders of flora and fauna of the world, the word "rights" has a completely different meaning from that in the positive, legal sense. (109, emphasis Baudet)

Baudet argues that this does not mean that human beings have no duties toward animals or the environment, but that the "rights talk impoverishes moral thinking rather than enriching it" (109).

The peril of the metaphorical application of scientific and legal terms in an ethical discourse is that ethically charged metaphors ossify when taken out of their specific fields. In his book *The Rights of Nature*, the environmental historian Roderick Frazier Nash develops a model of ethical extension based on the natural rights discourse, assuming that in an ethical past only self, family, tribe, and region were regarded to be ethical subjects; in an ethical present these cover the nation, races, humans, and some animals, and in an ethical future they encompass plants, life, rocks, ecosystems, the planet, and finally the universe (Nash 5). Nash is aware of the shift of meaning of the term *rights*. Granting that this shift has caused confusion: "while some use the term in a technical philosophical or legal sense, others take it to mean that nature, or parts of it, has intrinsic worth which humans ought to respect" (4). Nash sees Snyder as a "leader in this new nature worship" (114) and argues that Snyder "identified nature as an oppressed minority whose rights civilization violated" (115). Nash also claims that Snyder "rooted his defense of nature in the bedrock of the American political tradition" (115). However, I would argue that the metaphorical use of scientific and legal terms undermines the very notions of politics and history because, as Baudet argues, "[t]he fundamental problem of 'rights' talk is thus that rights (all rights, in all circumstances) are always open to multiple interpretations" and their application "requires a political choice" (112). Rights are linked to political struggles and traditions and are valid in territories. This is why Nash's notion of intrinsic rights of the universe is not only inadvertently anthropocentric (or rather terracentric) but also a politics masquerading as apolitical scientific truth.

Snyder's line "*Solidarity*. The People" contains two key terms of emancipatory struggle, but what do they mean? The term *people* is often used to denote the citizens of a national state, as in the opening of the American Constitution: "We the people." When the people of a country understand themselves as citizens rather than subjects, their struggles create common values and a shared history—a people. Institutions grow representing and safeguarding those values. In Snyder's global sense, however, the term changes its meaning, obfuscating its historical dimension and the struggles behind it. The same goes for *solidarity*. The Merriam-Webster online dictionary defines *solidarity* as "unity (as of a group or class) that produces or is based on community of interests, objectives, and standards." The realization of those interests, objectives, and standards means that they have to be created and asserted in a process of struggle or competition with other groups. The common struggle or competition then forms the basis of a dynamic solidarity in the traditional sense. In Snyder's use of the term, however, solidarity among people, animals, and plants is static and means to accept the order of an ideal world of intrinsic rights.

On the other side of the discursive spectrum, we find Callenbach's novel *Ecotopia*, which was highly popular in the United States and abroad and inspired the emerging German Green Party ("From Capitalism to Ecotopia"). In 1981, Callenbach published a "prequel," *Ecotopia Emerging*, about the events leading to Ecotopian secession. Ecotopians create a new nation by interpreting their national heritage leading to conflictual imaginaries; there is no universal dream, and there are mechanisms of inclusion and exclusion. Harvey criticizes such "exclusionary politics of nationalism and communitarianism" because "memories built around place cannot easily be shared with outsiders" (305). While Harvey is wrong in the sense that "a shared national identity [can] in fact bridge the differences in a diverse and cosmopolitan society" (Baudet 214), he is right in the sense that every political determination is built on a negation (*omnis determinatio negatio est*) and is by definition conflictual. Pure ecological reason without struggle or conflict of interests is a mirage.

A new political party, the Survivalists, are "creating a new sense of community and of shared biological and social destiny" (*Ecotopia Emerging*, 9). The new party's name has an established meaning, but the old survivalists are criticized for not understanding that "[p]ower grows out of social cohesion, not the barrel of a gun" (37). However, the Ecotopians are not pacifists: a militia, the Home Guard, is being established, and it has a military intelligence section (286, 293). The possibility of a civil war is debated (144), and one group of activists proposes to install nuclear mines in major American cities to avert a military attack. The Ecotopian movement here may have been inspired by the American War of Independence. The revolution is a dynamic process of adaptation and formation, but neither an invocation of a mythical essence nor of intrinsic rights. Struggle and involvement create solidarity and eventually form a new people. For their fight for self-determination, Ecotopians use the heritage of the nation they emerged from: Ecotopians see their politics rooted in the League of the Iroquois (44), the Federalist Papers (133), and Jefferson (272). When the Ecotopians plan to introduce an electronic town hall, they link it to Ancient Greece and town meetings of colonial days (120). The first president of Ecotopia, Vera Allwen, declares in one of her "fireside chats" (111) that "Governments are created to serve people, not the other way round" (263), resounding Jefferson's Declaration of Independence.[6] The American and Ecotopian notion of nationality is not ethnic or linguistic but rather is based on a common cause. Hobsbawm calls this the "revolutionary concept of the nation as constituted by the deliberate political action of its potential citizen [which is] still preserved in a pure form in the USA" (88). Ecotopia then brings back this historic (American) nation, which contemporary postcolonial and environmental discourse has reduced to a mere construction.

The idea of a new nation is based on a vision of the future that is too divergent to be compatible with the novel's present United States. The common imaginary and loyalty toward the old system forming its legitimacy disintegrates, and Allwen declares: "At such times old institutions become null and void" (261). In order to have a broad appeal and to form a new people, environmental ideas need to transcend their common middle-class connotations. One of the activists, a lumberjack living in a trailer park states: "Most of the people were loggers or handymen or construction workers—good folks, but not much in the way of money. . . . They didn't have any goddamn hippies or artsy-fartsy types. People chopped their own wood, fixed their own cars, and made their own livings" (41). The points of divergence are the Ecotopian rejection of capitalism, and in particular the automobile: "life without private cars is unthinkable for American people" (124), and "the biggest difference between them and us . . . is that we know the automobile is the enemy and they don't" (149). However, in their visions of the future, the American past is also mirrored, invoking the traditional town and the railway suburb; Ecotopian cities are "compact, energy-conserving mini-cities" characterized by "strong neighborhoods, compact, well-defined, and self-reliant, each one offering its inhabitants the basic necessities: dwellings, workplaces and stores" (67) and connected by "a network of fast trains or streetcars" (68).

The Survivalists promote a steady-state economy with a shrinking population, not permitting migration. Callenbach mentions the fact that Okie migrants were turned back at the California border during the Great Depression. However, this practice was declared unconstitutional then, but the Survivalists draw the conclusion that "though a state border was not a bar to unlimited immigration, a national border certainly would be" (136). These proposals are controversial today, but in the 1970s and 1980s they were in environmental mainstream: For example, in the zero population growth movement. Snyder also proposes "the only real solution: reduce population" by "correct[ing] traditional cultural attitudes that tend to force women into child-bearing" (*Turtle Island* 92).

The Ecotopians have a mutualist economic vision. Worker ownership was an aim of the union movement of the nineteenth century, and the Ecotopian ideal of the extended family merges traditional extended families and countercultural experiments of collective living (125). Likewise, the Ecotopian vision of the good life has a countercultural base. For example, in community gardens people "will have a lot of fun by learning to do things in better ways—but you will also produce a lot of inexpensive, fresh, tasty pure food [and] get to know people while doing it" (181). Not surprisingly, the spiritual life of Ecotopians is a conglomerate of traditional American Christianity and elements of countercultural flirtations with paganism. An evangelical preacher interprets the Garden of Eden ecologically: "For it was not the eating that was the Original Sin. All creatures are created as eaters" (128). The group of activists engaging in ecological sabotage, however, gets inspiration from the Old Testament: "Ye shall reap as ye sow" (213). Traditional holidays are remade in the spirit of their pagan origin because the "ancient solar festivals that fell on the solstices and equinoxes . . . had degenerated into what we know as Christmas and the Fourth of July for the solstices and Easter and Thanksgiving for the equinoxes [but] had lost all their original sacredness" (264–65).

Ecotopians develop the imagined community of their old nation in such a divergent way, that the question of self-determination emerges: "We must form our own new nation" and "we must take the same step our forebears took when the policies of the British government became so intolerable that they were forced to dissociate themselves from it" (*Ecotopia Emerging*, 319). The Ecotopian activists are told that "you have become a new people, with a new language and a new way of understanding, even if you speak with English words" (75). The people of the new nation have no "natural" essence, nor is the nation based on an individual choice of identity or on intrinsic rights, nor does it include all living beings. Rather, it emerges from the solidarity formed in collective struggle in a specific historical moment, drawing on a particular history and geography. *Ecotopia Emerging* is an example for a multilevel approach in environmentalism. Global environmental concerns are translated into local activism as well as nation building; the new structures are based on existing historical, mythological, and political contexts, which create a foundation for environmentality.

Conclusion

The slogan "Save the Planet" has a hollow ring to it not only because it lends itself to greenwashing, but because its global appeal lacks an institutional basis, invokes no shared traditions, myths, or imaginaries, relates to no shared cultural practices of nature use, and reflects no transformations through work or struggle generating solidarity. The globalist left has subscribed to such bloodless rhetoric exactly because it actually is bloodless—not stained by colonial and other abuses. However, it is also bloodless in a metaphorical sense of being apolitical and dispassionate. The old environmental slogan that "there is no free lunch" is also true for this globalist turn. Environmental globalism has become an ally in the neoliberal "starving the beast" attack on the state. In addition, the globalist left abandons its raison d'être, the idea of solidarity through struggle for particular class interests, seen in Snyder's semantic dilution of the term. Globalism creates an inadvertent colonialism, ignoring the liberating role national narratives had in overcoming colonialism as well as the fact that anti-fascist resistance was also often framed in national terms (Hobsbawm 146–48). In Latin America, the terms *nación* and *nacionál* are used frequently by both left and right without colonial guilt but with the connotation of collective empowerment. The globalist turn of the left was thus not caused by its internationalist ideals but by guilt, the conflation of internationalism with transnationalism, and a lack of political pragmatism. There was an alternative, however—a different trajectory of the left political imagination, as the socialist state of Ecotopia shows.

Eco-globalism tends to conflate diverging human interests into a single one—humanity—and further dilutes human interests with its anti-anthropocentrism. The price for ignoring the political arena is a patronizing "nature knows best" authoritarianism that disturbs not only social relations but also human relations to their particular environment. It is oblivious to the fact that state sovereignty is a prerequisite for citizenship in the form of shared and institutionalized control of a territory, as well as participation in shared imaginaries, uses of natural spaces, and affective engagement in nature—elements that are coded as landscape. Eco-globalism replaces those particular narratives and structures with uniform concepts and plans, such as the Sustainable Development Goals of the United Nations. These plans are then implemented into national plans, trickling down into various fields such as education, into national school curricula, and further into textbooks and classrooms. In this top-down approach, debates are replaced by moral imperatives created by an unaccountable guardian class, turning citizens in their different roles, such as teachers and students, into implementers of plans. Globalization is an economic process driven by class interests; it does not entail frames of political participation, cultural practices, or aesthetic sensibility, and is therefore antagonistic to an environmentalism that respects particular human agency.

Notes

1. The idea of political organization that fundamentally opposes supranationalism and multiculturalism—the idea of the nation-state—has been declared "outdated" and "irrelevant" by an overwhelming number of commentators. Yet, while supranationalism and multiculturalism have dominated politics and academia over the last several decades, their popularity is questionable and debates about national identity divide most European countries at present (Baudet 3).

2. It could be argued that regulatory environmentalism or "green state" has mainly displaced early twentieth-century environmental mythologies and narratives. One may counter this argument by arguing that environmental policies do not make a green state and that the disappearance of mythologies is a postmodern characteristic. But the real question here is about the control and scale of administration: Are regulations and administrative practices an expression of the political will of citizens of a territory guided by particular values and traditions, or are administrative authorities just implementers of globalist or supranational plans? The latter case points at a potential conflict between environmentalism and democracy.

3. Robert Tucker dismissed Trotsky's view that Stalin was not the real author of the national question and other writings.

4. See Bigell (2015) for a discussion of German community and allotment gardens.

5. In contrast, the collection of essays in the field of cultural geography, *Nordic Landscapes: Region and Belonging on the Northern Edge of Europe* (Jones and Olwig), contains half a page of such references.

6. Refers to Franklin Delano Roosevelt's Fireside Chats, transmitted on the radio between 1933 and 1944.

Works Cited

Arnstein, Sherry R. "A Ladder of Citizen Participation." *Journal of the American Institute of Planners*, vol. 35, no. 4, Fall 1969, pp. 216–24.

Baudet, Thierry. *The Significance of Borders: Why Representative Government and the Rule of Law Require Nation States*. Brill, 2012.

Bigell, Werner. "Allotment and Community Gardens: Commons in German Cities." *Spaces In-Between: Cultural and Political Perspectives on Environmental Discourse*, edited by Sigurd Bergmann and Mark Luccarelli, Brill Rodopi, 2015, pp. 102–30.

Buell, Lawrence. *The Environmental Imagination: Thoreau, Nature Writing, and the Formation of American Culture*. Harvard UP, 1996.

Callenbach, Ernest. *Ecotopia Emerging*. Banyan Tree Books, 1981.

———. "From Capitalism to Ecotopia: A Successionist Manifesto." 2006, www.ernestcallenbach.com/lectures. Accessed 20 April 2015.

Council of Europe. "European Landscape Convention—Explanatory Report." 2000, conventions.coe.int/Treaty/EN/Reports/Html/176.htm. Accessed 20 April 2015.

Cronon, William. *Uncommon Ground: Rethinking the Human Place in Nature*. W. W. Norton, 1996.

Ely, Christopher. *This Meager Nature: Landscape and National Identity in Imperial Russia*. Northern Illinois UP, 2002.

Glotfelty, Cheryll, and Harold Fromm. *The Ecocriticism Reader: Landmarks in Literary Ecology*. U of Georgia P, 1996.

Harvey, David. *Justice, Nature, and the Geography of Difference*. Blackwell, 1996.

Häyrynen, Maunu. "A Kaleidoscopic Nation: The Finnish National Landscape Imagery." *Nordic Landscapes: Region and Belonging on the Northern Edge of Europe*, edited by Jones and Olwig, pp. 483–510.

Heise, Ursula. *Sense of Place and Sense of Planet: The Environmental Imagination of the Global*. Oxford UP, 2008.

Hobsbawm, E. J. *Nations and Nationalism since 1780*. Cambridge UP, 1990.

Jones, Michael, and Kenneth Olwig, editors. *Nordic Landscapes: Region and Belonging on the Northern Edge of Europe*. U of Minnesota P, 2008.

Lenin, Vladimir Ilyich. "Critical Remarks on the National Question." 1913, www.marxists.org/archive/lenin/works/1913/crnq/. Accessed 1 Sept. 2015.

———. "The Right of Nations to Self-Determination." 1914, www.marxists.org/archive/lenin/works/1914/self-det/. Accessed 1 Sept. 2015.

Nash, Roderick Frazier. *The Rights of Nature: A History of Environmental Ethics*. U of Wisconsin P, 1989.

Olwig, Kenneth R. "Recovering the Substantive Nature of Landscape." *Annals of the Association of American Geographers*, vol. 86, no. 4, Dec. 1996, pp. 630–53.

Schama, Simon. *Landscape and Memory.* Knopf, 1995.

Snyder, Gary. *Turtle Island.* New Directions, 1974.

———. "Ecology, Literature, and the New World Disorder." *ISLE, Interdisciplinary Studies in Literature and Environment*, vol. 11, no. 1, Winter 2004, pp. 1–14.

Soper, Kate. *What Is Nature?* Blackwell, 1995.

Sörlin, Sverker. "Monument and Memory: Landscape Imagery and the Articulation of Territory." *Worldviews: Environment, Culture, Religion*, vol. 2, no. 3, 1998, pp. 269–79.

Stalin, Joseph. "Marxism and the National Question." 1913, www.marxists.org/reference/archive/stalin/works/1913/03.htm. Accessed 20 April 2015.

Tucker, Robert C. *Stalin as Revolutionary, 1879–1929: A Study in History and Personality*. W. W. Norton, 1973.

Tilly, Charles. "Citizenship, Identity and Social History." *International Review of Social History*, vol. 40, no. S3, Dec. 1995, pp. 1–17.

Žižek, Slavoj. *Demanding the Impossible.* Polity Press, 2013.

Part II

Contextualizing the National

Constraints and Possibilities

Chapter 5

Belonging

Population Genetics, National Imaginaries, and the Making of European Genes

Venla Oikkonen

Introduction

National narratives and imaginaries typically celebrate the roots of the nation: the moments that can be construed in retrospect as foundational to the emergence of the nation as a coherent historical entity. Since the eighteenth century in particular, national narratives have often drawn on the natural sciences—paleontology, geology, comparative anatomy, evolutionary theory—to promote the uniqueness and coherence of the national community. Ancient hominid remains have played a key role in attempts to establish ancient roots for the nation through science. Ancient remains have provided a means of ascribing great antiquity to the modern national population by connecting it to the imagined prehistoric landscape of the region (for examples, see Goulden; Oikkonen 73–129; Sommer).

Since the 1990s, human population genetics—the study of genetic variation among human populations—has served increasingly as a rhetorical and imaginative resource for national narratives. For example, the various national genome initiatives that have appeared since the late 1990s generally operate on the premise that the national population is a meaningful unit of genetic analysis. Helen Busby and Paul Martin have explored this dynamic in the context of the United Kingdom; Amy Hinterberger in the case of Quebec, Canada ("Investing"); and Aaro Tupasela in the context of Finland. Technological developments have also increasingly enabled the analysis of DNA retrieved from ancient human remains. By conjoining population genetic study of human genetic diversity and paleontological examination of ancient human remains, ancient DNA research has appealed to those wishing to establish a material trajectory between modern and ancient human populations.

In this chapter, I interrogate how human population genetics, and especially ancient DNA research, has shaped how the evolutionary roots of nations and national communities may be conceptualized. The central argument is that modern nations and prehistoric populations are not easily compatible. Yet, as I will show, population genetics and ancient DNA are repeatedly invoked to establish appealing narratives of national or ethnic belonging across the political continuum. These narratives have included, on the one hand, empowering personal accounts of ethnic roots produced through genetic ancestry tests, as Alondra Nelson has shown and, on the other hand, populist nationalist accounts of "authentic" national communities, as Anne-Marie Fortier has demonstrated. I am interested in the ambiguity of communal origins produced through population genetics and ancient DNA: population genetics can be invoked and appropriated to support various kinds of local, global, and national communities as well as a range of political positions. In what follows, I explore how the discrepancy between modern national and ancient human populations, and the ambiguity of population genetic belonging, challenge the evolutionary rootedness of national communities, and how such ambiguity affects how national belonging can be imagined through population genetics and ancient DNA. In particular, I focus on the tensions between national, continental, regional, and personal genetic belonging.

I address these questions through the case of "Ötzi the Iceman," the 5,300-year-old natural mummy discovered in Tyrol close to the Austrian-Italian border in 1991. The chapter explores the discursive and technological means through which Ötzi was variedly rendered Austrian, Italian, Tyrolean, and European as his bones, clothes, equipment, and stomach contents underwent scientific analysis. The primary focus is on the impact of genetic analysis on Ötzi's role as a prehistoric, geographically located individual. I use the public and scientific debates about Ötzi's genetic place in human evolution and the peopling of Europe to examine the cultural appeal and conceptual limits of genetic knowledge. As my focus is on conceptual issues arising from the conjoiner of ancient DNA and national frameworks, the chapter does not engage in an in-depth analysis of these debates but uses selected examples to illustrate key questions that Ötzi's discovery mobilized. Throughout the chapter, I approach ancient human DNA as an epistemically contested site through which ideas of local, national, continental, and personal genetic belonging are debated and negotiated. The case of Ötzi sheds light on both the appeal and complications of crafting evolutionary national narratives through a past that precedes nation-states by millennia.

Human Population Genetics

Human population genetics studies genetic variation between and within human populations. Historically, population genetics has often focused on the analysis of noncoding DNA (DNA that does not control physiological or behavioral characteristics) and nonrecombining DNA (DNA inherited from only one parent). Most important sources of such genetic material were the noncoding sections of mitochondria—tiny organelles located outside the cell nucleus and inherited from the mother—and the nonrecombining section of the Y-chromosome inherited from the father. As changes in mitochondrial and nonrecombining Y-chromosomal DNA result primarily from mutations, mitochondrial and Y-chromosome DNA were used as a so-called *molecular clock*. The idea is that the more differences there are between two DNA sequences, the longer the evolutionary distance between the populations they represent. The approach has been used to build evolutionary trees to trace when particular species or populations diverged in evolutionary history.

The growing availability of high-throughput sequencing technologies since about 2005 has also increasingly enabled genome-wide approaches. While genome-wide approaches vary, they often identify and compare SNPs (single nucleotide polymorphisms; that is, molecular sites were people vary)—especially markers associated with particular populations—across a person's overall genetic makeup. Whereas mitochondrial and Y-chromosome analyses have produced evolutionary trees that rely, respectively, on exclusively matrilineal and patrilineal genealogies, genome-wide techniques engender evolutionary histories that seek to encompass the reshuffling of genetic material within populations.

Population genetics has provided a culturally powerful means of reimagining the relationships between modern human populations and the place of each population in human evolution. Many of these projects have centered on the idea of national community and national belonging as rooted in evolutionary history, as is evident in the plentitude of national genome projects and biobank initiatives that seek to capture the genetic nature of the national population (for examples, see Kent et al.; Mitchell and Waldby; Nash 101–35). Yet this national framing is awkward for several reasons.

First, there is a discrepancy between national and evolutionary frameworks in terms of their temporal and spatial investments. Evolutionary history involves the migrations of human populations across continents over millennia, and the gradual divergence of populations, a process that does not typically involve clear temporal breaks or geographical boundaries. The slow view of change characteristic of the evolutionary framework seldom coincides with the considerably shorter timeframe of national narratives. Likewise, populations studied in population genetics do not generally follow neat national borders, since current national borders are mostly of modern origin. This underscores that the national population is not a naturally existing entity and may not be meaningful in an evolutionary context. National communities emerge as evolutionary communities only *within a particular temporal and spatial framing*. If the temporal or spatial parameters are changed, different kinds of communities—regional, transnational, continental, global—emerge as primary to the national community.

Second, population genetics is not a fixed approach, but a dynamic set of techniques and materials that are used to tease out various sets of differences and similarities depending on the kinds of questions that scientists are trying to answer. Amy Hinterberger ("Investing") and Amade M'charek have both shown how the very concept of population remains unfixed in order to operate as a methodological tool. Through the example of forensic genetics, M'charek demonstrates that the concept of population undergoes various technological and methodological adjustments in order to connect a DNA sample from a crime scene to an ethnic population (21–55). As for the use of population genetics to narrate national origins, a seemingly minor change in the methodological and technological setting of such analysis may engender forms of genetic belonging that contradict the idea of the national community as a coherent entity. What counts as *sameness* in one research setting emerges as *difference* when the setting is changed, as difference and sameness are tied to the choice of technology and computer software, availability of samples, and access to existing genetic databases. My discussion of Ötzi highlights the consequences of these issues for genetically grounded belonging.

In the analysis that follows, I use the case of Ötzi to demonstrate how this ambiguity of genetic population haunts the coherence of national narratives of belonging. I show how population genetics nevertheless remains an appealing rhetorical and affective resource for national imaginaries due to the epistemic power assigned to DNA in contemporary culture. While with population genetics, the practices of marking differences and similarities are relative—that is, differences are always situated and technologically bound—in popular discourse DNA is made to stand for permanence, indisputability, and precision. DNA thus tends to appear as the ultimate proof of origins, boundaries, and belonging. Through this cultural appeal of genetic discourse, the ambiguity of evolutionary populations and belonging often becomes erased and domesticated.

Ancient DNA

In the 1980s, many researchers turned toward mummified remains and museum specimens to retrieve DNA. The first two important cases were Higushi et al.'s extraction of mitochondrial DNA from a 140-year-old quagga, an extinct species related to zebra, and Svante Pääbo's analysis of mitochondrial DNA from an Egyptian mummy. With the development of a technique for DNA amplification known as *polymerase chain reaction* (PCR), genetic material retrieved from old remains emerged as a highly interesting object of study in the early 1990s. Many of the early studies—such as a claimed analysis of dinosaur DNA—were later shown to be products of contamination by modern DNA left by archeologists, museum workers, or geneticists themselves. Nevertheless, toward the end of the 1990s several significant studies of ancient DNA had been published, including Handt et al.'s analysis of Ötzi's mitochondrial DNA in 1994, and Krings et al.'s analysis of a mitochondrial sequence from Neanderthal remains in Germany in 1997. With the increasingly routine use of high-throughput sequencing technologies in the past decade, ancient DNA studies have proliferated (see Hofreiter et al.; Perry and Orlando; Rizzi et al.). A large number of genetic studies of considerably old remains, such as Rasmussen et al.'s analysis of the 9,000-year-old human remains known as Kennewick Man (the Ancient One) in Washington State, have been published. Instead of relying on mitochondrial DNA, these technologically advanced studies have employed genome-wide techniques.

Apart from providing new knowledge on extinct species and past populations, ancient DNA promised to complicate the evolutionary trees produced by population genetics. Population genetics had largely operated on DNA collected from living people. Variations within modern samples have been used to construct evolutionary histories that show when particular populations or species diverged. The appeal of ancient DNA lay in its promise of material concreteness. Instead of having to rely on extrapolation from modern samples, scientists could see what ancient sequences looked like. One advantage was that ancient samples could point to now-extinct variations that could not be detected through modern samples. The idea of a direct material connection between modern populations and a prehistoric ancestor had obvious cultural appeal. By conjoining the materiality of ancient bones with the imagined material precision of DNA, the study of ancient remains appears to establish a firm and indisputable link between us and our genetic roots. Without ancient DNA, those roots would remain largely theoretical and statistical. However, the assumed concreteness of the connection between modern and ancient samples is somewhat misleading, as the connection relies on methodological choices, statistical software, availability of samples, and selection of SNPs for analysis (see Oikkonen 73–129 for further discussion).

Biological material discovered in melting permafrost has provided an important source of ancient DNA, as ice can preserve DNA without significant degradation. The discovery of Ötzi in the Alps in 1991 was a key event in the scientific use of naturally frozen remains in the study of human evolutionary history. Ötzi's body was remarkably well-preserved under the ice and therefore a unique source of information, though the body's condition was not necessary to human population genetics. Advanced sequencing technologies developed in the past decade have enabled scientists to retrieve DNA from astonishingly small samples. In 2010, Rasmussen et al. analyzed DNA from human hair discovered in permafrost in Greenland to construct the genome of a 5,000-year-old man ("Extinct Palaeo-Eskimo"). Also, in 2010, Krause et al. and Reich et al. constructed the evolutionary history of a previously unknown hominin population—the Denisovan—based on DNA retrieved from a finger bone and tooth discovered in a cave in Siberia. Crucially, discoveries like Ötzi or the Denisovan appear to challenge the sense of temporal distance that organizes the cultural view of prehistory as a far-gone realm. In his discussion of Ötzi, David Turnbull argues that *cryopreservation*—the preservation of biological material, such as DNA, in ice—unsettles prevalent assumptions of temporality and spatiality in foundational ways. Turnbull shows how the discovery of hominin remains in melting ice engenders unexpected constellations of time and space, and how a range of technological maneuvers, such as different types of scientific analysis and narrative framings, are brought together to produce a coherent account of human evolutionary history.

The Discovery of Ötzi

In September 1991, two German hikers came across a frozen corpse protruding from the ice close to the Austrian–Italian border in the Ötztal Alps. The body was initially thought to be a deceased hiker, but a closer examination a few days later revealed that the body was much older. Subsequent radiocarbon dating established the age of the remains, dubbed "Ötzi" or "the Tyrolean Iceman," at about 5,300 years. What made the discovery so remarkable was the well-preserved state of the body: to date, Ötzi is the oldest known natural mummy discovered in Europe. He even had red blood cells still in his body.

Since the discovery, Ötzi has undergone extensive scientific study including, for example, an analysis of the contents of his stomach, indicating when and what he ate before his death (Dickson et al.; Oeggl et al.; Rollo et al., "Last Meals"); analysis of the pollen present in the food, locating his death in the spring (Oeggl); analysis of the isotopic composition of his tooth enamel, indicating where he grew up and where he lived in the surrounding regions (Müller et al.); and an analysis of so-called Beau's lines on his nail, suggesting several bouts of sickness during the last six months of his life. Aspöck et al. showed that Ötzi had an intestinal parasite—a whipworm—whilst Maixner et al. identified the strain of *Helicobacter pylori* in his gastrointestinal track. Scientists have also presented a number of theories on how Ötzi died, including hypothermia, loss of blood from an arrow wound, a blow to the head, and ritual killing; and why he was undertaking the arduous trip across the mountains: Was he hunting, or herding, or perhaps fleeing? His sophisticated clothing and equipment, which included a prestigious copper ax and medicinal supplies, have given rise to various theories on his social role and rank. Who was Ötzi, where did he come from, and where did he belong in human evolutionary history?

Genetics played a key role in addressing these questions. The first genetic studies examined Ötzi's mitochondrial DNA, a focus that reflected the technological state of ancient DNA research at the time. Handt et al.'s 1994 study was able to locate and amplify one section of noncoding mitochondrial DNA that was not too badly degraded or contaminated by other

DNA. The paper concluded that Ötzi's mitochondrial sequence "seems to fit within the European gene pool" while being "closest . . . to the individuals from the Alpine region" (1778). Furthermore, the paper states that Ötzi's sequence has "been found in 7 of 155 individuals from northern Germany, Denmark, and Iceland and twice among 100 British Caucasoids" (1778). In the wake of advances in sequencing technologies in the mid-2000s, this initial study was complemented by several new studies, including Rollo et al.'s more detailed analysis of Ötzi's mitochondrial DNA in 2006 based on new samples retrieved from his intestines ("Fine Characterization"), and Ermini et al.'s sequencing of his whole mitochondrial genome in 2008. These analyses showed that Ötzi belonged to a previously unknown branch of the mitochondrial subclade K1, a result that was confirmed by Endicott et al.'s 2009 study.

In 2012, almost twenty years after Handt and colleagues' initial mitochondrial analysis, Keller et al. were able to sequence Ötzi's nuclear genome. The new study traced a number of SNPs associated with physiological characteristics, such as eye color, blood group, lactose intolerance, and susceptibility to coronary heart disease. While the mitochondrial analyses had suggested that Ötzi was connected to populations around the Alps, the sequencing of his nuclear genome pointed to recent common ancestry between him and present-day populations of the Mediterranean islands of Sardinia and Corsica. The study also identified Ötzi's Y-chromosome haplogroup as G2a4–L91, a haplogroup that is particularly common in southern Corsica and northern Sardinia. Sikora et al.'s 2014 population genomic analysis of Ötzi, along with several other European ancient remains and additional samples from modern European populations, provided further details and corroboration.

National, Regional, or Continental Belonging?

Although the genetic studies of Ötzi's mitochondrial and nuclear DNA deployed the technical language of populations, haplogroups, and SNPs, such studies were engaged in conceptualizing Ötzi's prehistoric existence in terms of ethnic, racial, and regional affiliations. This becomes clear already in Handt and colleagues' 1994 paper, which suggested that "comparisons of DNA sequences from the body with contemporary populations may reveal aspects of his ethnic affiliation" (1775). This is in line with the discourses and framings of population genetics and ancient DNA studies at the time (Oikkonen 73–129). As we saw above, the genetic studies that emerged after

2005 provided increasing detail and specificity about Ötzi's genetic origins. Yet, as I will argue next, pinning Ötzi down to a national or regional identity is a complicated issue, and genetics can engender only a specific, epistemically situated view into Ötzi's national, regional, and ethnic belonging.

First of all, the question of Ötzi's national affiliation is closely tied to the shape of modern nations. What is interesting about Ötzi's case is that his body was found on the section of the Austrian-Italian border where the precise location of the border was unmarked due to the long-standing presence of thick ice. Consequently, Ötzi was first assumed to be found on the Austrian side and was sent to Innsbruck but was soon deemed to have been discovered in Italy, and arrangements were made to move his body eventually to the South Tyrol Museum of Archaeology in Bolzano. Turnbull observes that "[t]he question of Ötzi's retrospective nationalization was so intense that it led to an official surveying and marking of the border. It was determined that Ötzi was spatially located 92 meters on the Italian side of the border. After intense negotiations he was rechristened with an Italian identity" (160; see also Spindler 66–69). Ötzi's ambiguous national identity was reflected in media accounts. For example, *The Guardian* described Ötzi as "the 5,000-year-old Austrian iceman" in 1995, while an article in the British paper *The Observer* published in 1994 called him "an Italian Iceman" (McKie, "Italian Iceman," 5). In addition to national identities, Ötzi has also been given regional identities such as the "oldest of Tyroleans" (Anastas A108). My point here is not to suggest that one assignment of identity is right and the others wrong—that is, whether Ötzi was Italian or Austrian or simply Tyrolean. Rather, I want to highlight that national categories of belonging simply do not make sense in the context of prehistoric events 5,000 years ago.

Furthermore, even modern borders are not clear and unambiguous. Borders are multiple. For example, different forms of surveillance and border control, or disparate personal, communal, and institutional practices of border crossing define borders differently, as Sarah Green as well as M'charek et al. have shown. In the case of Ötzi, his renaming as "Italian" did not simply correct an error, but rather made visible the multiplicity and ambiguity of borders. Although Ötzi's discovery site turned out to be located on the Italian side of the unmarked border, the melting waters from the discovery site drained to the Austrian side, suggesting that the site was in fact part of Austrian Tyrol, and that the current border was a misevaluation made possible by the ice cover. Turnbull argues that this resulted in "a topographic reality incompatible with a political reality in which Ötzi resides in an

Italian museum" (160). To complicate issues further, borders have histories. In Ötzi's case, South Tyrol had been annexed by Italy after World War I; before that it had belonged to the Austrian-Hungarian Empire. Crucially, feelings of resentment still lived in parts of Tyrol, registered, for example, by a 1998 account in *The Washington Post* noting that "the date of the transfer [from Innsbruck to Bolzano] was kept secret, partly because of threats from Austrian nationalists who have never recognized the South Tyrol annexation" (Haller A19). This shows that in debates about genetics and national identity, it is pivotal to recognize that nations are historical entities with their own intertwined and often complicated histories. The power of population genetics to engender national belonging is thus challenged not only by the discrepancy between the modernity of nation-states compared to the antiquity of evolutionary landscapes. It is also complicated by the tension between the temporality of the nation—the emergence of a nation as a process that takes shape in relation to other nations—and the temporality of species-level evolutionary processes, such as human evolution. These national and evolutionary temporalities become entangled in problematic ways when scientists use historically evolved cultural concepts or administrative terms relating to ethnicity, kinship arrangements, or societal identity, to define scientific or technical terms such as population, as Amy Hinterberger ("Categorization"), Nina Kohli-Laven, and Tutton et al. have shown.

Second, there is a clear tension between national and continental frameworks of genetic belonging. While the media liked to frame Ötzi as "Italian" or "Austrian," they also portrayed him as "European." For example, the British newspaper *The Guardian* suggested in 1995 that based on Ötzi's genetic likeness with modern European samples, "he was, above all, a European" (*The Guardian* 26); a 2003 article in the British paper *The Observer* referred to Ötzi as a "Stone Age European" (McKie, "Secrets," 7); and a recent article in *The New York Times* maintains that Ötzi "has provided a trove of information about the life of Europeans at that time" (Wade). I suggest that the simultaneous presence of European, national, and regional frameworks in public discourses about Ötzi arise, to a considerable extent, from technological and material practices. Depending on the kind of population genetic analysis deployed, Ötzi's identity, as a prehistoric individual, shifts. One crucial factor is the temporal scope: the further back we zoom in evolutionary history—say, 10,000 to 5,000 years ago—the more likely we are to focus on events that led to the larger patterns of migration within the European continent, a temporal focus that encourages framing prehistoric identities as continental rather than national. Conversely, working within a temporal frame closer to the present—say, what happened between 5,000 and 2,000 years ago—often encourages emphasis on movements around local boundaries such as rivers or mountain ranges, many of which became enmeshed in the project of constructing national borders during the past centuries.

Likewise, the point of comparison employed in population genetic analyses matters. Comparisons with modern, geographically localized samples are likely to foreground an ancient sample's geographic locatedness in terms that resonate with national frameworks of belonging, while comparisons with other ancient samples often highlight much broader geographic scope, thereby resonating with a continental framing. Furthermore, SNPs chosen for analysis play a significant role. Some SNPs are associated with broad areas—Africa, for example—while others are considered to be more regionally specific. All in all, the line between continental, national, and regional frameworks is not clear-cut. Instead, these alternative forms of belonging appear or disappear through relatively minor revisions of the analytical apparatus. This reflects M'charek's carefully documented observations that population genetic practices are a matter of situated and pragmatic negotiations.

Enacting Personal Genetic Ties

Ötzi has become connected to modern and ancient populations in multiple and changing ways that are more than a matter of technologies becoming increasingly accurate over time. While technological innovation certainly has played a role, Ötzi's multiple and shifting genetic connections also reflect specific approaches within population genetics. For example, as we saw above, mitochondrial analyses suggested a genetic connection to the Alpine region and Y-chromosome analysis pointed to a genetic connection to Corsica and Sardinia because they examined different genetic material—mitochondrial DNA inherited through a maternal lineage and Y-chromosome DNA inherited through a paternal lineage. Crucially, mitochondrial and Y-chromosome analyses are culturally appealing because they seem to suggest a direct and irrefutable material connection between modern populations and an ancient individual.

The idea of an irrefutable and unique material connection between modern and ancient people gained particular momentum with the increasing interest in the genetic roots of specific modern DNA sequences at the turn of the twenty-first century. In the case of Ötzi, researchers and commentators have attempted to connect the iceman to modern individuals. These attempts reflect a larger cultural trend of seeking to root people within the patterns of prehistoric human migrations on *the level of the individual*. For example, commercial genetic ancestry tests have been marketed online directly to consumers since about 2000. Such tests promise to engender concrete material ties by comparing the customer's DNA sample (retrieved with the help of a test kit sent through mail) to a database of DNA samples and established mitochondrial and Y-chromosome haplogroups. As scholars like Henry Greely, Jennifer Wagner, and Lee et al. have shown, the sense of concrete material ties that the tests promise is misleading, as the tests typically focus only on a small percentage of a person's genetic makeup and the results are products of particular situated methods and available databases.

The interest in creating specific connections between prehistoric and modern individuals was present in the discourses surrounding Ötzi. In his popular book *The Seven Daughters of Eve* (2001), geneticist Bryan Sykes, who was part of the team that authored the 1994 mitochondrial paper, tells the story of how he connected Ötzi's mitochondrial DNA to a living person, an Irish woman (and friend of Sykes) named Marie Moseley, who lived in Dorset in the United Kingdom. (Sykes is also the director of one of the first commercial genetic ancestry testing companies, Oxford Ancestors, launched right before *The Seven Daughters of Eve* was published.) Intriguingly, Sykes maintains that Moseley experienced the connection between her and Ötzi as emotionally charged, and that such emotional investments arose from the understanding that the connection between them was material and thus irrefutable (7–8). For my analysis, the important point is not whether Moseley actually felt this way, but that Sykes's account of the event represents the connection between modern and prehistoric individuals as a source of intimate emotions and belonging. This suggests that population genetics, when applied on the level of the individual, resonates strongly with cultural ideas of personal belonging.

This move toward belonging as personal also underlies a 2013 study of the Y-chromosome haplogroup G in Tyrol by Burkhard Berger and colleagues. The study used blood samples from 3,700 men, along with self-reported genealogical information, to evaluate the presence of various G subgroups in Austrian Tyrol. While only a small section of the article focused on Ötzi's haplogroup, it was this part of the results that interested the media. For example, the *Discover* magazine website sported the headline: LIVING RELATIVES OF ÖTZI THE ICEMAN MUMMY FOUND IN AUSTRIA (Draxler). Echoing the language of mainstream news outlets such as NBC News (Boyle) or the BBC, the text referred to the nineteen Austrian men with Ötzi's haplogroup as "newly-found living relatives," "family members," "long-lost relatives," and "descendants of the Ötzi family" (Draxler). Such use of familial language rendered the connection between Ötzi and each of the nineteen modern Austrian men private and potentially affectively invested, while insisting that the kinship relationship embodied a material reality that could not be refuted. This celebrated material connection is made even more special through the foregrounding of the specific type of genetic material—Y-chromosome DNA inherited from the father—used in the study. (The specificity of genetic material—mitochondrial DNA—was also central to the affective politics of Sykes's account of Marie Moseley.) Interestingly, the case of the modern Tyrolean men differed from the case of Marie Moseley in a crucial way: the men were not named, nor were they apparently informed about the results. Yet the very idea of a personal (rather than communal) genetic connection to the prehistoric past appears to carry such strong cultural resonance that the anonymity of the men seemed trivial in cultural discourses around the study.

All in all, this turn to personal ancestry complicates evocations of national genetic belonging. While both the Irish mitochondrial descendant and the Austrian (Tyrolean) Y-chromosomal descendants emerge as ethnically and geographically located individuals, they are not related to Ötzi through their national identity: most Irish people and most Austrians (or Tyroleans) are not genetically connected to Ötzi in any meaningful way. While personal genetic belonging and national genetic belonging may sometimes coincide and reinforce one another, Ötzi's case shows that this is not necessarily the case, and in fact, national and personal frameworks often contradict each other. Moreover, the various forms of genetic belonging are all tied to specific technologies, such as mitochondrial, Y-chromosome, or genome-wide techniques of analysis. Interestingly, this multiplicity of technologies is most clearly visible in personal belonging, as the connection between a prehistoric and a modern individual is typically conceived through mitochondrial or Y-chromosome analysis. At the same time, the claims to material specificity in personal belonging suggest that national belonging, too, relies on specific situated technologies.

Conclusion

The chapter has shown that a prehistoric human like Ötzi can be construed alternatively within the frameworks of continental, national, regional, and personal genetic belonging. In the discourses surrounding Ötzi's discovery and genetic study, he appears as an early European who represents the role of Neolithic people in establishing the foundations of European societies and a European way of life. Ötzi also emerges as an early "Austrian" and an early "Italian" to whom modern national populations can arguably be traced. He is also constructed as an "authentic" Tyrolean, who tread the same laborious paths across the Alps as modern Tyroleans 5,300 years later. Finally, he is the ancestor of geographically located modern individuals whose private family histories are represented as arising from the intimate life of Ötzi. All these forms of belonging are potentially emotionally charged, resonating strongly with cultural discourses that seek to root communities and individuals in the distant past.

This multiplicity of continental, national, regional, and personal belonging suggests that it might be very hard for one version of belonging—such as national belonging—to take precedence over the others. Or, to put it slightly differently, such precedence is always situated and temporary, rather than arising from the biological qualities of Ötzi's remains. I have argued that Ötzi is rendered continental, national, or regional through technological and material practices as well as through cultural narratives and imaginaries. Seen from this viewpoint, Ötzi is a socio-technical and material *assemblage* that has come into existence through an evolving range of scientific practices, transnational collaboration between research teams, legal definitions (such as national borders and national autonomy) and circulating cultural narratives.

The case of Ötzi shows that population genetics can be invoked to engender culturally powerful narratives of belonging because ancient DNA is perceived widely as a concrete material point in the past where modern belonging can be anchored (see Oikkonen 73–129, for further discussion). At the same time, accounts of national, continental, or regional evolutionary roots rely on constant epistemic and rhetorical work to downplay and erase the alternative levels of genetic analysis and alternative narratives of belonging that Ötzi also enables. While population genetic knowledge and ancient DNA can produce trajectories that appear as material and irrefutable, it is important to remember that genetic analysis of SNPs or geographical distribution of haplogroups cannot tell us anything about emotional attachments, societal or political affinities, or the complicated and intertwined processes through which national and regional communities have emerged and transformed over time.

In fact, the ways in which Ötzi became a source for imagining roots in multiple narrative frameworks raise more questions than they settle. What counts as roots in an evolutionary genetic framework? What is belonging when conceived through genes and prehistoric migration patterns? What is the relationship between national community and land, or national community and time in an evolutionary framework? How should the temporal and spatial borders of communities be defined if communities are examined as evolutionary entities? Crucially, the ultimate ambiguity of these issues is precisely what makes possible the multiple frameworks of genetic belonging that surround ancient human DNA. The ambiguity enables national genetic belonging to emerge and coexist simultaneously with continental, regional, or personal genetic belonging in socio-technical practices and cultural imaginaries.

Works Cited

Anastas, Benjamin. "Mountain High: Three Provinces, Two Countries, One Region—Could the Alpine Wonderland of Tyrol Be the Model Modern State?" *The New York Times*, 30 March 2008, p. A108.

Aspöck, H., et al. "Parasitological Examination of the Iceman." *Iceman and His Natural Environment: Palaeobotanical Results*, edited by Sigmar Bortenschlager and Klaus Oeggl, Springer-Verlag, 2000, pp. 127–36.

BBC. "Link to Oetzi the Iceman found in living Austrians." 10 Oct. 2013, www.bbc.com/news/world-europe-24477038. Accessed 4 July 2017.

Berger, Burkhard, et al. "High Resolution Mapping of Y Haplogroup G in Tyrol (Austria)." *Forensic Science International: Genetics*, vol. 7, 2013, pp. 529–36.

Boyle, Alan. "Scientists say Ötzi the Iceman has living relatives, 5,300 years later." *NBC News*, 14 Oct., 2013, www.nbcnews.com/sciencemain/scientists-say-otzi-iceman-has-living-relatives-5-300-years-8C11392771. Accessed 17 Oct. 2018.

Busby, Helen, and Paul Martin. "Biobanks, National Identity and Imagined Communities: The Case of UK Biobank." *Science as Culture*, vol. 15, no. 3, 2006, pp. 237–51.

Dickson, J. H., et al. "The Omnivorous Tyrolean Iceman: Colon Contents (Meat, Cereals, Pollen, Moss and Whipworm) and Stable Isotope Analysis." *Philosophical Transactions of the Royal Society of London*, vol. 355, 2000, pp. 1843–49.

Draxler, Breanna. "Living Relatives of Ötzi the Iceman Mummy Found in Austria." *Discover*, 16 Oct. 2013, blogs.discovermagazine.com/d-brief/2013/10/16/living-relatives-of-otzi-the-iceman-mummy-found-in-austria/. Accessed 4 July 2017.

Endicott, Phillip, et al. "Genotyping Human Ancient mtDNA Control and Coding Region Polymorphisms with a Multiplexed Single-Base-Extension Assay: The Singular Maternal History of the Tyrolean Iceman." *BMC Genetics*, vol. 10, no. 29, 2009, doi:10.1186/1471-2156-10-29.

Ermini, Luca, et al. "Complete Mitochondrial Genome Sequence of the Tyrolean Iceman." *Current Biology*, vol. 18, no. 21, 2008, pp. 1687–93.

Fortier, Anne-Marie. "The Indigenisation of 'The People of the British Isles.'" *Science as Culture*, vol. 21, no. 2, 2011, pp. 153–75.

Fowler, Brenda. "World of Ancient Iceman Comes into Focus." *The New York Times*, 19 Dec. 1995, p. C1.

Greely, Henry T. "Genetic Genealogy: Genetics Meets the Marketplace." *Revisiting Race in a Genomic Age*, edited by Barbara A. Koenig et al., Rutgers UP, 2008, pp. 215–34.

Green, Sarah. "Borders and the Relocation of Europe." *Annual Review of Anthropology*, vol. 42, no. 1, 2013, pp. 345–61.

Goulden, Murray. "Boundary-Work and the Human-Animal Binary: Piltdown Man, Science and the Media." *Public Understanding of Science*, vol. 18, no. 3, 2009, pp. 275–91.

The Guardian. "Conan the Siberian." 2 Sept. 1995, p. 26.

Haller, Vera. "Modern Marketing Embraces Iceman: Bronze Age Mummy Found on Glacier Moved to Italian Museum Amid Hoopla." *The Washington Post*, 12 April 1998, p. A19.

Handt, Oliva, et al. "Molecular Genetic Analysis of the Tyrolean Ice Man." *Science*, vol. 264, 1994, pp. 1775–78.

Higuchi, Russell, et al. "DNA Sequences from the Quagga, an Extinct Member of the Horse Family." *Nature*, vol. 312, 1984, pp. 282–84.

Hinterberger, Amy. "Categorization, Census and Multiculturalism: Molecular Politics and the Material of Nation." *Genetics and the Unsettled Past: The Collision between DNA, Race, and History*, edited by Keith Wailoo et al., Rutgers UP, 2012, pp. 204–24.

———. "Investing in Life, Investing in Difference: Nations, Populations and Genomes." *Theory, Culture & Society*, vol. 29, no. 3, 2012, pp. 72–93.

Hofreiter, Michael, et al. "The Future of Ancient DNA: Technical Advances and Conceptual Shifts." *BioEssays*, vol. 37, 2015, pp. 284–93.

Keller, Andreas, et al. "New Insights into the Tyrolean Iceman's Origin and Phenotype as Inferred by Whole-Genome Sequencing." *Nature Communications*, vol. 3, 2012, doi:10.1038/ncomms1701.

Kent, Michael, et al. "Building the Genomic Nation: 'Homo Brasilis' and the 'Genoma Mexicano' in Comparative Cultural Perspective." *Social Studies of Science*, vol. 45, no. 6, 2015, pp. 839–61.

Kohli-Laven, Nina. "French Families, Paper Facts: Genetics, Nation, and Explanation." *Genetics and the Unsettled Past: The Collision between DNA, Race, and History*, edited by Keith Wailoo et al., Rutgers UP, 2012, pp. 183–203.

Krause, Johannes, et al. "The Complete Mitochondrial DNA Genome of an Unknown Hominin from Southern Siberia." *Nature*, vol. 464, 2010, pp. 894–97.

Krings, Matthias, et al. "Neandertal DNA Sequences and the Origin of Modern Humans." *Cell*, vol. 90, 1997, pp. 19–30.

Lee, Sandra Soo-Jin, et al. "The Illusive Gold Standard in Genetic Ancestry Testing." *Science*, vol. 325, 2009, pp. 38–9.

Maixner, Frank, et al. "The 5300-Year-Old Helicobacter Pylori Genome of the Iceman." *Science*, vol. 351. no. 6269, 2016, pp. 162–65, doi:10.1126/science.aad2545.

M'charek, Amade. *The Human Genome Diversity Project: An Ethnography of Scientific Practice.* Cambridge UP, 2015.

M'charek, Amade, et al. "Topologies of Race: Doing Territory, Population and Identity in Europe." *Science, Technology, & Human Values*, vol. 39, no. 4, 2014, pp. 468–87.

McKie, Robin. "In the End, a Little Softness Goes a Long Way with an Italian Iceman." *The Observer*, 7 Sept. 1994, p. 5.

———. "Secrets of a Stone Age Rambo." *The Observer*, 4 May 2003, p. 7.

Mitchell, Robert, and Catherine Waldby. "National Biobanks: Clinical Labor, Risk Production, and the Creation of Biovalue." *Science, Technology & Human Values*, vol. 35, no. 3, 2010, pp. 330–55.

Müller, Wolfgang, et al. "Origin and Migration of the Alpine Iceman." *Science*, vol. 302, no. 5646, 2003, pp. 862–66, doi:10.1126/science.1089837.

Nash, Catherine. *Genetic Geographies: The Trouble with Ancestry.* U of Minnesota P, 2015.

Nelson, Alondra. *The Social Life of DNA: Race, Reparations, and Reconciliation after the Genome.* Beacon Press, 2016.

Oeggl, Klaus. "The Diet of the Iceman." *The Iceman and His Natural Environment: Palaeobotanical Results*, edited by Sigmar Bortenschlager and Klaus Oeggl, Springer-Verlag, 2000, pp. 89–115.

Oeggl, Klaus, et al. "The Reconstruction of the Last Itinerary of 'Ötzi,' the Neolithic Iceman, by Pollen Analysis from Sequentially Sampled Gut Extracts." *Quaternary Science Reviews*, vol. 26, no. 7–8, 2007, pp. 853–61.

Oikkonen, Venla. *Population Genetics and Belonging: A Cultural Analysis of Genetic Ancestry.* Palgrave Macmillan, 2018.

Pääbo, Svante. "Molecular Cloning of Ancient Egyptian Mummy DNA." *Nature*, vol. 314, 1985, pp. 644–45.

Perry, George H., and Ludovic Orlando. "Ancient DNA and Human Evolution." *Journal of Human Evolution*, vol. 79, 2015, pp. 1–3.

Rasmussen, Morten, et al. "Ancient Human Genome Sequence of an Extinct Palaeo-Eskimo." *Nature*, vol. 463, 2010, pp. 757–62.

———. "The Ancestry and Affiliations of Kennewick Man." *Nature*, vol. 523, 2015, pp. 455–58.

Reich, David, et al. "Genetic History of an Archaic Hominin Group from Denisova Cave in Siberia." *Nature*, vol. 468, 2010, pp. 1053–60.

Rizzi, Ermanno, et al. "Ancient DNA Studies: New Perspectives on Old Samples." *Genetics Selection Evolution*, vol. 44, no. 21, 2012, doi:10.1186/1297-9686-44-21.

Rollo, Franco, et al. "Fine Characterization of the Iceman's mtDNA Haplogroup." *American Journal of Physical Anthropology*, vol. 130, 2006, pp. 557–64.

———. "Ötzi's Last Meals: DNA Analysis of the Intestinal Content of the Neolithic Glacier Mummy from the Alps." *PNAS*, vol. 99, 2002, pp. 12594–99.

Sikora, Martin, et al. "Population Genomic Analysis of Ancient and Modern Genomes Yields New Insights into the Genetic Ancestry of the Tyrolean Iceman and the Genetic Structure of Europe." *PLOS Genetics*, vol. 10, no. 5, 2014, p. e1004353, doi:10.1371/journal.pgen.1004353.

Sommer, Marianne. "Mirror, Mirror on the Wall: Neanderthal as Image and 'Distortion' in Early 20th-Century French Science and Press." *Social Studies of Science*, vol. 36, no. 2, 2006, pp. 207–40.

Spindler, Konrad. *The Man in the Ice: The Amazing Inside Story of the 5000-Year-Old Body Found Trapped in a Glacier in the Alps*. Translated by Ewald Osers, Phoenix, 1995.

Sykes, Bryan. *The Seven Daughters of Eve: The Science that Reveals Our Genetic Ancestry*. W. W. Norton, 2001.

Tupasela, Aaro, et al. "Constructing Populations in Biobanking." *Life Sciences, Society and Policy*, vol. 11, no. 5, 2015, doi:10.1186/s40504-015-0024-0.

Turnbull, David. "Out of the Glacier into the Freezer: Ötzi the Iceman's Disruptive Timings, Spacings, and Mobilities." *Cryopolitics: Frozen Life in a Melting World*, edited by Joanna Radin and Emma Kowal, The MIT P, 2017, pp. 157–77.

Tutton, Richard, et al. "From Self-Identity to Genotype: The Past, Present, and Future of Ethnic Categories in Postgenomic Science." *What's the Use of Race? Modern Governance and the Biology of Difference*, edited by Ian Whitmarsh and David S. Jones, The MIT P, 2010, pp. 125–46.

Wade, Nicholas. "Ötzi the Iceman's Stomach Bacteria Offers Clues on Human Migration." *The New York Times*, 7 Jan. 2016, www.nytimes.com/2016/01/08/science/otzi-the-iceman-stomach-bacteria-europe-migration.html. Accessed 7 June 2017.

Wagner, Jennifer K. "Interpreting the Implications of DNA Ancestry Tests." *Perspectives in Biology and Medicine*, vol. 53, no. 2, 2010, pp. 231–48.

Chapter 6

National Time, Literary Form, and Exclusion

The United States in the 1920s

BRUCE BARNHART

The nation is a form that frames possibilities for itself and its citizens. Like aesthetic forms, the nation works by way of selection, reducing and limiting the range of possible actions and events. The nation provides a certain amount of stability and security for its citizens by its use of power to place limits upon the unexpected, constraining and curtailing those events that are figured as most threatening to the productive possibilities of the nation-state and its citizens. In its work to secure some possibilities and curtail others, the nation is necessarily engaged in shaping temporality. Possibilities always depend upon the way in which the present is connected to the future, and in its function as guarantor of both stability and possibility, the nation is heavily invested in determining the nature of the links between the present and the future. The nation gives its citizens a meaningful form in which to carry out their lives, and part of this form is temporal. Any meaningful national form necessarily depends upon a set of meaningful and orderly connections between the past, the present, and the future.

In emphasizing the temporal aspects of national form, I follow in the wake of scholars like Benedict Anderson, Homi Bhabha, Franco Moretti, and Fredric Jameson. All of these scholars emphasize the dependence of national form on a particular construction of time.[1] This is clearest in Benedict

Anderson, who sees the nation as an imaginative form held together by a temporal framework in which different individuals share the same time. In his 1983 work, *Imagined Communities: Reflections on the Origin and Spread of Nationalism*, Anderson famously defines the nation as an "imagined political community." He writes that the nation is "*imagined,*" because "the members of even the smallest nation will never know most of their fellow-members, meet them, or even hear of them, yet in the minds of each lives the image of their communion" (6). This imaginative communion depends crucially on a particular form of temporality, a form of what Anderson refers to as "empty, homogenous time," a time in which different members of a national community can experience themselves as sharing the same temporal movement with each other. National subjects imagine themselves as carrying out their daily activities simultaneously with other members of the same nationality: this coordination depends upon a shared conception of temporality.

For Anderson, the emergence of this form of temporal experience is brought into being by a particular literary form: the novel. According to Anderson, the novel is the cultural form that allows for the emergence of the modern nation-state. What is important about the novel is that it creates and codifies an experience of time in which the reader can imagine the actions of different individuals in different places as taking place simultaneously. The form of the novel allows readers to see how otherwise unaffiliated or unconnected characters or individuals share the same time. Anderson argues that this experience is the basis for the emergence of the nation as a form in which individuals who will never meet are imagined as part of the same community. In its manipulation of events to create a meaningful narrative, the novel engenders a particular experience of time, one in which individuals can imagine their participation in the temporal unfolding of the nation as it moves inevitably into the future.

Anderson stresses the ability of novels to provide a homogenous temporal form for the coexistence of different members of the national community, but in this essay, I want to think about another aspect of the way in which novels and national communities configure time: the way in which they construct the future. I want to argue that national form depends more upon the valence of the future it imagines for itself than it does upon the imagined simultaneity of its different members. Both the novel and the nation posit a future that gives a particular community its temporal orientation. The way in which the novel or the nation posit this future has much to do with the way in which any community imagines its own boundaries. In the United States, there is a strong tendency to posit a future imagined as a necessary and predictable extension of the present, a future unthreatened by contingency. This form of the future is linked to a pervasive American tendency to see otherness and immigration primarily as a threat, rather than as a set of new possibilities.

My focus in this essay is on the role that a particular construction of American time plays in determining American attitudes toward immigrants and immigration. America is a nation in which immigration plays an incredibly important role, both in the practical economic and social history of the nation and in the way the nation conceives of itself. Americans will often describe themselves as a "nation of immigrants," and American identity is virtually unimaginable without the waves of immigrants arriving in the eighteenth, nineteenth, and twentieth centuries.[2] Despite this fact, American history is characterized by recurring periods of intense xenophobia and hostility to immigration. Indeed, the present is just such a period, as can be seen in the political profit that the Donald Trump administration has made out of fostering hatred toward Islamic and Mexican immigrants. The shape and form of the current hostility toward immigration has deep roots in American history, and as several historians have noted, is a very close parallel to the hysteria over immigration that occurred in the 1920s.[3] (In fact, one of the key architects of the Trump immigration policy, then-attorney general Jeff Sessions, repeatedly referred to the most draconian legislation of the 1920s as a model for what he would have liked to achieve in the present.[4])

In order to diagnose this recurring American antipathy to otherness and its dependence on a particular construction of time, this essay focuses on the 1920s, a period in which the United States experienced an intense anxiety concerning both foreign immigration and the status of the nation's temporal path into the future. Smack-dab in the middle of this decade, one finds three telling events: the passage of the 1924 Johnson-Reed Act, the most draconian immigration bill in American history, and the publication of two novels symptomatic of American attitudes towards time, otherness, and immigration. In 1925, F. Scott Fitzgerald published *The Great Gatsby* and Anzia Yezierska published *Bread Givers*. Both novels are deeply implicated in the period's heightened attention to shifting sets of possibilities and to its desire for a bulwark against the most threatening of these possibilities. Both novels are working with the materials of the American imagined community, reflecting on and shaping the temporality at work in narratives of American identity.

In their own different ways, each novel provides a complex portrait of the relationship between American conceptions of time and American hostility to otherness. This essay treats these novels as cultural forms capable of exposing, critiquing, and/or reinforcing the temporal ideologies and narrative structures at work in nativism, xenophobia, and other forms of nationalist exclusion. In my reading of these two novels, I want to suggest two things: (1) that in these two novels, we see the key mechanisms for shaping time at work in a persistent form of American xenophobia (a form active in both the 1920s and in the present), and (2) that both the nation and the novel most influence xenophobic habits of mind by virtue of their power to shape time.

One of the key resources in this essay's investigation of temporality, the nation, and the novel is the work of Hannah Arendt. In *The Human Condition*, *The Origins of Totalitarianism*, and elsewhere, Arendt diagnoses a persistent form of hostility to otherness and unpredictability that depends upon presenting the movement of time as if it were obeisant to laws of necessity and predictability. Arendt's critique of xenophobia, anti-Semitism, and other forms of totalitarian thought posits a link between fictions of necessity, and hostility to any alteration in established narratives of identity. This link is at work in the nativism of the American 1920s. It is also at work in the American present, and indeed part of the implicit argument of this essay is that this connection is a persistent possibility in all constructions of the nation. This essay begins with a consideration of Hannah Arendt, and then moves on to look at treatments of temporality and otherness in *The Great Gatsby* and *Bread Givers*. My aim is a diagnosis of the temporal mechanisms at work in forms of American national identity predicated on xenophobia and hostility to immigration. The strong suggestion of this essay is that similar mechanisms are at work in national forms in other geographical regions.

Hannah Arendt

The link between cultural modes of shaping time and hostility to immigration is forcefully articulated in the work of Hannah Arendt. In *The Origins of Totalitarianism*, in *The Human Condition*, and elsewhere, Arendt consistently maintains that a particular conception of temporal movement is a core constituent of all totalitarian, reactionary, and xenophobic worldviews. For Arendt, plurality and unpredictability are at the very core of human existence in the social world. Any productive social or political institution must first of all embrace these essential conditions of human existence.

Arendt's devotion to this core truth drives her to relentlessly critique forces that work to constrain or suppress plurality and contingency. One of the most persistent of these forces is the tendency to present the movement of time as if it were a necessary movement subject to historical or natural laws. Any narrative or other construction of temporality that presents time as a series of necessary moments progressing away from unpredictability, contingency, and the unexpected is hostile to plurality and to the essence of social existence.

For Arendt, the defining condition of the social world is plurality. She is most explicit about this in *The Human Condition*, where she defines the world as an intense interplay of different perspectives and of interlocking social roles. To be an actor in the social world is to play a role seen and interpreted by a wide variety of spectators, each of whom is likely to interpret and respond to the role in original and unpredictable ways. The result is that each agent or individual is shaped and determined by a crisscrossing plurality of social perspectives, their identity a shifting composite of responses and interpretations.

The central defining character of the human in this plural world is a certain form of spontaneity or unpredictability: an ability to break with tradition, precedent, and expectation that Arendt refers to as *natality*. For Arendt, natality is the inherent capacity of humans to break with existing temporal patterns and to act, think, or create in ways that are startling or unexpected. In *The Human Condition*, she describes this as a strong form of beginning. She writes that: "It is in the nature of beginning that something new is started which cannot be expected from whatever may have happened before. This character of startling unexpectedness is inherent in all beginnings." (176) This is natality: the constant possibility of new thoughts, actions, and social forms. What characterizes the human condition more than anything else is the potential for new beginnings, for breaking the chain that binds different moments together.

In her critique of totalitarianism and of totalitarian mental habits, Arendt identifies a powerful refusal to countenance or cognize this central fact of human existence. Injustice, terror, and xenophobia are always linked to what Arendt describes as "a negation of the significance of human behavior" (8). This negation takes place both in the physical world, and in the intellectual or theoretical world. Arendt gives us both the practices of imprisonment and extermination that physically negate "the significance of human behavior" as well as the intellectual practices that construct narratives or theoretical frameworks that negate "the significance of human behavior" by leaving no intellectual or temporal space for the essential unpredictability of this behavior.

In *The Origins of Totalitarianism*, Arendt characterizes the repressive regimes of Joseph Stalin and Adolf Hitler as violations of this unpredictability and as a kind of war on natality itself. Both Stalin and Hitler strove violently to suppress or eliminate the human capacity for unprecedented and unpredictable actions. In their war on human unpredictability, Hitler and Stalin depended on a vast apparatus of physical repression and violence, but they also depended on versions of narrative identity that mute human unpredictability. A crucial part of totalitarian forms of intellectual violence are narratives that portray temporality as a succession of necessary moments untroubled by unpredictability or contingency.

Arendt describes these narratives as coercive forces that prescribe certain "laws of movement." The totalitarian impulse to quash natality and unpredictability works by way of a prescriptive temporality, a force that compels obedience to its laws of temporal movement by presenting "society as the product of a gigantic historical movement which races according to its own law of motion" (463). This totalitarian hostility to natality and spontaneity posits "its own beginning and its own end," restricting human action by requiring obedience to its temporal movement (465). What is clear here is the power of temporality as a fearful reaction against natality. Arendt describes this as the fear "that with the birth of each human being a new beginning might raise and make heard its voice in the world" (473). In response to this fear, totalitarian systems embody a forceful temporal movement that sweeps the individual along with it.

For Arendt, totalitarianism works by subordinating everything to a powerful and relentless temporal movement that suppresses individuality and the possibility of a new voice or a new birth emerging. The justification for terror, for suppression of human spontaneity, and for laws directed against immigration is not the whim of a tyrannical leader or any fear grounded in a rational assessment of loss. Instead, repression is justified by appeal to the necessity of a temporal movement posited as the central rationale of a whole way of life.

The anti-immigrant forces of the 1920s worked to present a narrative of American identity as just this kind of temporal movement, a necessary movement into the future threatened by immigrants seen as capable of a new beginning that might derail this movement. Two politicians central to this anti-immigrant nativism gave their name to the 1924 legislative act enshrining anti-immigrant feelings as law: Congressman Albert Johnson and Senator David A. Reed. These two figures exemplify an American fear of new beginnings that wants to restrict immigration on the basis that immigrants are incompatible with the proper narrative movement of the American nation. Johnson and Reed saw immigrants from Southern Europe, Eastern Europe, and Asia as a threat to the established narrative of the United States, and as a challenge to their vision of a white, protestant nation moving along a predetermined path toward a prosperous future. Albert Johnson denounced these kinds of immigrants as "abnormally twisted" and "un-american," signaling their unfitness to participate in the temporal movement of the American nation.[5] After the passage of the Johnson-Reed Act radically restricted immigration to the United States, Congressman Reed exulted that with the act's passage, "the racial composition of America at the time is thus made permanent" (Serwer). In the terms given to us by Arendt, what Johnson, Reed, and other nativist political leaders represent is a defense mechanism against the unpredictability and precarity of the world. The nativists' vision of American identity negates the plurality of a world we share in common and the natality bound up with human unpredictability and action. Elements of this narrative vision and of its mode of imagining the future can be seen in the 1924 Johnson-Reed Act, in F. Scott Fitzgerald's 1925 novel, *The Great Gatsby*, and in Anzia Yezierska's novel *Bread Givers*.[6]

The Great Gatsby

All of the factors considered by Arendt are at play in F. Scott Fitzgerald's 1925 novel. *The Great Gatsby* is a novel about time, it is a novel about inclusion and exclusion, and it is a novel that betrays the sharp anxieties about American identity in the 1920s.[7] The novel's form is shaped by what Arendt would refer to as the clash between forms of otherness that threaten to disrupt established narrative identities and forms of temporal necessity that function as defensive mechanisms against such threatening disruptions. In *The Great Gatsby*, we can see this dynamic in the way that the narrator and the narrative itself both struggle to contain the disruptive energies of an interloper in the rarefied social atmosphere of upper-class American society.

Fitzgerald's novel tells the story of Jay Gatsby, a figure who grew up poor but who eventually amassed a fortune capable of allowing him to compete for the hand of a wealthy, well-established upper-class woman. This woman is Daisy Buchanan, a figure with the right kind of family, the right kind of social connections, and the right kind of bank account. Jay Gatsby is an outsider in the social world of Daisy Buchanan, and the novel narrates the clash between upper-class society and Gatsby's attempt to insert himself into this society. The end result of this clash is Gatsby's death and the recounting of his tale by Nick Carraway. Carraway is the novel's narrator, a figure who comes from the same social world as Daisy Buchanan but doesn't have the same amount of wealth.

The conflict at the heart of the novel has much to do with social and economic class, but race also plays an important role in this conflict. Jay Gatsby grew up as James Gatz, and in order to get anywhere near Daisy, he has to leave behind a name that marks his foreignness. Fitzgerald's novel is a reflection upon the temporal path of the American nation at a time in which large numbers of immigrants from Southern and Eastern Europe are entering the country. As James Gatz, Gatsby's entry into the privileged upper class is blocked by prejudice, just as it was for Americans of Southern or Eastern European descent. As the historian Mae Ngai notes, these kinds of Americans were seen as "unassimilable"—descendants of "the 'degraded races' of Europe, incapable of self-government" (19). Understood in this context, Gatsby figures as both a lower-class interloper in an upper-class world, and a suspiciously foreign interloper in an Anglo-Saxon and Protestant world. Gatsby's suspiciously un-protestant-sounding original last name and his close business connections with Jews and Greeks marks him as figure closely associated with the "hordes" of foreign immigrants dominating political debate at the time in which *The Great Gatsby* was written and published.

In the upper-class Anglo-Saxon social world of the novel, full of individuals and families with the right kind of last names and the right kind of family and racial history, Gatsby just does not seem to fit. From the perspective of the upper-class world he struggles to enter and from the perspective of the novel's narrator, Gatsby's actions are out of sync: he doesn't speak properly, he doesn't have the right kind of social manners, he has a strange sense of propriety, his parties are not exclusive enough, and he has a bizarre sense of temporality.[8] In short, Gatsby is an outsider with an outlandish sense of how the present should be connected to the future. He is out of step with a proper American sense of time, an interloper who threatens to disrupt the ongoing movement of American temporality. He is threatening because he makes the established links between the present and the future seem less secure. His presence and persistence make the established American narrative seem more malleable and more precarious. In the terms that Arendt gives us, Gatsby suggests the possibility that "a new beginning might raise and make heard its voice in the new world" (*Origins* 473). As a manifestation of Arendt's "new beginning" or "new voice," Gatsby represents a challenge to existing forms of temporality and the possibility of new or revised rhythms of identity and social relation.

The 1920s were a period of intense nativism, a period in which the flow of immigrants from Southern and Eastern Europe outpaced the flow of immigrants from Northern and Western Europe. Unlike immigrants from Northern and Western Europe, these new immigrants were seen as a threat to social cohesion and national integrity. The historian Mae Ngai describes the period as governed by a "crisis atmosphere," in which labor groups and patriotic organizations "warned that 'hordes'" of inassimilable immigrants were on their way, threatening to overwhelm traditional and properly American patterns of living and working (20). Immigrants from Southern and Eastern Europe were associated with undesirable ideas and radically different political notions: Jewish immigrants from Eastern Europe were seen as bearers of Bolshevisim, and Italian immigrants were seen as bearers of anarchism. Like Gatsby, these immigrants figure as rival temporal trajectories, individuals with different conceptions of how the present should be linked to the future. They are threatening because they challenge the implicit temporal program of the nation; their presence and temporal difference threatening to transform the promised American future from a settled and certain goal into a question up for debate, one possible and contingently posited future among a variety of possible futures.

The panic over foreign immigration in the 1920s culminated in a Congressional act radically restricting immigration and setting up national quotas that heavily favored immigrants from nations with racial populations seen as more readily assimilable to the American way. This was the Johnson-Reed Act of 1924, also known as the National Origins Act, a part of American history crucial to the anti-immigrant movement of the 1920s and still a touchstone for key figures in the anti-immigrant movement in the present. The Johnson-Reed Act not only enforced a restrictive sense of American identity and possibility, but also, as historians of U.S. immigration have demonstrated, established the pattern for subsequent immigration laws and conceptions of immigration flows, borders, and national integrity. Mae Ngai convincingly argues that the act's passage brought two new and persistent forces into discourses and practices of American national integrity: First of all, it "created a new class of persons within the national body—

illegal aliens"; secondly, it "created a new emphasis on control of the nation's contiguous land borders, which emphasis had not existed before" (57). So, the 1920s mark the inauguration of a new emphasis on policing borders, restricting the influx of foreign persons and ideas, and making sharp distinctions between proper and assimilable American persons and improper and unassimilable "foreigners."

One of the virtues of Fitzgerald's 1925 novel is that it lays bare some of the dynamics cultivating and perpetuating the cultural investment in nativism and exclusion, as well as in the deeply felt need to police the geographical and imaginative borders of the nation. *The Great Gatsby* allows us to see the ways in which attachment to a preordained temporal progression toward a certain future fosters antagonism toward individuals and groups seen as having different notions of how the present and future should be shaped. Jay Gatsby—aka James Gatz—is one of these individuals with a different notion of how the present moves into the future, and the homology between him and the Eastern and Southern immigrants that stirred the anxieties of the 1924 Congress suggests that Fitzgerald's narration of Gatsby's entry into and violent expulsion out of the upper class is also an attempt to make narrative sense of national identity.

The novel is narrated from the point of view of Nick Carraway, and Nick's task is to bring some order to the disordered narrative intrusions of Gatsby. Nick narrates the novel with a strong desire for "the world to be in uniform and at a sort of moral attention forever" (6). Despite his friendship with Gatsby, Nick shares the social commitments of the upper-class world to which he belongs, and he ultimately shapes Gatsby's story in accordance with his sense that "Gatsby represented everything for which I have an unaffected scorn" (6). Carraway's task as narrator of the novel is to bend or shape the narrative of Gatsby's life so that it conforms to the already established temporal pattern of the American national community. Carraway works to narrate Gatsby's life in ways that minimize its challenge to belief in a secure American future and that suppress its tendency to attenuate belief in any firmly secured links between the present and the future.

The novel's narrative performs these operations in a number of ways, but I want to focus on just one of them: the novel's reliance on a kind of prolepsis or anticipation that foretells Gatsby's fate before his story properly begins. This narrative operation works to dismiss Gatsby as a real set of new possibilities, and to figure him as a dead end, an example of the chaos that results from violating the narrative laws of the nation.

Prolepsis

In the novel's first few pages, before any actual encounter with Gatsby, Carraway tells readers that the ending of the story and of Gatsby's fate is already known in advance. On the novel's second page, Fitzgerald writes: "Gatsby turned out all right in the end" (6). Gatsby turns out dead in the end, so this is not the happiest ending, but it does perform a certain reassuring function in so far as it confirms belief in a secure and well-established temporal framework. Gatsby turns out "all right," because his story's ending is made to match the expectations established by the novel's opening and those established by deeper, epistemic expectations about a future with clear connections to the present.

The beginning of Fitzgerald's novel momentarily leaps ahead to the novel's ending, a literary strategy fairly common in novels, a strategy known as *prolepsis*.[9] The literary theorist Gerard Genette defines prolepsis as a "narrative manoeuver that consists of narrating or evoking in advance an event that will take place later" (40). Prolepsis is a narrative maneuver, but it is not only a literary maneuver. Nations and communities are narratives as well, and prolepsis is a way of thinking about time at work in the social and political world, as well as in the literary world. We see this a little bit more clearly in the definition of prolepsis given by the Oxford English Dictionary: "the action or fact of representing or regarding something done in the future as already done or existing." Citizens and subjects in the social world often engage in this form of representing or regarding the future. Prolepsis is a way of thinking about time, a rather prevalent habit of mind at work in the way national communities understand themselves. Prolepsis is at work in the social world as well as in literary form.

Fitzgerald's novel begins by positing a future toward which its narrative movement will orient itself; nations do something similar. The similarity between novelistic beginnings and national ones is captured by J. Hillis Miller in his 1987 work *The Ethics of Reading*. According to Miller, the imaginative act that founds a community always has "an implicit teleology":

> This inaugural act . . . is the prolepsis of a story not only with a beginning, but with a middle and an end. Like all founding legislation or drawing up of a social contract it makes a promise: if you follow this law you will be happy and prosperous; if you do not, disaster will follow. (29)

Following Miller, we could say that the nation gives itself narrative cohesion by giving itself an ending. To imagine oneself as a national subject is to imagine oneself as on the narrative path toward this ending.

All futures are some kind of projection out of the present, but not all futures are the result of a prolepsis that "represents or regards something in the future as already done or existing" ("Prolepsis"). What we see in *The Great Gatsby* is a proleptic habit in which the future is imagined as a certain and already determined point of orientation. What we see in the literary and cultural formations of the 1920s is a tendency for a proleptically posited future and a settled path toward this future to serve as regulating ideals working to minimize the threat of the unexpected, the unfamiliar, and the inassimilable foreign. *The Great Gatsby* is proleptic but so are xenophobic and nativist narratives of American identity. Just as Carraway tells us that Gatsby will turn out all right in the end, anti-immigrant politicians tell us that the United States will turn out all right in the end, reassuring Americans by utilizing a narrative in which a promising future is established in advance. There is, then, a politics of prolepsis, a struggle over the way in which the present is linked to the future that is also a struggle over who counts as proper participants in the American movement toward a prosperous future.

The kind of proleptic future at work in *The Great Gatsby* serves as an endpoint for a fixed narrative that works to enforce belief in one prescribed path toward a prosperous future, outside the boundaries of which lay only chaos and dissolution. The expectation fostered by such a temporality is that the unexpected or unforeseen can only be seen as threats to a secure passage into the promised and alluringly prosperous future. In Miller's account, the proleptic narrative of community holds out both the promise of a happy ending and a clear set of laws or narrative steps guaranteeing arrival at this future ending. Those who violate these laws invite "disaster" for themselves and the community, a fact that makes the exclusion of those with "inassimilable" temporal rhythms seem absolutely necessary. In Fitzgerald's novel, Gatsby's actions have violated the expectations of proper society, but his death conforms to expectations that deviations from the fundamental law of American narrative propriety can only lead to unproductive ends.

The prolepsis we encounter at the beginning of Fitzgerald's novel announces that Gatsby's end is determined in advance, preparing the reader both for Gatsby's death and for an ending that reconfirms a fixed and pre-established temporal pattern that binds the national "we" together. And this is exactly what the famous last sentence of the novel delivers: "So we beat on, boats against the current, borne back ceaselessly into the past" (189).

In the wake of Gatsby's death, the pattern of his life can be assimilated to a repeating temporal pattern that "we," a rhetorical American community, all share. After Gatsby's temporal aberrations have been purged by way of his violent termination, the narrative workings of Fitzgerald's novel transform his tale into a reassuring confirmation.

Measuring all temporal movement against a prescribed pattern, the narrative movement of the novel first rejects Gatsby's aberrant conception of time and social movement by transforming him into the deadest of dead ends and then, following his death, stamps the pattern of inevitability upon his remembered life. In doing so, it participates in larger social patterns in which "inassimilable" immigrants are similarly rejected for their different conceptions of time and social movement, whether real or imagined. The narrative operation of Fitzgerald's novel functions as a kind of protective wall that purges the dissonant energies of Gatsby and, by extension, of those Americans with different social senses of possibility and futurity.

These proleptic and exclusionary aspects of the novel are symptomatic of a persistent set of mental and temporal habits at work in the American imagination. These are not the only aspects of the novel, nor are they the only temporal strategies at work in American culture. They are, however, enduring and persistent patterns, part of the deep structure of the American imagination. The narrative operations used to violently end Gatsby's interference in the social world of proper Anglo-Saxon Americans and to transform his life into a story that reassures readers of the persistence of a stable temporal pattern undergirding the flux of everyday life, are also narrative operations that function in the larger discourse of American identity to justify the exclusion of those imagined as lacking a proper sense of American movement toward a prosperous future. Nativism and xenophobia are not just beliefs or sets of practices, they are also commitments to a particular narrative shape of the American nation.

Bread Givers

Published the same year as *The Great Gatsby*, Anzia Yezierska's *Bread Givers* is a novel more overtly concerned with immigration and the assimilability of recent immigrants from Southern and Eastern Europe. The main character, Sara Smolinsky, is the daughter of Jewish immigrants from Poland and, unlike Gatsby, she does little to cover up her immigrant roots. Although she does successfully integrate herself into the American education system,

Sara is consistently read as outside of properly established ethnic and cultural currents. Her family's "Old World" Jewishness puts her at odds with cultural expectations, including temporal expectations embodied in established rhythms of work, study, and leisure. Like Gatsby, Sara Smolinsky represents a form of otherness frightening to many Americans in the nativist 1920s, and, like Gatsby, she encounters an established temporal narrative hostile to her version of American identity. This temporal narrative exerts an immense pressure on Sara to renounce her past and to strive furiously to adapt or assimilate to "American" modes of existence.

Much distinguishes Fitzgerald's account of Gatsby from Yezierska's account of Sara Smolinsky, but the most telling difference between the two novels is that of point of view: *The Great Gatsby* is narrated by Nick, whereas *Bread Givers* presents the point of view of Sara herself. This point of view gives us a different perspective on the temporal structure of American identity and its hostility to immigration. In *The Great Gatsby*, the narrative structure of the novel participates in the hostility toward immigration, working to write Gatsby's aberrant possibilities out of the ongoing story of American identity. In *Bread Givers*, the narrative shows us Sara struggling with the hostility and antipathy to immigrant experience built into dominant American forms of temporality. Although Sara feels compelled to adapt herself to this temporality, the novel gives us Sara's strong sense of resentment concerning what this temporality forces her to give up.[10] Both Sara and the novel itself are ambivalent about the temporality to which she is forced to conform.

The bulk of the novel is dedicated to Sara Smolinsky's struggle to become a schoolteacher. Breaking with her parents' expectations, Sara works her way through high school and college, supporting herself economically as she doggedly pursues a vision of herself as an independent woman and full-fledged member of the American educational system. From the moment that Sara dedicates herself to this goal, her life becomes more and more oriented toward the "implicit teleology" of American narrative identity (Miller 29). She feels the prolepsis and promise of the American future as a tangible presence within herself and this presence reorients and restructures her sense of herself and her place in the world.

As Sara works her way toward her goal, she becomes symptomatic of the close connection between national narratives and personal narratives. As Priscilla Wald writes, "National narratives actually shape personal narratives by delineating the cultural practices through which personhood is defined" (4). One of the ways in which cultural practices shape personhood is by inculcating in subjects particular attitudes toward temporality, giving individuals a template for how to coordinate their present, past, and future. The nation provides individuals with a framework within which to understand and coordinate the different temporal vectors of their lives. As Sara Smolinsky "becomes American," she takes on the American impulse toward prolepsis, a temporal orientation in which a fixed future determines the present and what takes place in it. Sara Smolinsky's path toward success shows us the nation at work as a kind of temporal discipline, shaping possibilities and the path that one takes to realize these possibilities.

Bread Givers presents Sara's choice of future vocation as a kind of epiphany, an overwhelming event in which Sara is both struck by the vision of becoming a schoolteacher and is simultaneously drawn into the ongoing temporality of American identity. The vision provides her with both an image of her future self, and of the path toward this future self. The vision that "flashe[s]" in Sara's imagination is a narrative one, a "story from the Sunday paper" that shows a woman like her stringing different temporal moments together into a tightly knit narrative of success: "A girl—slaving away in the shop. . . . Then suddenly she began to study in the night school, then college. And worked and studied, on and on, till she became a teacher in the schools" (153).

Sara has just fled from her parents' home, and after disheartening visits in which she sees the desultory fate of her two sisters, Sara walks through New York without any path or goal. Untethered from the expectations of her family, Sara is walking through the world without any narrative governing her movement from one moment to the next. She is in search of a temporal path, and the force of the narrative presented in the newspaper overwhelms her, pulling her out of her past and her real present and placing her within the imaginative structure of a properly American path toward a properly American future. This is not a moment of self-determination, but an instance of interpellation or socialization.[11] Sara is socialized by a narrative from the media; this entails her being pulled in to the forceful movement of American temporality. Cornelius Castoriadis captures this link between socialization and temporality when he writes that: "In and through the process of socialization, the psyche absorbs or internalizes the time instituted by the given society" (385). As Sara's epiphany strikes her, she looks forward to becoming "a real person," but she has become a different kind of subject as she is socialized in this moment. Her psyche absorbs American time and the rhythmic ordering of her thoughts, feelings, and actions takes on a different orientation.

In taking on this new orientation, Sara Smolinsky submits herself to a certain kind of sacrificial logic, subordinating everything in the present to the attainment of her future goal. Driven by an inner compulsion, Sara sees every present moment only in terms of the way it leads toward the projected future. Sara understands herself as following a set of absolutely necessary protocols that inflexibly govern the use of her time. She has absorbed a fixed temporal orientation to a future goal, and as a result, she forces herself to sacrifice or suppress crucial aspects of her past and present life.

One of the hardest impositions that this temporal regime forces upon Sara is the denial of her family. Sara is happy to escape her father and his insistence upon obedience to Old World traditions, but her new temporal path also forces her to isolate herself from her mother and sisters as well. This is clearly illustrated in the novel's depiction of Sara's mother's first visit after Sara leaves home. Her mother has defied her husband's wishes and has traveled hours from her rural town to visit Sara in the city. She has brought Sara a feather bed and can only stay for a "few minutes" before starting her long trip back home (171). In the presence of her mother's expansive "goodness," Sara feels the poverty of her own narrow path, and the contrast between herself and her mother makes Sara "hate . . . [herself] for [her] selfishness" (170). At this moment, Sara realizes how much she has given up by binding herself to the strict temporal laws of American success. Stricken by guilt, she asks what she can do to repay her mother's kindness. All her mother asks is that Sara come visit her soon, but Sara refuses this request, telling her that she "can't take time" to make such a visit. She uses the language of necessity in telling her mother that "Every little minute must go to my studies" (171). Driven by the force of her submission to the temporal protocols of American identity, Sara denies her mother and her love for her. Sara has internalized the rhythms of American striving and the spirit of time-calculation that goes with these rhythms, and from within this temporal regime sees the denial of her mother as a necessary imperative, a kind of law of temporal movement.

From the perspective of Hannah Arendt, we can see Sara's denial of her mother and of her own devotion to her mother as a function of a kind of temporal "law of necessity" at work in the narrative of American identity. Sara finds herself swept along by a temporal logic that seems to move of its own accord, driving her to ration her time in ways that go against her deepest feelings. She desperately wants to become a full member of American society, and she experiences the totalitarian impulse of this society's temporality when it strikes her as "the product of a gigantic historical movement which races according to its own law of motion" (463). The laws of motion of American identity in the 1920s bear within them a certain hostility to anything from outside of their prescribed beginning and ending, and here Sara is compelled to renounce those aspects of her cultural identity that don't match the rhythms of this narrative movement. In the nativist vision of the 1920s, Sara's family represents the feared possibility of a "new beginning," a challenge to the preestablished beginning and end of American identity. By adapting herself to this vision's strict temporal laws of motion, Sara suppresses the set of possibilities that her familial and cultural past have left at work within her.

Like Gatsby, Sara is forced to confront a narrative temporality at war with natality and with possibilities seen as "foreign" to American identity. In *The Great Gatsby,* we see a set of narrative maneuvers working to construct Gatsby as a dead end by eliminating him as a possible alteration to the established narrative of American identity. In *Bread Givers,* we see this narrative construction working *within* Sara Smolinsky, working not to eliminate Sara's participation in American society, but to eliminate that within her that most works to threaten American society with the possibility of a new beginning.

The tyrannical temporal logic at work within Sara is a kind of compulsion, which she exerts over herself. As Hannah Arendt writes, these kinds of laws or rules "rely on the compulsion with which we can compel ourselves; . . . this inner compulsion is the tyranny of logicality against which nothing stands but the great capacity of men to start something new" (*Origins* 473). In a society powerfully shaped by aversion to natality and its power to restart and reshape established narratives, Sara shapes her inner being to the dictates of a fixed temporal movement that functions as protection against this power of restarting. Through Arendt's frame, we can see *Bread Givers* as an illustration of the ways in which a powerfully prescriptive temporal narrative "with its own beginning and its own end" can impose itself on the inner life of individuals. Sara Smolinsky is subjected to a construction of temporality hostile to human unpredictability, a narrative that wants to suppress the unexpected possibilities that Sara and her fellow immigrants bring to the United States.

In the unfolding of Sara Smolinsky's narrative destiny, we see the temporal mechanisms of the American nation as it works to maintain its imaginative shape and cleave to its proleptically posited future. Unlike Gatsby, Sara Smolinsky is written into the imagined community of the American nation, adopting its temporal movement as her own. As a result, she becomes a complex figure for American possibility, a reflection on both the limitations and potentials of an American temporality that posits tight links between the present and the future. Sara Smolinsky is both empowered by her adaptation of American temporality and diminished by its rebarbative scope. She takes her place within the educational system and she does gain a measure of independence, self-assurance, and economic self-determination. At the same time, she mourns that which she has left behind on the stringent path to success: Another way of life, a different structure of feeling, and a different set of possibilities.

Sara's character inhabits the nexus of the American nation's engagement with otherness and natality, and the ambivalence of the novel's ending resonates with a deep ambivalence within the American nation. This is the ambivalence between the nation's role in fostering possibility and the nation's role in providing stability and security. Every nation needs a temporal path binding its citizens together and enabling its movement into a prosperous future, but the greater the investment in a fixed form of this temporal path, the more it works to circumscribe new possibilities. This tension between possibility and stability is inherent in national form.

Despite this ambivalence at work in *Bread Givers*, the juxtaposition of Yezierska's novel with Fitzgerald's novel and with the harshly xenophobic Johnson-Reed Act of 1924 outlines a sharp critique: a critique of the American overinvestment in secure links between the present and the future. In the fate of James Gatz, of Sara Smolinsky, and of the tens of thousands of immigrants denied entry to the United States, we see the nefarious effects of the proleptic impulse at work in both the novels and in the nativism of the period. In both Yezierska's narrative and Fitzgerald's narrative, we can see the ways in which a proleptic investment in a predetermined future works to suppress natality and foster hostility to otherness and immigration.

Both *Bread Givers* and *The Great Gatsby* expose the temporal mechanisms at work in the potent nativism of the 1920s. In both novels, we see the exclusionary impulse of a national narrative invested in necessity and in a proleptic or predetermined future. This tendency of American national form to posit a stable, well-established temporal narrative with a fixed future still exists. The nativism of 2019 is not identical to the nativism of 1925, but similar conceptions of time and of national form are at work in each situation. These forms of temporality and their exclusionary impulses are endemic to American national form. And, I would like to suggest, this kind of play with time is endemic to national form in general, whether in North America, Europe, or elsewhere.

Notes

1. For a useful survey of the literature on time and the nation, see Tim Edensor's "Reconsidering National Temporalities." Edensor is critical of uses of Ben-

edict Anderson that overemphasize the nation as a singular, strictly linear temporal form. In this essay, I am critiquing one among many temporal tendencies in the United States and in national form in general.

2. See Higham, King, and Ngai.

3. Eric Schewe, "The Historic Echoes of Trump's Immigration Ban," *JSTOR Daily*, 7 Feb., 2017. See also Priscilla Alvarez's 2017 interview with Alan Kraut in *The Atlantic*.

4. See Adam Serwer, "Jeff Sessions's Unqualified Praise for a 1924 Immigration Law," *The Atlantic*, 10 Jan., 2017.

5. See Daniels, *Guarding the Golden Door*.

6. In my use of Arendt to critique the logic of American nativism, I am not suggesting that the United States is a totalitarian nation. I am suggesting, however, that there are totalitarian tendencies at work in American nativism. In this context, it is worth noting the link between American nativism and German National Socialism that James Q. Whitman describes in *Hitler's American Model*: Nazi planners looked at American laws on immigration and miscegenation as explicit models for their own policies.

7. For readings of *The Great Gatsby* as a novel about time, see Barnhart (2014), Berman, Holquist, and Stallman. For readings of the novel that emphasize its entanglement with questions of immigration, race, and national identity, see Michaels and Nies.

8. Gatsby famously believes that the past can be repeated. See p. 116.

9. Both Mark Currie and Paul de Man see this kind of prolepsis as a constitutive feature of the novel. See Currie's *About Time*; de Man's "The Contemporary Criticism of Romanticism" (esp. p. 19); and Barnhart's "Prolepsis and Parabasis."

10. This is a point well represented in the writing on Yezierska's novel, a point made particularly strongly by Renny Christopher's "Rags to Riches to Suicide." Christopher characterizes the novel as a "narrative of unfulfilling transformation" and makes a strong case for the novel as a sharp critique of narrow forms of American identity.

11. See Chip Rhodes's reading of the novel, in which he argues that Sara merely exchanges one ideology for another. Unlike Christopher (see previous note), Rhodes sees the novel as an ideological justification of Sara's "choice" rather than as a critique. I argue that the novel betrays a deep ambivalence about Sara's chosen path.

Works Cited

Alvarez, Priscilla. "A Brief History of America's 'Love-Hate Relationship' with Immigration." *The Atlantic*, 19 Feb. 2017.

Anderson, Benedict. *Imagined Communities*. Verso, 1991.

Arendt, Hannah. *The Human Condition*. U of Chicago P, 1970.

———. *The Origins of Totalitarianism*. Harcourt Brace Jovanovich, 1979.

Berman, Ronald. *The Great Gatsby and Modern Times*. U of Illinois P, 1994.

Barnhart, Bruce. "Prolepsis and Parabasis." *Novel*, vol. 42, no. 2, 2009.

———. *Jazz in the Time of the Novel.* U of Alabama P, 2014.

Castoriadis, Cornelius. "Time and Creation." *World in Fragments*. Translated by David Ames Curtis, Stanford UP, 1997.

Christopher, Renny. "Rags to Riches to Suicide." *College Literature*, vol. 29, no. 4, Fall 2002, pp. 79–108.

Currie, Mark. *About Time: Narrative, Fiction and the Philosophy of Time*. Edinburgh UP, 2007.

Daniels, Roger. *Guarding the Golden Door*. Macmillan, 2005.

de Man, Paul. "The Contemporary Criticism of Romanticism." *Romanticism and Contemporary Criticism*. Johns Hopkins UP, 1993.

Edensor, Tim. "Reconsidering National Temporalities." *European Journal of Social Theory*, vol. 9, no. 4, 2006.

Fitzgerald, F. Scott. *The Great Gatsby*. Simon & Schuster, 1992.

Genette, Gérard. *Narrative Discourse*. Translated by Jane E. Lewin, Cornell UP, 1980.

Higham, John. *Strangers in the Land: Patterns of American Nativism, 1860–1925*. 2nd ed., Rutgers UP, 1988.

Holquist, Michael. "Stereotyping in Autobiography and Historiography: Colonialism in *The Great Gatsby*." *Poetics Today* vol. 9, no. 2, 1988, pp. 453–72.

King, Desmond. *Making Americans: Immigration, Race, and the Origins of the Diverse Democracy*. Harvard UP, 2002.

Michaels, Walter Benn. *Our America: Nativism, Modernism, Pluralism*. Duke UP, 1995.

Miller, J. Hillis. *The Ethics of Reading*. Columbia UP, 1987.

Ngai, Mae. *Impossible Subjects: Illegal Aliens and the Making of Modern America*. Princeton UP, 2004.

Nies, Betsy L. *Eugenic Fantasies: Racial Ideology in the Literature and Popular Culture of the 1920s*. Routledge, 2002.

"Prolepsis, *N*." *Oxford English Dictionary Online*. 2nd ed. Accessed July 2018.

Rhodes, Chip. "Education as Liberation: The Case of Anzia Yezierska's 'Bread Givers.'" *Science & Society*, vol. 57, no. 3, Fall 1993, pp. 294–312.

Schewe, Eric. "The Historic Echoes of Trump's Immigration Ban." *JSTOR Daily*, 7 Feb. 2017.

Serwer, Adam. "Jeff Sessions's Unqualified Praise for a 1924 Immigration Law." *The Atlantic*, 10 Jan. 2017.

Stallman, R.W. "Gatsby and the Hole in Time." *Modern Fiction Studies*, vol. 1, no. 4, Nov. 1995, pp. 2–16.

Wald, Priscilla. *Constituting Americans: Cultural Anxiety and Narrative Form*. Duke UP, 1995.

Whitman, James Q. *Hitler's American Model: The United States and the Making of Nazi Race Law*. Princeton UP, 2017.

Yezierska, Anzia. *Bread Givers*. Persea Books, 1999.

Chapter 7

Taking the Boundaries with You

Italy and the National in the Work of Luigi Di Ruscio, an Italian Migrant Writer in Norway

Sergio Sabbatini

Since its birth in 1861, Italy has been a nation with a weak self-identity, and this weakness is reflected in the development of its language and letters. The Italian literary canon starts with Dante, and it is his fourteenth-century Tuscan dialect that became the basis for the modern Italian language. In Italy, literature was the chosen instrument of intellectual elites and romantic critics for unifying a country in which only 2 percent of the population actively used that language or could read that very literature. In his monograph, *La letteratura degli italiani*, Franco Brevini discusses the price that Italian writers outside of Tuscany had to pay when they employed this literary Italian—a sort of Esperantic dead language based on Tuscan dialect—in order to convey the flavors of their most intimate emotions, their connections to home, their familiar experiences, their everyday lives—all events naturally expressed orally in their native dialects.

It is interesting and exemplary, then, that as an Italian immigrant in Norway, the poet and novelist Luigi Di Ruscio (1930–2011) chose to express himself in the standard literary Italian language and find inspiration in the classic Italian literary canon. His writerly preference for literary Italian coexisted with his use of Norwegian with his family in Oslo, as well as the dialect of Fermo in the Marche region when he visited his hometown in Italy during his holidays. In fact, Di Ruscio, a poor immigrant from the Marche, chose in the 1950s to recall and reuse a literary canon based on elitist Italian national discourses established one hundred years before by a political and intellectual minority. Despite his origins and his active militancy in international movements such as factory workers' associations and the Communist Party, literary Italian appears to have sustained his identity in a foreign country. At the same time, through the act of writing, he exhibited a marked relationship to both international and national discourses as he recreated a new and personal language.

In this chapter I consider the persistence of national discourses in the work of Di Ruscio who lived, worked, and wrote in Norway from the moment he moved there in 1957 until his death in 2011. In addition, I highlight the idiosyncrasies in the work of this Italian author living outside of Italy and analyze his linguistic strategies as a migrant writer who had to deal with the issues and conceptions of national identity/identities.

Di Ruscio moved to Norway at the end of the 1950s, not only for economic reasons, but also for political ones. He was born in the little town of Fermo in the Marche region in central Italy and was a militant in the Italian Communist Party, making it difficult for him to find a job in a postwar Italian province ruled by the Christian Democratic Party. His solution was to move to Oslo where his uncle had lived and worked for a short time; perhaps Di Ruscio had planned only a short stay, but he ended up working in a metallurgical factory (Christiana Spigerverk) for forty years. In his works, he returns several times to the struggle of the Norwegian workers organizations that won the battle for the forty-hour workweek, giving him the opportunity to focus on his writing during the entire weekend. He actually dedicated all his weekends to the act of writing in his Norwegian home—an activity he had already begun in Italy at the beginning of the 1950s. For Di Ruscio, writing was a moment completely detached from his everyday Norwegian life, a pursuit that took him back to his original country, Italy, and its language and literature. Yet, none of his family members understood Italian. As he tells us in his own words, Norwegian was the language he spoke with them and with his colleagues:

> In any case the narration of the events in Oslo will be complicated by the language issue and the narrator can only use the Italic language. Here everything is expressed in the Norwegian language that I understand perfectly; however I'm half-illiterate

> in the Norwegian language in the sense that I read and speak Norwegian perfectly but do not know how to write it. On the contrary, I can read and write Italian very well, but I speak it now very badly: I will try to translate the Nordic word—simultaneously into the language that the undersigned is quite capable of writing—but I never read Italic grammar, let alone Norwegian. Writing is complicated also because I live in one room and kitchen with my wife and a son. And lately we have had a daughter too, and I no longer know where to plant the typewriter for the several novels I am working on, and I no longer know when I can type the metal letters that swoop down on paper without waking with keystrokes the people piled above us and also under. The nest on the third floor is now too full. We risk falling anytime now. The wife accuses the typewriter, now in perpetual motion here from Friday night to Monday. It will not stop since the Nordic working class has freed all our Saturdays. (Di Ruscio 19–20; translations are mine; original Italian passages are found in endnotes)[1]

While his everyday life was in Norway, his artistic work was strongly anchored to Italy and its literary tradition. In fact, his literary career took place only in Italy, the country where his works were published and where his literary contacts resided. Indeed, he never published in Norway or in Norwegian and one might say that he rebuilt his Italian home through his writing. It is possible to see here, as Sante Matteo notes, the image of writing as the writer's only home—something that is found in many texts pertaining to migrant writing (Matteo 243). Matteo further remarks that "migrant writers" are not "minor" writers, giving voice to the marginalized "other" who does not feel at home in either the world left behind or in the new world they have migrated to, but rather they should be seen as "major" writers who voice the displacement that all human beings feel as we cross or are crossed by shifting social, political, racial, and gendered borders (247). In effect, Di Ruscio lacked the status as a writer to justify his migration and his state of in-betweenness.

Italian critics labeled him as *poeta operaio* (worker poet)—close to the political left-wing movements—a label acknowledged by Di Ruscio himself. Indeed, one of his most famous novels is titled *Palmiro*, after Palmiro Togliatti, the mighty head of the Italian Communist Party during and after World War II, but it is far too reductive to summarily place Di

Ruscio in a minor literary category and leave it at that. His first poem collections were reviewed by great poets such as Franco Fortini and Salvatore Quasimodo. He has also often been called a *poeta neorealista*, and some consider him close to the so-called *Neoavanguardia* (new avant-garde) movement in Italian literature that started with the Gruppo 63 (founded in 1963), though his writing is never as dry and intellectual as that of its main representatives and is instead notably realistic and true to life. But neorealism does not fit either. He reminded Italo Calvino of Céline because of "his will to download a dark aggression in his word flow" (qtd. in Ferracuti). Further, his novels are also often marked by a Joycean stream of consciousness, and some scholars have also found an affinity to the works of the Czech writers Hrabal and Hasek because of his reckless and funny language (Ferracuti). Surrealism is also a key to reading Di Ruscio's novels, due to his love of analogies, free associations, digressions, and nonsense. While Andrea Cortelessa speaks about a "jazzy way of writing" (qtd. in Ferracuti), Di Ruscio himself, an autodidact in the world of literature, tells us that he found inspiration in the works of Gramsci and Anceschi, Cesare Pavese and Italian neorealism, together with the work of his fellow Marchigiano poet Leopardi—"with my poems I had become 'a tale of laughter and amusements' " (Di Ruscio 17).[2] Dante, Foscolo, Belli, and the first works of Montale and Ungaretti count among other crucial influences—yet, as mentioned earlier, Di Ruscio is primarily viewed as a worker poet while the significance of his achievement as an Italian writer has been underemphasized. In fact, generally speaking, until recently all literature written by Italian migrants has been seen as minor literature.

More recently, a postcolonial perspective on Italian literature has begun to shed some light on the works of Italians who emigrated, as well as the literature of today's immigrants in Italy who have chosen Italian as their writing language. There is, in fact, a sort of amnesia about the long history of Italian emigration together with that of Italian colonialism, which only now has begun to be discovered, along with the focus on migrant or multicultural Italophone literature of today (see the debate on *letteratura italiana della migrazione* in Gnisci or in Quagliarelli). In *Borderlines*, Jennifer Burns notes that the social position and the "hybrid" condition of the migrant author make her/his access to both the tools of production (language included) and the channels of distribution problematic, while the low profile of these texts results in persistent difficulties in reaching—at the very least—a relatively wide and varied reading public. Nonetheless, because of its marginal position, the migration narrative has the potential to suggest alternative models and introduce new elements, simultaneously challenging and pushing out the limits set by the canon. In this sense, narratives of migration, one of the forms of "minor literature" (qtd. in Burns) described by Deleuze and Guattari, can be considered the only ones capable of becoming truly "major" or innovative (or "revolutionary") works, precisely because of their condition of "deterritorialisation" (Burns 231).

In *La neve nera di Oslo* (*The black snow of Oslo*) we see that Di Ruscio's state of displacement as an Italian in Norway comes back constantly, together with the alienation connected with his condition as a poet—although things are typically seen with an ironic distance, a trait typical of peripheral writers:

> I heroically put up with the mockery of the Italian poet who works in a factory in Oslo, metallurgical poets in Norway have never existed; however, with the Italians everything is possible. I was also called a *spaghettaro*, a spaghetti *poet*, the spaghetti that my Nordic wife cooked in terror for fear of making a mistake with the pepper, salt, vitriol and moldy canned chilis and Madonna Santa.[3] (Di Ruscio 26)

La neve nera di Oslo is a first-person narrative in which Di Ruscio uses a stream of consciousness technique full of puns, parodies, and allusions to tell us about his life in Norway: His hellish work in the spike factory, his pride in being part of an international working class, his family—his wife Mary and four children—and his situation as a writer in a sort of linguistic isolation. To these he adds personal, political, and philosophical considerations, and the problem of his identity is also crucial: "The problem of my identity: a 'yours truly' Italian that has lived in Italy for only 27 years and the last 43 years he has lived in Norway, collapsing constantly in his Italianitude [Italianness]" (32).[4]

At this point in the narrative he is now retired and writes and works as a full-time poet and the feeling of displacement he feels is the same as he felt before leaving Italy in the 1950s. At that time, he was somehow soothed by reading foreign literature in translation; now in Norway he tries to hold on to his "Italianitude" by visiting the library of the local Italian Cultural Institute:

> When I was Italic, I almost always read only translated books—the cosmopolitan character of the Italian intellectual—because not to die I had to do everything to strengthen my identity and I found

> the "italianitudine"; I went to the Italian Cultural Institute to defend it, my "italianitudine." Here, in the communal libraries, I found Italian books that were exclusively by Italian authors, searching through the pages, among the books. An identity based on Carducci, Pascoli, D'Annunzio would have been a repugnant thing. In this Ibsen, Kierkegaard, Strindberg are better, much better.[5] (Di Ruscio 37–38)

Here, he refers always to an *italianitudine* ("Italianitude"), which as an expression of the national spirit of *modern* Italy must be different than *italianità* (Italianness or the Italian spirit). In line with the latter, he calls himself *italico*—Italic—but still never *italiano*, Italian.

Accordingly, the worker poet is reluctant to read his work at the Italian Cultural Institute in Oslo. The new dentures that will prevent him from reading properly serve as an excuse, but the larger issue is his reluctance to "becoming a well-known poet in Oslo, where I would want to live in complete secrecy" (Di Ruscio 38).[6] He does not wish to be the instrument of a national culture associated with Fascism, as evidenced by his contrasting his situation to that of the poet Amelia Rosselli, who was also born in 1930 and moved to Italy from France in the 1950s, at the same time that Di Ruscio had moved to Norway. Rosselli used Italian as the language of her poetry and became well known, even though Italian was the language of the Fascists who killed her father, a language that was not even her mother tongue. For Di Ruscio, working in Italian was a personal choice that helped obscure his public persona: "I write in Italian and even here in my house where no one will ever read what I write" (Di Ruscio 47–8).[7] Thus, for Di Ruscio, the act of writing has become a sanctuary where the poet finds asylum from the hell of the factory and the boredom of family routines.

Still, his family is a comfort; there is also a lot of love for his wife Mary and his children, especially the young one, Adrian, who, depicted in the narrative as an image of Di Ruscio himself as child, runs to greet his father when he returns home at the end of the workday. But there was anguish as well. Mary was always threatening to throw his manuscript to the winds, as she once actually did, scattering his chaotic unnumbered text all over their modest apartment. But overshadowing the succor and difficulties of his familial relationships there was Norway, a place that seemed to him as far and different from his Italy as was conceivable:

> How did I end up in Norway? About Norway I knew only Ibsen and while I was reading him I thought that if Norway had a similar poet, then it had to be a beautiful country. As a kid I loved the books of polar adventures. When Thomas Mann was stripped of his German citizenship, he said that where he was, there was Germany. It also happens to yours truly, transplanted further north than anyone in the whole history of literature, dragging an extremism almost suckled by village breasts, an opposition that serves mostly to show that diversity is still possible.[8] (Di Ruscio 82)

Transplantation to the far north was an act of literary and political will that tested his resolve, particularly as he aged, but the reasons for his flight from Italy remained utmost in his mind. Lamenting his inability to assimilate in Norway, he realized nonetheless that even when writing his last book, *La neve nera*, the Italy he rejected had not changed:

> I had been Italian in Italy until 1957, for 27 years; now I am 78 years old and I should be more Norwegian than Italian. That is the terrifying problem of clinging to identity. Nonetheless, certain aspects of Italianitude have become really repulsive to me. Perhaps the idea that there are two Italies is true: a Sanfedist and reactionary majority broken to all corruptions, versus the other Italy, the modern, enlightened Italy that arises at certain times as a tiny minority. The first becomes more and more unbearable and disgusting to me as the second becomes numerically insignificant.[9] (Di Ruscio 92–93)

As he struggles to recover his Italianness to no avail, he must also come to terms with how alien Norway feels. He visits Oslo Cathedral and takes in the painting of the Last Supper. He finds that Jesus and the disciples are blond and beautiful, but Di Ruscio can only find himself in the character of Judas, short and black haired. Even his wife betrays his patrimony; she takes back her maiden surname after having problems using Di Ruscio in Norway. He writes, "Even his fellow workers know perfectly well that he is not normal, being as he says an Italic. His wife keeps telling him to stop writing poems and apply for the Norwegian citizenship and to get normalized before dying" (Di Ruscio 105–06)![10] Yet he cannot. He is still filled with his Italian "linguistic universe," which is actually *fermano*, from his hometown of Fermo:

> I transplanted all my Ferman linguistic universe to Oslo while it was disappearing in Fermo because of these endless mass communications. Transportation has been facilitated by the fact that this entire linguistic universe takes up very little space, not even a handbag is necessary, I passed the frontiers like a king without customs hassles . . . the linguistic universe is my soul, the souls pass borders very easily. Thomas Mann when the Nazis took away his German citizenship declared in an interview that where he was there too was also Germany. Where is yours truly is also our entire Italianitude. My soul filled with this linguistic universe is stubbornly chasing me.[11] (Di Ruscio 106–07)

As noted earlier, Franco Brevini writes about the difficulties non-Tuscan Italian writers faced when they had to use the canonic Italian literary language to convey the flavors of their most intimate emotions connected to their homes, their familiar experiences, their everyday experiences—all events naturally expressed orally in their native dialects.

Di Ruscio tackles these shortcomings by manipulating and changing the canonic Italian literary language by using nonsense, mistakes, Freudian slips, repetitions, and he sees lapsus as a truth shouted by the unconscious. In *La neve* he ironically calls himself "*la vergogna delle lettere italiche*," or "the shame of Italic literature," but later he insists "*continuare ad ogni costo la sgrammaticatura delle carte*," that he must "continue at all costs the ungrammatical qualities of the writings" (Di Ruscio 95). Here Di Ruscio resembles another famous Italian emigrant writer, Luigi Meneghello, who also plays with the ungrammatical character of the vernacular. As Lorenzo Chiesa explains, for dialectophones such as Meneghello and Di Ruscio, one:

> can only write in Italian . . . through an operation of cutting—which in different ways echoes a common primordial repression, namely that of our dialect—followed in its turn by some kind of sewing, of re-composition, on which, in general, we could define as, with different intonations, neologistic. The originality of this kind of writing is therefore based on a "twisting" technique that complicates the original meaning of some words (or expressions) whilst continuing to let it glimpse in the background. (326)

Emanuele Zinato notices Di Ruscio's resemblance to Meneghello, as he sees in Di Ruscio's language games and in his permanent digression strategy a way to unveil and deconstruct the collective unconscious of the Italian people (3). Those are the same writing strategies that Brevini again finds in another author from the same region of Di Ruscio, Dolores Prato, in her most famous novel *Giù la piazza non c'è nessuno.* There, as in Di Ruscio, he finds "a stubborn disarticulation of the rhetoric structures of the Italian tradition and a quest for irregularities, exceptions, eccentricities that she found in dialect, in regional Italian, in the spoken language against the written one: a revolt against the literary Tuscan that was imposed onto her in the nuns' boarding school" (qtd.in Paolini Giachery 10, my translation). Di Ruscio enumerates a stimulating list of his frequent language slips in his unpublished work *Brodo comico*, which gives us an example of his typical language manipulation:

> not to clear but to brighten, not consumerism but communism, not drilled but transformed, not we touched on but we went out, not al dente but ardent, not led to but smashed, not drafts but beatings, not error but horror, not I but God, not parody but poetry, not mistaken but gag, not the end of the "mimmennium" but the end of the millennium, not quashed but bullshit, not the procession of the pork of God but the procession of the body of God.[12] (*Brodo comico, Zibaldone norvegese*, qtd. in Ferracuti)

In conclusion, as a poor, working-class immigrant from the Marche to 1950s Norway, Di Ruscio managed to sustain his identity in a foreign country in part by recalling and reusing a literary canon based on elitist Italian nationalistic discourses established one hundred years before by a political and intellectual minority. Despite his common origin and his active militancy in international global movements such as factory workers associations and the Communist Party, literary Italian was an increasingly important part of his identity. But in choosing the techniques of surrealism—nonsensical phrasing and linguistic manipulation—as tools in an attempt to manage and control a literary tradition, Di Ruscio alienated both sides of his true self—both the revolutionary socialist and the struggling migrant. As he said to his Italian critics, "Dear professors in belles-lettres, I write very ugly literature and don't bust my balls"[13] (qtd. in Ferracuti). It is interesting here to remember how Julia Kristeva, in *Strangers to Ourselves*, analyzes the condition of those foreigners and immigrants who refuse the culture and rules of their hosts, and reconstruct on the new territory the institutions of their country of origin (noted in Masolini 253). This practice, as Kristeva observes, clearly has more to do with reinvention, subversion, and creative narration than with preserving ancient traditions and thus is similar to the writing strategies of Luigi Di Ruscio, and along with him of other dialectophone "minor" writers who engage and struggle with the legacy of the canonic Italian literary language.

Notes

1. In ogni caso la narrazione degli avvenimenti in Oslo si farà complicata per la questione linguistica, il narratore può adoperare solo la lingua italica e qui tutto si esprime in norvegese lingua che io capisco alla perfezione però della lingua norvegese io sono per metà analfabeta nel senso che leggo e parlo alla perfezione il norvegese ma non lo so scrivere, al contrario, l'italiano lo leggo e scrivo molto bene ma lo parlo ormai molto male, comunque il verbo nordico cercherò di tradurlo simultaneamente nella lingua che il sottoscritto è abbastanza capace d'iscrivere, mai letta una grammatica italica e figuriamoci quella norvegese, la scrittura si complica maggiormente perché io con mia moglie e un figlio e ultimamente mi è nata anche una femmina abitiamo in una camera e cucina e ormai non so più dove piantare la macchina da scrivere per i romanzi consecutivi e non si sa più quando battere le letterine metalliche che piombano sulla carta senza svegliare con le battiture il popolo accumulato sopra di noi e anche sotto abitando al terzo piano il nido è ormai troppo pieno rischiamo di precipitare da un momento all'altro, la consorte mette sotto accusa la macchina da scrivere ormai volta in un moto perpetuo qui dal venerdì sera al lunedì non si ferma più avendo la classe operaia nordica liberato tutti i nostri sabato.

2. *con le mie poesie ero diventato* "argomento di riso e trastullo."

3. Sopporto eroicamente l'irrisione del poeta italiano che lavora in una fabbrica di Oslo, poeti metallurgici in Norvegia non sono mai esistiti però con gli italiani tutto è possibile. Venivo chiamato anche poeta spaghettaro, spaghetti che mia moglie nordica cucinava con terrore per paura di sbagliare con il pepe, sale, vetriolo e conserve ammuffite e peperoncini e la Madonna Santa.

4. Il problema della mia identità: un sottoscritto italiano che però ha vissuto in Italia per solo anni 27 e gli ultimi 43 anni li ha vissuti in Norvegia profondando continuamente nella propria *italianitudine.*

5. Quando ero italico leggevo quasi sempre libri tradotti, il carattere cosmopolita dell'intellettuale italiano, per non morire ho dovuto fare del tutto per rafforzare la mia identità ed ho trovato l'italianitudine, andavo all'istituto di italianistica a difenderla, la mia italianitudine. Qui nelle biblioteche popolari trovavo

libri italiani che erano esclusivamente di autori italiani, cercare tra le pagine, tra i libri una identità basata su Carducci, Pascoli, D'Annunzio sarebbe stata cosa troppo ripugnante, in questo caso è meglio molto meglio Ibsen, Kierkegaard, Strindberg.

6. Cerco di evitare di diventare un poeta nominato anche ad Oslo dove vorrei vivere in una completa clandestinità

7. Scrivo in italiano e perfino qui a casa mia nessuno potrà mai leggere quello che scrivo

8. Come sono capitato in Norvegia? Di norvegese conoscevo solo Ibsen e mentre lo leggevo pensavo che se la Norvegia ha un poeta simile deve essere un paese bellissimo, da ragazzino amavo i libri delle avventure polari, quando a Thomas Mann fu tolta la cittadinanza tedesca disse che dove era lui era tutta la Germania, succede anche al sottoscritto trapiantato più a nord di tutta la storia delle lettere trascinando un estremismo quasi poppato dalle mammelle paesane, una opposizione che serve più che altro a dimostrare che una diversità è ancora possibile.

9. Sono stato italiano in Italia sino al 1957, sino a 27, ora ho anni 78, dovrei essere più norvegese che italiano, c'è quel problema terrificante dell'identità, però certi aspetti dell'italianitudine sono diventati veramente ripugnanti, forse è vera la questione delle due italie, una maggioranza sanfedista e reazionaria rotta a tutte le corruzioni, l'altra Italia, quella avanzata, illuminata che in certe epoche è una minoranza ristrettissima, la prima mi diventa sempre più insopportabile e schifosa più la seconda diventa numericamente insignificante.

10. Gli operai sanno bene che sono italico, di conseguenza non troppo normale di testa. Mia moglie continua a dirmi di smettere di scrivere le poesie e prendere la cittadinanza norvegese e prima di morire normalizzati!

11. Tutto l'universo linguistico fermano l'ho trapiantato ad Oslo mentre a Fermo a causa delle infinite comunicazioni di massa spariva. Il trasporto è stato facilitato dal fatto che tutto questo universo linguistico occupa pochissimo spazio, non è stata necessaria neppure una borsetta, ho trapassato le frontiere come un Re senza noie doganali . . . l'universo linguistico è l'anima mia, le anima trapassano le frontiere come niente fosse. Thomas Mann quando i nazisti gli tolsero la cittadinanza tedesca dichiarò in una intervista che dove era lui era anche la Germania. Dove è il sottoscritto è anche tutta la nostra italianitudine. L'anima mia riempita dall'universo linguistico mi insegue caparbia.

12. Non chiarire ma chiarore, non consumismo ma comunismo, non trapanò ma trasformò, non strusciammo ma uscimmo, non al dente ma ardente, non sfociate ma sfasciate, non le bozze ma le botte, non errore ma orrore, non io ma Iddio, non parodia ma poesia, non sbaglio ma bavaglio, non la fine del mimmennio ma del millennio, non cassate ma cazzate, non la processione del porco d'Iddio ma del corpo d'Iddio.

13. Carissimi professori in belle lettere, io scrivo lettere bruttissime e non rompetemi i coglioni.

Works Cited

Brevini, Franco. *La letteratura degli italiani. Perché molti la celebrano e pochi la amano*. Feltrinelli, 2010.

Burns, Jennifer and Polezzi Loredana, editors. *Borderlines. Migrazioni e identità nel Novecento*. Cosmo Iannone Editore, 2003.

Chiesa, Lorenzo. "Luigi Meneghello: 'I-taglia,' between 'dispatrio' and 'bad' dialect." *Borderlines. Migrazioni e identità nel Novecento*, edited by Jennifer Burns and Polezzi Loredana, Cosmo Iannone editore, 2003, pp. 325–33.

Di Ruscio, Luigi. *La neve nera di Oslo*. Ediesse, 2010.

Ferracuti, Angelo. Preface, *La neige noire d'Oslo/The Black Snow of Oslo*. Anacharsis, 2014, irisnews.net/luigi-di-ruscio-la-neve-nera-di-oslo-la-neige-noire-doslo/.

Gnisci, Armando. *Creolizzare l'Europa: Letteratura e migrazione*. Meltemi Editore, 2003.

Matteo, Sante. "Lamefricatalia: Italian Lessons in Elision, Truncation, and Contraction." *Borderlines. Migrazioni e identità nel Novecento*, edited by Jennifer Burns and Polezzi Loredana, Cosmo Iannone editore, 2003, pp. 239–51.

Masolini, Alessandra. "Between an Irish God and Anglo-Saxon Faces." *Borderlines. Migrazioni e identità nel Novecento*, edited by Jennifer Burns and Polezzi Loredana, Cosmo Iannone editore, 2003, pp. 253–59.

Paolini Giachery, Noemi. "Il primo, sconosciuto romanzo di Dolores Prato." *Campane a Sangiocondo*. Avagliano editore, 2009.

Quagliarelli, Lucia, editor. *Certi confini. Sulla letteratura italiana dell'immigrazione*. Morellini editore, 2010.

Zinato, Emanuele. "For Said, Against Said: Between Literary Criticism and Contemporary Italian Studies." *Postcolonialitalia: Postcolonial Studies from the European South*, 17 Feb. 2014, www.postcolonialitalia.it/index.php?option=com_content&view=article&id=57:per-said,-contro-said&catid=27:interventi&Itemid=101&lang=it.

Chapter 8

Monuments Carved in Film[1]

Developing Civic Awareness through the Memory of Fallen Anti-Mafia Activists

Stefano Adamo

Introduction

Placido Rizzotto and Peppino Impastato were two young Italian Mafia victims whose names were long forgotten until their stories became the subject of two films released in 2000: *Placido Rizzotto*, by Pasquale Scimeca, and *One Hundred Steps*, by Marco Tullio Giordana. The two films are today seen as part of a wider cultural movement prompted by the Mafia terrorist attacks of 1992 to 1993, which aimed at developing a strong anti-Mafia sentiment in the Italian population. Taken together, these films and the cinematic trend to which they belong are also said to have contributed to building a different sense of national identity in opposition to the culture, values, and behaviors that allow the Mafia to thrive. The present chapter elaborates on these claims by relating the cultural impact of these films to their stylistic and narrative means, and it shows that they break away from the conventions of the Mafia film tradition, particularly of American cinema, in at least three significant ways. First, by dismissing the entertaining gangster-movie style of traditional movies, these films encourage viewers to question the individualistic myths that surround the Mafia and to consider its social downsides. Second, by focusing on little-known activists rather than prominent Mafiosi and their institutional opponents—police officers, prosecutors, etc.—they counter a deep-rooted notion according to which Mafia members may well use violence against each other, but do not generally hurt their surrounding community. Third, by emphasizing the pathetic aspects of their stories, these films elicit an emotional response that may leave a deeper trace of the story's meaning than more spectacular films of the kind. In addition to formal analysis, the chapter contains an overview of the critical and popular reception of these films, which adds support to claims about their cultural impact.

It is generally recognized by the scholarly community that *One Hundred Steps* (*I cento passi*, 2000) and *Placido Rizzotto* (2000) belong to a series of films that have introduced significant changes in the representation of the Mafia at the turn of the twenty-first century (Small; Pastorino, "Tano"; Marcus; Pugliese; Albano 117–18). In a seminal paper on this topic, Millicent Marcus has identified *Il giudice ragazzino* (1994) as the film that marked "the transition from the cinema politico genre of the 1970s and the 1980s to the more poetic, nuanced, anthropological approach of the late 1990s" (292). A short list of such films, however, should also include *The Escort* (*La scorta*, 1993), which uses an action-movie style to expose the corruption and inefficiency that taint the very forces that should fight the Mafia (Marangi and Rossi 133; Albano 82); *An Eyewitness Account* (*Testimone a rischio*, 1997), in which the true story of an eyewitness to a Mafia execution who has to give up his identity to save his life turns into a metaphysical narrative with a Kafkaesque flair (Albano 88–90); as well as *To Die for Tano* (*Tano da morire*, 1997) and *Johnny Stecchino* (1991), which taken together overturn traditional Mafia film motifs in favor of a humorous and derisive approach (Small 41; Albano 81–82). In this cinematic wave, *Placido Rizzotto* and *One Hundred Steps* stand out for having achieved unparalleled cultural influence. *One Hundred Steps*, for example, was hailed as "[holding] out the hope of doing for the anti-Mafia movement in Italy what *Schindler's List* did for a wider public consciousness of the Holocaust" (Pugliese 1110). Similarly, *Placido Rizzotto* has been regarded as a revival of Italian engagé filmmaking, reminiscent of postwar neorealism (Marcus; Boylan).

Both public authorities and the public at large granted these two films significant attention at the time of their release (Albano 113–14). The first screening of *Placido Rizzotto* took place in the context of the Venice Film Festival on the day of the eighteenth anniversary of the assassination of General Carlo Alberto Dalla Chiesa. The date must have been no coincidence because Dalla Chiesa appears in the film as a young carabinieri captain investigating the disappearance of Rizzotto. The anti-Mafia president Giuseppe Lumìa and Dalla Chiesa's son, Nando, also attended the event, as well as many Sicilian mayors, which clearly suggests that the first release of *Placido Rizzotto* represented something more than the mere promotion of one of the many films of the festival (Porro). The official preview took place a month and a half later in the presence of the then-president of the Republic, Carlo Azeglio Ciampi. The opening of *One Hundred Steps* took place at the same Venice Film Festival. The film was in competition, and the screenwriters Claudio Fava and Monica Zappelli shared the best screenplay award with director Marco Tullio Giordana. A few months later, *One Hundred Steps* won five David di Donatello awards and was nominated for six *nastri d'argento* (the silver ribbon awards), winning for best screenplay. The list of prizes that the film either won or was nominated for includes thirty-three items.

Whether it was for the number of awards they received, or for the political and media attention they raised, it is undeniable that the two films played a decisive role in resurrecting the memory of their respective main characters (Bianconi; Macaluso; Cavallaro; Tornabuoni). It is significant, for example, that Maurizio Porro, in his chronicle of *Placido Rizzotto* opening in Venice, defined Rizzotto as "a crime-fighting unknown soldier." In contrast to this, today one can even find wine bottles—those produced on estates confiscated from organized crime—dedicated to Placido Rizzotto and Peppino Impastato (Fiano).[2] The different levels of renown of these two characters before and after the release of the films becomes apparent when comparing two of the most popular Mafia history books released before and after 2000, respectively. In *Storia della Mafia* by Salvatore Lupo, first published in 1993, Placido Rizzotto is mentioned twice: first in a list of three union organizers killed by the Mafia in the 1940s and later in a summary of his violent death described in six and a half lines (233–34). Peppino Impastato is evoked in eleven lines in the context of a description of a women's rebellion against the Mafia. In fact, the focus of the paragraph is more on Impastato's mother, Felicia Bartolotta, than on him (302). In *Cosa Nostra* by John Dickie, published in 2004, a whole section is dedicated to Peppino Impastato (363–76); less space is given to the story of Placido Rizzotto, which is told in half a page and in the context of the history of the *Corleonesi*, the Corleone Mafia family.[3] Nevertheless, his figure stands out as the only non-Mafioso victim of the postwar rural Mafia to appear in the book with his full name (352–53).

Finally, a simple query on Google Ngram Viewer checking for the frequency with which the names of Placido Rizzotto and Peppino Impastato appear in Italian-language books published around the year that the two films were released only confirms the strength of their cultural impact.

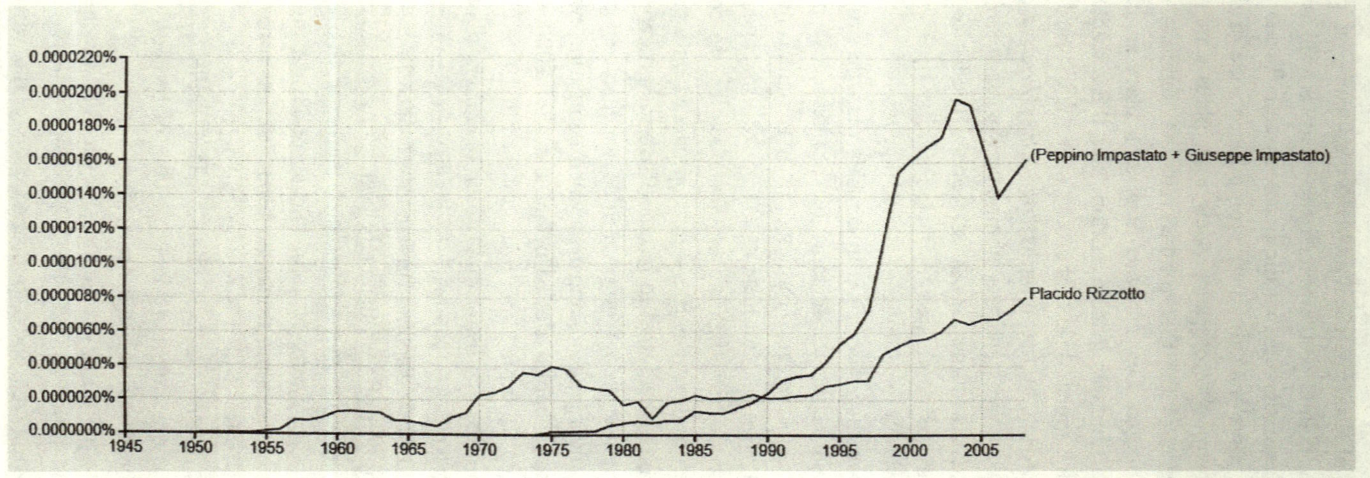

Figure 8.1. Relative frequency of *Placido Rizzotto* and *Peppino Impastato* in Italian Publications from 1945 to 2008.

In sum, the screenwriters of *Placido Rizzotto* and *One Hundred Steps* presented the stories of two relatively unknown characters, but the films made Rizzotto and Impastato highly recognizable figures, and imposed their life stories and intended meanings on the consciousness of the public. In an essay on *Placido Rizzotto*, Amy Boylan has observed that in the years following World War II, the memory of the resistance came to symbolize a new way in which Italians wanted to think of themselves as a nation, emphasizing discontinuity with the fascist past. She deliberates:

> Perhaps there is a movement to construct a new national—or at least regional identity—based on anti-Mafia activism by reviving the memory of fallen heroes like Peppino Impastato and Placido Rizzotto, as well as evoking a comparison between anti-fascist and anti-Mafia struggles? This nascent identity, then, would exist in opposition to the culture created by the Mafia and the solidified values and behaviours that allows the Mafia to operate unchallenged. (318)

In the pages below, I follow up on Marcus's and Boylan's suggestions about the power of these films to inspire a new sense of identity based on the opposition to the values and behaviors that allow the Mafia to thrive. Specifically, I show through what formal and narratological means the authors have achieved such a significant result. As a first step in this direction, I expand upon the common biographical and identity traits of the two characters that the films have emphasized.

Common Aspects of the Identity of the Two Characters

The characters of Placido Rizzotto and Peppino Impastato, as the two films represent them, show some typical features of cultural icons. On the surface, both had a rebellious character, died at a young age, and lived and carried out their political activity in areas of high Mafia concentration such as Cinisi and Corleone. Both had direct knowledge of the most important Mafia bosses of their time, from Cesare Manzella to Tano Badalamenti, from Michele Navarra to Luciano Leggio (aka Liggio). Peppino Impastato was even a son of a "man of honor," and godchild of the boss of Cinisi, Cesare Manzella.[4] In other words, the two young men were antagonistic to the power system surrounding them and, most importantly, died in a very violent way, which powerfully resonated with viewers when the movies came out, just eight years after the tragic attacks on magistrates Giovanni Falcone and Paolo Borsellino. Additionally, the two boys identified themselves with those segments of the Italian left that, aside from their underlying differences, have always championed the rule of law as a value in itself and contrasted with some deeply rooted Italian cultural traits, such as "amoral familism" in Banfield's sense. At the time of his death (1948), Placido Rizzotto was a local leader of the Italian Socialist Party, as well as secretary of the Corleone labor union headquarters and of the local branch of the veteran's association ("Rapporto sull'assassino" 110). As a union organizer, he stood out for his campaigns against illegal employment and worked hard to implement the so-called ""Gullo decrees" of 1944, a legislation package aimed at granting farmers the use of uncultivated land. Peppino Impastato was an agitator and a restless young man. He found personal fulfillment in civil engagement, which he carried out first as an independent journalist, and later as a full-fledged anti-Mafia activist. He participated in many of the political battles of the 1970s, from feminism to environmentalism, in a period when Italian environmentalism meant fighting against rampant building speculation, as the film at one point suggests. He was close to the extra-parliamentary left-wing ideology and to groups such as il Manifesto and Lotta Continua. His rebelliousness was not an unusual personality trait in that period of widespread political agitation, but the painful family conflict that he went through in his struggle against the Mafia adds a sign of distinction to his temperament (Behan; Pastorino, "Peppino"; De Stefano).

Whatever the ideological underpinnings of their activism, however, Peppino Impastato and Placido Rizzotto tried to confront a local and tangible political order that was responsible for the state of subjugation and backwardness of a significant part of the Sicilian population. The movies *Placido Rizzotto* and *One Hundred Steps* not only capture all the aspects outlined above, but also add a mythical aura to the characters. The contrast between the realistic appearance of the narrative and the mythical shape of the story is one of the most effective ways in which the films impose the two characters on the attention and memory of the audience.[5]

Between Realism and Myth

Both *Placido Rizzotto* and *One Hundred Steps* start with a scene set at the time of their protagonists' childhood. The former opens with an evocation of a fascist campaign to annihilate the Mafia led by the so-called "iron prefect" Cesare Mori. In the desolate atmosphere of a rural dawn, police officers arrest Placido's father, Carmelo Rizzotto, accusing him of collusion with local Mafiosi. The audience has no way of figuring out whether Placido's father really is in contact with the Mafia or if he is simply a victim of Mori's summary justice—nor does the film ever return to this subject. The scene, however, reproduces an episode of real life (Paternostro 11) and functions as a hint at the aggressive, although retrospectively ineffective, anti-Mafia offensive undertaken by Fascism. Carmelo Rizzotto soon reappears in the role of an iconic narrator engaged in telling the story of his son to a contemporary audience with the help of some hand-drawn illustrations. The scene, which operates as a frame story, brings to mind the old-time oral storytellers, and adds an aura of legend to the life and death of the young Corleonese union organizer. From that moment onwards, the film presents a discontinuous succession of episodes—a structure similar to that of mystery plays—in which each episode reveals a new aspect of the character's life and temperament, while simultaneously showing the Mafia activities of the time.

One Hundred Steps has a similar construction. The film opens with the birthday party of Cesare Manzella at his country house, an event that takes place when Peppino Impastato is still a child. Manzella was an uncle of Peppino and brother-in-law of his father, Luigi. The scene serves the purpose of showing the kinship between the Impastato family and prominent members of the local Mafia, which adds meaning to the political and ethical choices that Peppino would make later in life. Shortly afterwards, the audience realizes that Peppino's childhood is marked by the violent death of Cesare Manzella, who was killed by a car explosion in 1963 in the context of the first Mafia war. Peppino responds to this event by seeking out Stefano Venuti, a painter and Communist militant of the Cinisi section of the Italian Communist Party. Peppino's decision shows that he is curious to hear a voice from outside the choir. The film shows Peppino's meeting with Venuti as a decisive moment in the life of the protagonist. On the one hand, the child reveals a courageous and determined character because he shows up at Venuti's place with the expectation of hearing the painter confess the assassination of Manzella. On the other hand, however, Pepppino is fascinated by the sincerity and mildness that Venuti conveys and even connects with the painter's ideas through a conversation on the Russian poet Vladimir Mayakovski. The scene ends with the child's face suggestively morphing into that of the grown-up Peppino, played by Luigi Lo Cascio.

Both films, therefore, begin with a prologue consisting of a crucial episode from the childhood of their main character, followed by a brief interlude regarding that character's *bildung*. This narrative scheme is likely to bring to the mainstream viewer's mind a characteristic feature of myths and popular legends eventually taken up by contemporary serial fiction (i.e., the fact that the hero has an immutable character and a marked destiny [Eco 230]).[6] The films show Placido Rizzotto and Peppino Impastato going through a revealing and emotionally shocking experience at one point in childhood and living the rest of their lives as a function of that experience. As a child, Placido Rizzotto witnesses the fascist attempts to suppress the Mafia through repressive laws and brute force. As if the filmmakers wanted to suggest a follow-up to the experience of fascist repression, Placido reappears after a scene as a partisan in World War II. The childhood of Peppino, in *One Hundred Steps*, is characterized by a constant sense of peril that surrounds his home, marked by the brutal death of his uncle Cesare Manzella. In this case too, the succession of the sequences prompts viewers to connect the experiences of the young Peppino with his activism within the Cinisi branch of the Italian Communist Party and his fellowship with Stefano Venuti. With the exception of a few glimpses into Peppino's poetic sensitivity and the strong bond of love and affection that ties him to his mother (Pastorino, "Peppino"; De Stefano 322), the films show nothing of these two characters that is not related to their anti-Mafia commitment.

While the two films do not tell the lives of their respective protagonists in an accurate way, there is a recognizable method in their inaccuracies, which reinforces the idea that the filmmakers' intention was to create emblematic figures rather than sketch realistic biographies.[7] For example, at the death of Caesar Manzella in 1963, Peppino was no longer a child but a teenager of fifteen. In the Sicily of the time, a boy of that age would have been well acquainted with the ways of the world and therefore less impressionable than the film suggests. As for *Placido Rizzotto,* one element that adds a legendary aura to the biography of the eponymous character is the frame story of the storyteller mentioned above. The frame story serves two functions: On the one hand, it adds to the film a didactic connotation; on the other, it generates in the audience a sense of Brechtian estrangement, which forces viewers to follow the story with the emotional detachment that may help judge it rationally.[8] An example of this technique is found in one of the first scenes of the film, when Placido attempts to rescue some of the partisans captured by German troops. The characters' movements are plastic and theatrical; the struggle between Placido and the other soldiers looks forced and unnatural. Moreover, the scene itself is highly emblematic because it displays the salient features of the protagonist's personality, such as abnegation of duty and human generosity. Rizzotto is also shown from the start as a sacrificial figure. In this sense, it is tempting to interpret the image in which the young man celebrates his homecoming at the end of the war by widening his arms and taking deep breaths in front of the rocky landscape that surrounds Corleone. Those open arms and the low shooting angle—a momentary expression of joy and comfort—foreshadow the via crucis the protagonist is about to undertake. The identification of the sacrifice of Placido with that of Christ becomes even more explicit in the scene of the Passion play, which, placed as it is at the center of the film, functions as a mise en abyme of Placido's own story.

Although *One Hundred Steps* is stylistically different from Scimeca's film, it still bears traces of a didactic intent; as is the case, for example, with the many scenes in which the film deviates from historical reality. In particular, both films dwell on the conflict between father and child as a reflection of an ideological and moral clash. By stressing the conflict of Placido and Peppino with their respective fathers, the filmmakers achieve two results. On the one hand, they convey the provocative idea that rebellion against the Mafia goes along with a rebellion against culturally established commonsensical norms (e.g., minding one's own business, not obstructing the powerful, submitting even to the most controversial local customs). On the other hand, they compel viewers to think about the conflict with the Mafia in terms of other highly recognizable forms of conflict (i.e., generational), which may help create a sense of empathy and identification with the characters.

Other aspects of both films suggest the presence of a didactic intent. Marco Tullio Giordana, the director of *One Hundred Steps*, makes this intent explicit by including the final shots of *Hands over the City* (*Le mani sulla città*, 1963) in the film-club scene. *Hands over the City* is a classic "denunciation" film, and one of the most accurate representations of the corruption phenomena at the heart of the housing speculation in the economic boom years. In *One Hundred Steps*, another significant scene in this regard depicts Cesare Manzella explaining to the rest of the family that the oil production must change. As an old farmer objects that replacing the terra cotta jars with stainless-steel tins would require a huge investment, Manzella retorts that "we will have the regional government give us the *piccioli* (money)." Through this scene, the film captures the transformation of the Mafia during the 1950s into a criminal organization tied to public administration: procurements and funding in exchange for electoral preferences and territorial control.

The finale of *Placido Rizzotto* is visually rendered as a newsreel: the arrest of Luciano Leggio and his accomplices for the assassination of the protagonist is shown in a black-and-white vintage texture and shot from angles that recall a news-footage style. In addition to the formal solutions adopted by Scimeca in this or that scene, *Placido Rizzotto* reveals itself capable of illustrating a structural aspect of the Mafia phenomenon in a scene when the *caporali*—illegal labor intermediaries—gather in a square to recruit day laborers. During that scene, the roll call is suddenly interrupted by a union organizer who halts the process by encouraging laborers not to submit to the labor system imposed by the Mafia, but to turn to the official employment office instead. The young man is a friend and colleague of Placido's. Like the main character, he acts in the name of legality in an environment in which labor is regulated by long-established customary rules enforced by the local Mafia. The scene is constructed to show a contrast between the state and what may be called an anti-state. In doing so, the film reveals an aspect of Mafia activities that has been fleshed out at an academic level only in recent times, that of governance, i.e., regulating and controlling the production and distribution of a given product or service in an illegal way (Varese 14). Economic regulation and territorial control define the Mafia not merely as a criminal organization, such as a drug cartel, but as a more complex organization aiming at governing both illegal and legal activities within a given territory in lieu of the legitimate government.

The various dramatic and figurative elements twined together in the two films preside over the three discursive strategies that distinguish *Placido Rizzotto* and *One Hundred Steps* from the most well-known Mafia movies—especially the American productions of the 1970s to the 1990s that still dominate the popular imagination. These strategies are the downsizing of the image of the Mafioso, a focus on the Mafia victims rather than the mobsters, and an emphasis on the pathetic aspects of the stories, rather than the most spectacular ones. The following is an analysis of each strategy.

Individualistic Myths and Collective Misery

Tony Montana, Vito and Michael Corleone, Al Capone, Jimmy Conway: the main characters of the most popular Mafia movies appear like supermen.[9] They have charisma, intelligence, a nose for business. Ironically, they are "wise guys," as Henry Hill, the diegetic narrator of *Goodfellas*, calls them. The same can be said of many characters of Italian Mafia films, from Mariano Arena of *Mafia* (*Il giorno della civetta,* 1968) to Tano Cariddi of *La Piovra (3–7)*, not to mention Salvatore Giuliano, the never-seen-but-ever-present character of the eponymous film.[10] The characters that stand out in *One Hundred Steps* and *Placido Rizzotto* are instead young activists, farmers who claim rights, women subjugated by the violence and arrogance of men. Mafiosi do not have any character trait that makes them stand out from those around them. They are "like any other person," to quote a well-known observation by Giovanni Falcone ("Lotta alle mafie-Osservatorio su criminalità e malapolitica" 9:30).

In *Placido Rizzotto*, Michele Navarra, the powerful Mafia leader of Corleone, looks like a minor country boss. His political activity under the aegis of the Christian Democratic Party is never shown, and his medical profession never features on-screen, although it is mentioned in the dialogue. The paramedic who kills the young Salvatore Letizia, an alleged witness to the murder of Rizzotto, is represented as a fainthearted and terrified little man—the opposite of a cold, professional killer. The character of Luciano Leggio, often referred to by the other characters as "*lo sciancato*" (the gimp), looks prematurely aged and older than Rizzotto although, in real life, Leggio was eleven years younger than him. Vincenzo Collura and Pasquale Criscione, Leggio's accomplices and actual killers of Rizzotto, look like two misfits at the mercy of individuals who manipulate them like puppets. They are the opposite of the highly efficient hit teams of American cinema.

In *One Hundred Steps*, we find similar choices. Here, too, the Mafiosi look anything but supermen. Cesare Manzella is a flabby country lordling; Luigi Impastato a simple man who lives in terror; Anthony, Peppino's American cousin, looks mild and even reassuring. The only exception is Tano Badalamenti who, in Tony Sperandeo's interpretation, preserves the assertive temperament and authoritative appearance of a traditional film gangster. However, the fact remains that Badalamenti's characterization impresses the audience in a very different way from traditional film gangsters. Whereas characters such as Michael Corleone or Al Capone look intimidating and their businesses convey a sense of grandeur, Tano Badalamenti merely resembles a vulgar and pretentious small-town bully.[11] The film tells us nothing about him; his businesses never appear on screen; his figure does not stand out for any unique ability—not even his criminal skills. The only occupation the audience sees him involved in is that of a cattle rancher.

The two films not only downsize the stereotypical image of the Mafioso, but they also eschew the magnification of individual qualities in positive characters. The heroic character of the protagonists transpires from the narrative structure of the film, not from the interpretation of the actors. In fact, the actors who played them were unknown to the public at the time the films were released but were chosen for their physical resemblance with their respective characters. As some critics have already noticed, the characters of Placido Rizzotto and Peppino Impastato appear in the films as simply human characters, with their peculiarities and weaknesses (Boylan 312–14; De Stefano 322). This choice is in line with the intention of both films to focus on the unknown, the weak, the victims of the Mafia (Boylan 313–14; Small 50). This choice constitutes the second critical discursive strategy of the two films, namely that of placing Mafia victims at the center of their respective stories.

The Centrality of the Victims

Around the time in which Placido Rizzotto disappeared, there were many other Mafia victims in the surroundings of Palermo (Paternostro 16; "Dirigente"; "Un'ora"). The infamous adage "the Mafiosi only kill each other" is obviously not true, but no traditional film had ever put victims other than politicians, Mafiosi, and law-enforcement members at the center of their narrative. The filmmakers of *Placido Rizzotto* and *One Hundred Steps* chose instead to emphasize this aspect and load it with emotional strength, even at the price of some inaccuracies.

In *Placido Rizzotto*, for example, the focus on innocent victims comes with inaccuracies that prove very useful in provoking a sense of indignation in the viewers. One of these is the scene in which Lia, aka Leoluchina Sorisi, the girlfriend of Rizzotto, beats her belly with her fists after being abused by Luciano Leggio. The scene is graphic and suggests a fit of self-punishment, as well as an attempt to interrupt a possible pregnancy. In real life, Luciano Leggio was found hiding in the house of Leoluchina Sorisi at the time of his arrest in 1964, an episode that turned Rizzotto's girlfriend into a controversial figure (Dickie 356). Likewise, the events surrounding the death of Salvatore Letizia in *Placido Rizzotto* are given more emphasis than what the chronicles of the time would have us to imagine.[12] The film shows Salvatore's father vehemently and even violently pressing Pasquale Criscione to turn himself over to the carabinieri. According to Dino Paternostro, the parents of the young boy did not press charges, nor did they report to Dalla Chiesa the names that Salvatore had mumbled in delirium in the hours that preceded his fatal hospitalization (40–42). It looks as if the film was trying to magnify the figure of an innocent victim such as Salvatore's father, attributing to him a more virtuous behavior than omertà. Finally, the end scene of *Placido Rizzotto* brings together, in a single frame, Pio La Torre and Carlo Alberto Dalla Chiesa, united, in the plot of the film as in real life, by a tragic correspondence between their respective fates and that of Rizzotto. It is not known whether La Torre and Dalla Chiesa ever met, but it does not matter: by showing that handshake, the film draws a parallel between Placido Rizzotto and more famous figures of Mafia martyrs. In doing so, the film pays a tribute to the memory of those who have fought the Mafia to the death.

In One *Hundred Steps*, Felicia Impastato, Peppino's mother, occupies a relatively large space. Throughout the film, the woman is always shown as a passive and patient victim of the situation and appears four times in the foreground during the funeral scene. In a scene that is especially memorable for Peppino's reading of Pasolini's poem "*Supplica a mia madre*" ("Prayer to my mother"), Felicia is shown carrying books and supplies to her son while he is living in a garage after having been kicked out by his father. In an interview book released by the Sicilian Documentation Center, "Giuseppe Impastato," Peppino's mother confirmed the authenticity of the event depicted in the film but also added that she would let Peppino enter the house behind her husband's back (*Bartolotta Impastato* 34).[13] Felicia Impastato was not the mild and sorrowful woman portrayed in the film. She was a brave and resolute woman, as she proved in the years following her son's death when she joined her family members in the struggle to keep alive the memory of Peppino and transform him into a symbol of anti-Mafia activism (Lupo 302; Dickie 376; Puccio-Den 34). The story of Peppino's time away from home could have been told in many ways. The film selects the moments in which Felicia catered to her son in his improvised lodging and omits those in which she snuck him back into their home against her husband's will. The character of Felicia portrayed in the film, however, is better suited to stir empathy and compassion in the audience, which is in line with the discourse strategy of *One Hundred Steps*, a film that does not aim to represent heroism as something exceptional but focuses on the tragedies of ordinary people.

From Thrill to Compassion

Traditionally, movies that tell stories of organized crime, based as they are on the actions of extraordinary characters staged in action-movie style, generate entertainment by thrilling the audience. In some cases, such feelings may be tempered by a sense of moral repulsion emanating from the endless episodes of murder, betrayal, and other violations of common ethical principles that these stories lump together.[14] *Placido Rizzotto* and *One Hundred Steps*, instead, attempt to engender a reaction of empathy and compassion in the audience as a result of the numerous scenes in which the action is suspended and, through a careful balance of music and images, viewers are invited to linger on the humane aspects of the story. The scene where Lia lies on her bed and strikes her womb as to destroy the consequence of the sexual abuse she suffered from Leggio clearly shows the film's aim at provoking the kind of sensations described above. I have already mentioned how inaccurate the construction of the character of Rizzotto's girlfriend is—a controversial figure such as Leoluchina Sorisi is transformed into a loyal partner. I should add that Lia's rape sequence comes along with the drama of her mother who, unable to overcome her inertia, involuntarily becomes an accomplice in the violence committed against her daughter. Amy Boylan wrote that "Lia's mother's actions can be read as an allegory of the self-destructive way many Sicilians have responded to the Mafia's overwhelming grip on their region" (314). In this case, however, the moral outrage that the filmmakers may have expected from the audience is provoked by acting upon the audience's emotions rather than by stimulating their critical thinking.

In *One Hundred Steps*, the funeral scene is accompanied by the notes of "A Whiter Shade of Pale" by Procol Harum, which is not only a hymn of the counterculture of the sixties and seventies, and therefore a representative song of that period, but also a song with characteristic features such as gospel influences, a minor chord, and a hegemony of the organ over the other instruments. All these features give to that musical piece and to the scene a remarkable emotional tension. *One Hundred Steps* is a "realistic" film in a traditional sense, meaning that it is relatively accurate in its historical reconstruction. Nevertheless, the film does not fall short of providing highly dramatic moments and theatrical inventions aimed at stimulating an emotional response in the viewers. One can think, for example, of the scene that gives the film its title, in which Peppino yells in contempt of the Mafia in front of the building where Tano Badalamenti lives. Or again at the use of music, as remarked by Gloria Pastorino, which accompanies the most significant moments of the film with diegetic and extra-diegetic songs that add a powerfully emotional tone to the story ("Peppino"). What I would like to emphasize, however, is that unlike Mafia films in which drama is presented as a spectacle of the macabre, the pathos of these two films leaves a deep mark in the viewers' consciousness. This accounts for their memorability. In this sense, even the emotional aspects of the two productions served an educational purpose.

Film Impact and Memory Building

The analysis carried out to this point suggests that the discursive strategies implemented in the two films have contributed to determining their cultural impact and, as a result, to constructing a public persona out of their respective protagonists. The way Placido Rizzotto and Peppino Impastato were killed suggests that the killers sought to eliminate not only the bodies of the two young men, but also their memory. The corpse of Placido Rizzotto was thrown into a sinkhole and only identified with certainty, thanks to DNA evidence, sixty years later. Luciano Leggio's intention was for the Corleone union organizer to join the numerous Mafia victims of the after-war years who were destined to disappear from the country's collective memory.[15] The newspaper *La Nuova Stampa* wrote in those days that the government would pay four million lire for the capture of the perpetrators of this and other crimes that had taken place in the area ("Dirigente" 1). Likewise, the CGIL, the most left-wing national labor union, allocated half a million lire as a reward to anyone who would provide useful information to find Rizzotto—still believed to be kidnapped—or to identify the individuals responsible ("Un'ora" 1). None of those incentives produced any results.

While the disappearance of Placido Rizzotto was immediately taken to be a Mafia execution by the authorities and the local population, that of Peppino Impastato was reported marginally by the newspapers, probably because of the simultaneous discovery in the center of Rome of the lifeless body of Aldo Moro, the president of the Christian Democratic Party. Moreover, the tones used to report the story sound surprising, if not outrageous, today. Many newspapers described Impastato as a depressed, self-destructive young man ("Ultrà" 13), if not a terrorist (Behan 148–49). Although the film is accurate in describing the funeral of the young activist as an event involving about a hundred people, most of the inhabitants of Cinisi responded coldly to the street procession (Behan 144; Puccio-Den 36). It took twenty-two years from the time of Peppino Impastato's death to obtain a formal recognition of the controversial ways in which the authorities treated his case (Russo Spena).[16] That time span was filled by unremitting activity on the part of the Impastato family and their friends to keep Peppino's memory alive and get justice (Puccio-Den; Behan 153–58). If, however, attendance at the annual commemoration of his death in his native Cinisi may be an indication of his popularity, it must be noted that for years that event had only been locally relevant. It turned into a national event, and an opportunity for broader civil demonstrations, only after the release of the film (Behan 177).

If we consider the impact of these films on the popularity of the two figures, we can only conclude that it has been decisive. One can recall the opinion of former magistrate Antonio Ingroia, quoted by De Stefano, according to whom "*One Hundred Steps* . . . was widely seen and discussed, and . . . has been used by anti-Mafia forces to raise awareness, especially among Sicilian youth, about organized crime" (326). The same author also recalls Paul Ginsborg's observation that Italian politics is characterized by a strange tendency to give rise to an "opposition of the martyrs." De Stefano writes: "When the organized Left is weak or embattled, exemplary heroes come forth to make personal sacrifices in defence of social justice and democracy. Peppino Impastato, according to Ginsborg, represented this tendency, which is imbued with 'Catholic symbolism'" (De Stefano 323).

Through the idea of Mafia martyrdom, *One Hundred Steps* and *Placido Rizzotto* have, over time, created a sort-of monument to the memory of two young Mafia victims using film in place of stone.[17] This was possible, in part, because the two films came out at a time in which the public was more sensitive than in the past to the anti-Mafia message contained in them, but also because the formal construction of the films combines aspects of popular cinema with violations of the expectations that are usually associated with Mafia film imagery. This balance of formal and narrative elements may have allowed the films to arouse the interest of a broad and heterogeneous audience, get their message across effectively, and stimulate the construction of a collective memory.

Notes

1. A previous version of this essay was published in Italian in the journal *L'avventura* (2, 2015) under the title "Vittime restituite alla memoria." I would like to thank the editors of the journal for granting me permission to reuse that material for the present essay.

2. It is also symptomatic of the popularity achieved by these two personalities that several municipalities have named streets after them, sometimes exploiting their fame for political opportunism (Gatti).

3. Corleone is a town in the province of Palermo with a mafia history that dates back to the post-World War II era. In the late 1970s, prominent Corleone mafiosi, such as Totò Riina and Bernardo Provenzano, launched a direct attack on the Palermo families to gain full control of the drug trade. The attack gave rise to the so-called second mafia war, which caused hundreds of deaths—including among non-mafiosi—and brought the corleonesi to the center of the mafia stage. The fact that Marlon Brando's character in *The Godfather* is from Corleone (his real name is Vito Andolini as we learn in part 2) may be a reference to the mafia ties that that town is known for, or perhaps purely coincidental.

4. This latter aspect constitutes an innovation of the Mafia film tradition as well, because there had never been films about Sicilians who rebel against the Mafia from within before.

5. I am here employing the terms in their narratological sense as synonyms of *syuzhet* (narrative) and *fabula* (story) respectively.

6. Comic book enthusiasts know, for example, that the biography of several 'superheroes' is marked by a tragic event experienced in their youth. Bruce Wayne, aka Batman, decides to dedicate his life to fighting crime after seeing his parents being killed by thieves at the exit of a movie theater. Peter Parker, destined to become Spiderman, witnesses as a child the shocking death of his uncle Ben. Matt Murdock, a teenager who would later become Daredevil, is struck by the death of his father, a boxer who pays with his life his refusal to be bribed. I owe these examples to Riccardo Capoferro (pers. comm. 3 March 2015).

7. One *Hundred Steps*, for example, contains twenty-seven inaccuracies (Vitale 43).

8. No less, there are moments of great emotional strength, such as when Rizzotto's girlfriend, Lia, torments herself after having been raped by Luciano Leggio.

9. These are the main characters of the following films: *Scarface* (1983), *The Godfather* (1972), *The Untouchables* (1987); *Goodfellas* (1990). On the influence of the Hollywood imagery on the Italian Mafia movie, see Marangi and Rossi (7).

10. On the ambiguities that have always accompanied the cinematic representation of the Mafia, see Marangi and Rossi (5) and Albano (11). Regarding Salvatore Giuliano, Francesco Rosi claimed to have contributed to fueling the legend, arguing that the purpose of the film was not to question the figure of the famous bandit, but to describe the human, political, and sociological aspects related to his story (Marangi and Rossi 34).

11. I am referring here to the characterization by Robert De Niro of the famous Chicago outlaw in *The Untouchables* (1987).

12. It is not even ascertained that the young Salvatore truly witnessed the crime (Dalla Chiesa, "Rapporto" 128).

13. This is also confirmed in a video available online (Studio legale Melpignano min. 2:41).

14. Moreover, that movies such as *Scarface* have inspired real-world criminals such as the Camorra clan of the "Casalesi" is well known, thanks to the success

of the book *Gomorra* (2006), in which Roberto Saviano devotes a whole chapter to the subject.

15. The newspaper *La Nuova Stampa* published a short list of labor union Mafia victims fallen in those years ("Dirigente" 1). Similarly, Paternostro has drawn a list of thirty-two people fallen between 1947 and 1948 (16). The list includes labor unionists, farmers involved in land struggles, and the victims of the Portella della Ginestra massacre. That same list of names can also be heard in the film twice, first by Placido Rizzotto himself, and at the end as part of the final speech by Pio La Torre, whose voice significantly reaches the audience from a distance. The notoriety reached by Placido Rizzotto thanks to the film is exceptional compared to that of the other Mafia victims of those years.

16. The report of the parliamentary committee of inquiry into the Impastato case states that "[the] murder was at the time considered a '"hindrance' " to get rid of as quickly as possible. [The case] was therefore categorized as a suicide, or accident in an act of terror, beyond any clear evidence" (Russo Spena 152).

17. It is worth remembering, however, that in recent years the Catholic Church has been at the center of two embarrassing episodes. In 2003, the archdiocese of Monreale set off the procession of Santa Fara, patron saint of Cinisi, on the same day in which the procession in memory of Peppino Impastato had taken place for the previous twenty-five years. The procession was moved to a different day only after the Impastato family released a communication to the press (Behan 177). More recently, the archbishop of Monreale, Salvatore Di Cristina, never uttered the word "Mafia" and twice mangled the name of Rizzotto, saying "Rizzuto" during the state funeral of the former union organizer celebrated in 2012 in the presence of the President of the Republic, Giorgio Napolitano, and other authorities. Some have interpreted the archbishop's apparently accidental false steps as a gesture of submission to the Mafia (Pipitone).

Works Cited

Albano, Vittorio. *La mafia nel cinema siciliano: Da In nome della legge a Placido Rizzotto*. Barbieri, 2003.

Banfield, Edward C. *The Moral Basis of a Backward Society*. Free Press, 1958.

Bartolotta Impastato, Felicia. *La Mafia in casa mia*. Intervista di Anna Puglisi e Umberto Santino, La Luna, 1987.

Behan, Tom. *Defiance: The Story of One Man Who Stood Up to the Sicilian Mafia*. I. B. Tauris, 2008.

Bianconi, Giovanni. "Quel film su Placido Rizzotto contiene falsità." *Corriere della sera*, 17 Oct. 2000, p. 19, archiviostorico.corriere.it/2000/ottobre/17/Quel_film_Placido_Rizzotto_contiene_co_0_0010173950.shtml.

Boylan, Amy. "Pasquale Scimeca's Placido Rizzotto: A Different View of Corleone." *Mafia Movies: A Reader*, edited by Dana Renga, U of Toronto P, 2011, pp. 312–19.

Cavallaro, Felice. "Il regista: dai politici cento passi indietro." *Corriere della sera*, 17 Oct. 2000, p. 19, archiviostorico.corriere.it/2000/ottobre/17/regista_dai_politici_cento_passi_co_0_0010173939.shtml. Accessed 5 Sept. 2015.

Dalla Chiesa, Carlo Alberto. *Michele Navarra e la mafia del corleonese*, edited by Francesco Petruzzella, La Zisa, 1990.

———. "Rapporto sui presunti assassini di Placido Rizzotto." Inviato da Corleone in data 30 maggio 1950, Petruzzella, *Michele*, pp. 123–32.

———. "Rapporto sull'assassinio di Placido Rizzotto." Inviato da Corleone in data 18 dicembre 1949, Petruzzella, *Michele*, pp. 109–22.

De Stefano, George. "Marco Tullio Giordana's *The Hundred Steps*: The Biopic as Political Cinema." *Mafia Movies: A Reader*, edited by Dana Renga, U of Toronto P, 2011, pp. 320–28.

Dickie, John. *Cosa nostra: Storia della mafia siciliana.* Laterza, 2004.

Eco, Umberto. *Apocalittici e* integrati. 2nd ed., Bompiani, 1965.

Editorial Board. "Un'ora di fermata nel lavoro di tutta Italia." *La Nuova Stampa*, 1 April 1948, p. 1.

———. "Dirigente della Federterra assassinato in Sicilia." *La Nuova Stampa*, 3 April 1948, p. 1.

The Escort (*La scorta*). Directed by Ricky Tognazzi. Claudio Bonivento Productions, 1993.

An Eyewitness Account (*Testimone a rischio*). Directed by Pasquale Pozzessere. Istituto Luce, 1997.

Fiano, Fulvio. "Don Ciotti-Regione, patto contro le mafie «I clan sono già qui." *Corriere della sera*, 25 July 2013, p. 2.

Gatti, Cinzia. "Via Giuseppe Impastato a Savona. Il fratello: 'Peppino lotterebbe contro operazioni immobiliari come il Crescent 2.' " *Savona News*, 18 Nov. 2014, www.savonanews.it/2014/11/17/leggi-notizia/argomenti/attualit/articolo/via-giuseppe-impastato-a-savona-il-fratello-peppino-lotterebbe-contro-operazioni-immobiliari-come.html. Accessed 30 March 2015.

Girone, Remo, performer. *La Piovra (3–7)*. RAI Radiotelevisione, 1987–1995.

The Godfather. Directed by Francis Ford Coppola. Paramount Pictures, 1972.

Goodfellas. Directed by Martin Scorsese. Warner Brothers, 1990.

Hands Over the City (*Le mani sulla città*). Directed by Francesco Rosi. Galatea Film, 1963.

Johnny Stecchino. Directed by Roberto Benigni. Cecchi Gori Group Tiger Cinematografica, 1991.

Law of Courage (Il giudice ragazzino). Directed by Alessandro Di Robilant. Rai 2, 1994.

"Lotta alle mafie-Osservatorio su criminalità e malapolitica." *Nemici della mafia. La solitudine del giudice Falcone (documentario tv, 1988) 2/4*. YouTube. 20 June 2012, goo.gl/CqYfFH.

Lupo, Salvatore. *Storia della mafia: Dalle origini ai giorni nostri*. Donzelli, 2004.

Macaluso, Emanuele. "Macaluso: Rizzotto assassinato anche perché socialista." *Corriere della sera*, 16 Oct. 2000, p. 17, archiviostorico.corriere.it/2000/ottobre/16/Macaluso_Rizzotto_assassinato_anche_perche_co_0_0010163813.shtml. Accessed 5 Sept. 2015.

Mafia (*Il giorno della civetta*). Directed by Damiano Damiani. Panda Societa per L'Industria Cinematografica, 1968.

Marangi, Michele, and Paolo Rossi. *La mafia è cosa nostra: 10 film sull'onorata società*. Gruppo Abele, 1993.

Marcus, Millicent. "In Memoriam: The Neorealist Legacy in the Contemporary Sicilian Anti-Mafia Film." *Italian Neorealism and Global Cinema*, edited by Laura E. Ruberto and Kristi M. Wilson, Wayne State UP, 2007, pp. 290–306.

One Hundred Steps (I cento passi). Directed by Marco Tullio Giordana. Istituto Luce, 2000.

Pastorino, Gloria. "Tano da morire di Roberta Torre tra musical, film di mafia e 'camp.'" *Intersections: Italy in Music, Art, Literature, and Cinema*, Terrazza Solferino, Turin, 6 June 2014.

———. "Peppino Impastato, poeta della libertà, a cento passi dalla morte." *Il cinema di Marco Tullio Giordana: Interventi critici*, edited by Federica Colleoni et al., Vecchiarelli, 2015.

Paternostro, Dino. *Il sogno spezzato: Placido Rizzotto e le lotte contadine a Corleone*. Città nuove, 1998.

Pipitone, Giuseppe. *Rizzotto, dopo 64 anni i funerali di Stato: "Corleone non è solo Riina e Provenzano*. IlFattoQuotidiano.it. 24 May 2012, www.ilfattoquotidiano.i/2012/05/24/rizzotto-dopo-anni-funerali-stato-corleone-solo-riina-provenzano/241168/. Accessed 19 Sept. 2015.

Placido Rizzotto. Directed by Pasquale Scimeca. Istituto Luce, 2000.

Porro, Maurizio. "Emoziona 'Placido Rizzotto,' sindacalista-eroe che sfidò i boss di Corleone." *Corriere della sera*, 4 Sept. 2000, p. 29, archiviostorico.corriere.it/2000/settembre/04/Emoziona_Placido_Rizzotto_sindacalista_eroe_co_0_0009045926.shtml. Accessed 5 Sept. 2015.

Puccio-Den, Deborah. "Mafia: état de violence ou violence d'état? L'affaire Impastato et la requalification concomitante des groupes subversifs et de l'État en Italie (1978–2002)." *Quaderni*, no. 78, 2012, pp. 23–43.

Pugliese, Stanislao G. "Review of *The Hundred Steps* by Fabrizio Mosca; Marco Tullio Giordana; Claudio Fava; Monica Zapelli." *The American Historical Review*, vol. 106, no. 3, 2001, pp. 1109–10, doi:10.2307/2692533.

Renga, Dana, editor. *Mafia Movies: A Reader*. U Toronto P, 2011.

Russo Spena, Giovanni. *Relazione sul "caso Impastato."* Commissione parlamentare d'inchiesta sul fenomeno della mafia e delle altre associazioni criminali similari, Camera dei Deputati, 6 Dec. 2000, legislature.camera.it/_dati/leg13/lavori/doc/xxiii/050/d000r.htm. Accessed 20 Sept. 2015.

Salvatore Giuliano. Directed by Francesco Rosi. Galatea Film, 1962.

Saviano, Roberto. *Gomorra*. Strade Blu, 2006.

Scarface. Directed by Brian De Palma. Universal Pictures, 1983.

Small, Pauline. "Giordana's I cento passi: Renegotiating the Mafia codes." *New Cinemas: Journal of Contemporary Film*, vol. 3, no. 1, 2005, pp. 41–54. doi:10.1386/ncin.3.1.41/1.

Studio legale Melpignano. *Felicia Impastato.wmv*. YouTube, www.youtube.com/watch?v=DMLABkrPFcc. Accessed 12 March 2015.

To Die for Tano (*Tano da morire*). Directed by Roberta Torre. A.S.P., 1997.

Tornabuoni, Lietta. "Cofferati 'La mafia uccide le idee.'" *La Stampa*, 13 Oct. 2000, p. 11.

"Ultrà di sinistra dilaniato dall'esplosivo: suicidio?" *La Stampa*, 10 May 1978, p. 13.

The Untouchables. Directed by Brian De Palma. Paramount Pictures, 1987.

Varese, Federico. "What is Organized Crime?" *Organized Crime*, edited by Federico Varese, vol. 1, Routledge, 2010. *Critical Concepts in Criminology*, federicovarese.com/sites/default/files/What_is_Organized_Crime-Introduction.pdf. Accessed 2 May 2014.

Vitale, Salvo. "Realtà e fiction ne 'I cento passi.'" *Antimafia 2000*, vol. 19, Feb. 2002, p. 43. antimafiaduemila.com/200805196176/articoli-arretrati/per-una-cultura-della-legalita-nd19.html. Accessed 15 May 2014.

Conclusion

Reframing the National?

Chapter 9

Nation as Home

Anthropological Foundations and Human Needs

ROSARIO FORLENZA

I long, as does every human being, to be at home
Wherever I find myself

—Maya Angelou

Introduction

Nations and nationalism have assumed an enormous importance in the political and social life over the past centuries and are still at the center of the political debate. Yet, the dominant contemporary intellectual attitude toward nations and nationalism is dismissive, to say the least. Mainstream social sciences, social theory and the humanities, as well as liberal opinion around the globe, see nations and nationalism as passing, transient things, remnants of the past, and the products of a specific moment in history.[1] It is assumed that under the forces of progress, cosmopolitanism, and globalization, nations, nation-states, and nationalism will retreat, decline, and eventually disappear. In short, the world has entered a "post-national" era (Appadurai 411; Hobsbawm 182).[2] In the understanding of the major theorist of "second modernity" and "cosmopolitan society," Ulrich Beck states:

> Now that the totalitarian encumbrance of Communism has been overcome, nationalism has taken shape as the remaining real danger to the culture of political freedom at the beginning of the 21st century. It is a revived anti-cosmopolitan nationalism which could give the sectarian acts of violence and eccentricities of extremists a terrible legitimation. Although nationalism is absolutely discredited by a history of endless suffering and bloodshed, it has undergone a remarkable resurrection since the end of the East-West conflict. ("The Cosmopolitan Condition" 38)[3]

Ernest Gellner and Benedict Anderson—foundational figures for the contemporary mainstream literature on nationalism—shared these views in their books, which are widely considered *the* main works in the field, and certainly representative of the series of works that, from the 1980s, started to return analytical attention in the wider social, political, and human sciences to the phenomenon of nationalism.[4] To understand the persistent popular appeal of nationalism and the idea of the nation, and to provide an alternative reading to the narrow and dismissive perspectives on the questions at stake, this chapter argues for the reassertion of the importance of latent or hidden background practices that are simply taken for granted both in ordinary life and in explicit scientific investigation and conception formation. The proposition defended here holds that the political imagination of nationalism and the persistence of national feelings require a problematization of the sociocultural, anthropological, and existential conditions underlying the nation: namely, the experience of home and the question of borders. While nationalism and the nation were historically contingent on specific instances of political modernity, this chapter argues that different historical conditions can nevertheless be understood by means of specific anthropological practices that are persistent.

Against Nations, against Nationalism

Benedict Anderson and Ernest Gellner share the same modernist paradigm and, consequently, both insist on the recent origins of nationalism as an ideology of legitimation for modern nation-states. However, the decisive symptoms of modernity they postulate vary. For Gellner, nationalism is an essential feature of modernization, which is the transition from the agrarian to the industrial society. The latter requires a state that can create a culturally homogeneous workforce. This, in turn, requires an educational system that transmits to the nascent political community the high culture of emerging national elites. As Gellner writes, in a vocabulary that has become part of a wider philosophy of history, nationalism is essentially

> the general imposition of a *high culture* on society, where previously *low cultures* had taken up the lives of the majority, and in some cases the totality, of the population. It means the general diffusion of a school-mediated, academy-supervised idiom, codified for the requirements of a reasonably precise bureaucratic and technological communication. It is the establishment of an anonymous impersonal society, with mutually substitutable atomised individuals, held together above all by a shared culture of this kind, in place of the previous complex structure of local groups, sustained by folk cultures reproduced locally and idiosyncratically by the micro group themselves. (*Nations* 57)

Conversely, Anderson traces nationalism to the dual forces of the printing press and capitalism (or print capitalism) combined with the growing usage of vernacular languages. Under such conditions, people could be mobilized in their ethnic and national self-identification into a nation and thus transcend division and the lack of social interaction through an "imagined political community." The now-classic concept of "imagined community" resonates with a likewise classic definition first formulated by Gellner in 1964: "Nationalism is not the awakening of nations to self-consciousness; it invents nations where they do not exist" (*Thought* 169). In fact, Anderson goes one step further and proposes to replace the term *invented* with *imagined.* In his view, Gellner still accepts a misleading distinction between "true" and "false" communities. To Anderson, this makes no sense at all. For Anderson, Gellner is "so anxious to show that nationalism masquerades under false pretences" that "invention" turns to "fabrication" and "falsity" and not, as would be more correct, to "imagining" and "creation." For Anderson, all communities "larger than primordial villages," and "perhaps even these," are "imagined." Therefore, "communities are to be distinguished not by their falsity/genuineness, but by the style in which they are imagined" (Anderson 6).

Anderson's ideas are by no means identical to Gellner's. However, as Arpad Szakolczai has written in a devastating and well-received critique, the two complement each other rather well "by spanning a space within the modern episteme." This includes constructivism and the "reduction" of the idea of the nation to "exclusive ethnic boundaries" ("The Spirit" 200). As Gellner writes, "Nationalism is a theory of political legitimacy, which requires that ethnic boundaries should not cut across political ones" (*Nations* 1). The main difference lies in their view on progress, which for Anderson, in the footsteps of Walter Benjamin, is essentially ideology, while for Gellner is a fact of history. But for Szacolczai, these "classic" critiques of nationalism derive from a "coherent position" that rests on a few basic points: A "belief in progress through industrialization," a "rejection of history and a fatalistic waiting for the Messiah," the embrace of "liberalism or socialism," or a combination of the two, and finally the vision of modernity as "the gate to earthly Paradise." Furthermore, this position is consistently formulated "against" nationhood, community, and nationalism. Most importantly, both Gellner and Anderson fail to recognize "any underlying meaning behind nation" ("The Spirit" 200), including the meaning of a home, and they ignore—precisely for their blindness to the question of home and to other background anthropological practices—that "attachment to a nation could be intrinsically human" (198). Rather, those who feel even the minimal sense of attachment and belonging to a nation are dangerous fools. To Anderson and Gellner, there is no community, no authentic reality, no meaning, no home—human beings are instead always free to invent and/or imagine ourselves and the world altogether.

Primordialism, Ethno-symbolism, and Modernism

Other approaches to nations and nationalism have challenged the reigning modernist and functionalist perspectives. The "primordialists" maintain that nationalists create a feeling of national "uniqueness" when they effectively tie the principle of self-determination to cultural symbols that are not subject to rational calculation, or what Clifford Geertz calls "primordial attachments":

> By a "primordial attachment" is meant one that stems from the "givens"—or, more precisely, as culture is inevitably involved in such matters, the assumed "givens"—of social existence: immediate contiguity and kin connection mainly, but beyond them the given-ness that stems from being born into a particular religious community, speaking a particular language, or even a dialect of a language, and following particular social practices. These congruities of blood, speech, custom, and so on, are seen

> to have an ineffable, and at times overpowering, coerciveness in and of themselves. (Geertz 109)[5]

National movements manipulate the "assumed givens" of a society and harness cultural symbols for political purposes. As Elie Kedourie put it, "nationalists make use of the past in order to subvert the present" (75). Kedourie further asserts that this method of creating a national movement is particularly efficient and effective when nationalists manage to incorporate religious symbolism into their narratives and road map: "This transformation of religion into nationalist ideology is all the more convenient in that nationalists can thereby utilize the powerful and tenacious loyalties which a faith held in common for centuries creates" (76).

Anthony Smith has tried to bridge modernism and primordialism by offering a synthesis known as "ethno-symbolism" (*Ethnic Revival*; *Theories*; *The Ethnic*; *National*; *Nationalism*; *The Cultural*). Thus, he has combined the modernist concern for the socioeconomic transformations that opened the way to a political order based on nation-states as institutions, and nationalism as an ideology with the recognition that national identity can appeal to individuals and communities only by tapping into and utilizing cultural symbols, the "assumed given" based on preexisting traditions, symbols, myths, religion, and practices. For Smith, nationalism is "an ideological movement for attaining and maintaining autonomy, unity, and identity on behalf of a population of whose members deem it to constitute an actual or potential 'nation' " (*National* 73). National identity, as defined by Smith, is a "continuous reproduction and reinterpretation of the pattern of values, symbols, memories, myths, and traditions that compose the distinctive heritage of nations, and the identification of individuals with that pattern and heritage and with its cultural elements" (*The Cultural* 19). Smith argues that the origins of nations and national identities can be traced back to premodern forms of collective identity, making ethnic myths and symbols crucial features of nationalism. These bring together "elements of historical fact and legendary elaboration to create an overriding commitment and bond for the community" (*Myths* 57), thus encapsulating the meanings and visions that lie at the basis of a national identity. In each generation, new elites rework, re-elaborate, and readapt the preexisting myths to modern inclusive narratives and discourses of national identity. In this sense, modern nationalism is the updated secular equivalent of the premodern sacred myth of ethnic selection.

Despite their differences, all approaches to nationalism are united in their insistence on the centrality of historical representation and narration within their explanatory schema, reflecting the need for nationalists to be able to tell a story about the nation and its importance. This story must resonate emotively with people, glorify the nation, and be easily transmitted and absorbed. In Kantian terms, the ability to represent a history in an extremely partial and easily digestible manner is a necessary condition of the very possibility of nationalism (Bell 67).

Furthermore, despite their differences, the various theoretical approaches—modernism, primordialism, and ethno-symbolism—are steeped in, and therefore eventually trapped into, positing a relation between ethnicity (an ambiguous and complex term) and nationalism. However, for Gellner and the modernists, the birth of a new social organization based on a specific economic structure of modernity and depending on the transmission of high culture to the community is more important in the genesis of nationalism than ethnicity. While Gellner highlights the importance and even the necessity of the political and cultural proximity of ethnic groups as an important cause of nationalism, Smith underscores the paramount role of preexisting *ethnies* on nationalism. The point here is that both approaches are based on an evolutionary reading of history, which seeks to trace the consequence or condition of possibilities between phenomena evidenced in the continuities and discontinuities between different periods of historical time. Consequently, both perspectives fail to capture the social, existential, and experiential basis on which national allegiance—as with other forms of political allegiance and participation—can be effectively built, as well as the historical circumstances under which that building can take place. The most crucial of such bases is the experience of home.

The Experience of Home

Home—the feeling of home, to have a home, or to share a home—is the solid and necessary basis for human life to have meaning. Nonetheless, "home" is completely absent from political thought and it is likewise duly underdeveloped in critical theory and social thought, with a few notable exceptions.[6] To assess the fundamental importance of home as the existential basis of a meaningful political unit, and to reinstate the centrality of the experience of home for social theory and political thought, this chapter will now elaborate and synthesize research and reflections in social and cultural anthropology, ethnography, philosophy, archaeology.

The point here is to reassert the importance of latent or hidden background practices, and of the conduct of life derived from them. It is a search for the fundamental background symbolic and material practices of human culture that underlie political, ideological, or legal dimensions. This is a crucial point voiced in the intellectual endeavors of Alfred Schütz, the "frame analysis" of Erving Goffman and Gregory Bateson, and the work of John Searle on the "background."[7] The same concern is present in the work of Edmund Husserl on the life-world; Martin Heidegger on background practices; Ludwig Wittgenstein and John L. Austin on ordinary language; Michel Foucault on the death of author, the genealogical method, and the problem of reflexivity; and in Eric Voegelin's idea that we always start in the between (*metaxy*). Furthermore, the same concern is present in powerful attacks of Søren Kierkegaard against the Hegelian system and in the return to the existential tensions of simple human being. It is a concern that implies, as Arpad Szakolczai has forcefully explained, a "reflexive," or rather self-reflexive, turn ("Citizenship" 59; *Reflexive*).

Home is not simply a metaphor. It is a concrete, existential fact, a sense of self-grounding. In many languages—from English to Russian, from German to French, from Italian to Hungarian—home is always associated with house ("Citizenship" 62). Home is, to follow Heidegger, a place where someone dwells. For him, to be human is to dwell. Dwelling in turn is the way in which human beings "are" humans on earth. Dwelling draws human being in a space—a place where things and the existence itself become true and meaningful in the complex interaction of earth and sky, life and death, gods and mortals. Dwelling is who we are, and dwelling happens in concrete space: "Spaces open up by the fact that they are let into the dwelling of man. To say that mortals are is to say that in dwelling they persist through spaces by virtue of their stay among things and locales" (Heidegger 159). Bachelard embraced this spatial and temporal dimension of intimacy by recognizing, as Janet Donohoe explains, that "the dwelling place of home is intimately connected to memory" and consequently retains our past and opens up "an immemorial domain" (27). To Bachelard, home and space are not simply physical dimensions, but a means to finding one's way of engaging the world. Heidegger and Bachelard highlight the "existential" nature of home, in the sense that "our way of being-at-home" secures a "sense of our own-ness" (Jacobson 222; see also Clingerman 42–43). At the same time, the perspective of Heidegger is quite problematic. The real character of the Dasein (Being-In), as revealed in the sixth chapter of *Being and Time*, is a basic disposition to anxiety that originates from the ontological unsettledness of the Dasein itself, or from the fact that one is not at home in the world (*Un-zuhause*). "From an existential-ontological point of view," Heidegger writes, "the not-at-home, must be conceived as the more primordial phenomenon" (qtd. in "Citizenship" 60). In other words, Heidegger does not start from a world based on home, and familiarity (from the recognition of the world as home) with the potential or actual threat of its dissolution, which is the condition of possibility of every human action and the prime mover to politics. Instead, he places isolation, anxiety, and homelessness as being at the real center of human existence, out of which, through the work of care, humans can secure a small clearing, which might even be understood as a retreat ("Citizenship" 60–61). Consequently, the welcoming senses of familiarity, dwelling, and rootedness in the world implied in the Dasein turn into a mirage of home.

To be at home means to be embedded in a dense pattern of relationships to people and place, which gives rise to an inherently meaningful experience of the world. This order is neither abstract nor imposed from without but crystallizes from the shared experience of people inhabiting a concrete location. Home involves the localization of meaning in a concrete setting and in the activities of everyday life—an experience thematized by anthropologists under the rubric of participation in a broader entity and this embodies an ongoing process of "cosmicization," or the rediscovery of the "rhythm which can harmonize us with everything," which is vital for both social life and individual well-being (Eliade 21).[8] Home is not a fixed structure, static and frozen, which shuts out the external world—it is a dynamic center that draws in experience and gives it meaning. It is a constellation of significance rather than a singular and unitary essence, or a process produced by localizing processes, which concentrate and stabilize values around a secure center. Two of the most crucial of these localizing processes are the cultivation of space and, perhaps even more importantly, the elaboration of symbolic boundaries and the physical creation of borders and frontiers that encircle a space.

Borders and Boundaries: Arnold Van Gennep

As Arnold Van Gennep wrote in his *Traité comparatif des nationalités*, which anticipated more recent development in the so-called "anthropology of border," it is precisely on borders that differentiations and the production of meaning and identity happen. It is in this liminal space, a familiar space, that nations are being built as a kind of home by fostering an identity that basically relates to a place (not necessarily to a geographical space). "Territory only acquires its full symbolic values when we know its boundaries," Van

Gennep writes in *Traité comparatif*, a forgotten classic in nationalism studies (151).[9] The idea of boundaries exists in all societies, from the primitive to the civilized. Different markers have been used to indicate boundaries: some natural, other artificial. These markers are often envisaged as sacred, and to cross a boundary is to perform magic, or a religious ritual. To cross a boundary is to move from one world to another, or from home to the world. Often, limits are invisible; an ideal line traced between two physical markers. Precision in delineating borders is a recent thing; in the past, what was common was not an ideal line, not a clearly defined geographical marker but rather a frontier, a border area that was neutral.[10]

Borders in a pre-institutional sense are boundaries that define a unity, a community, and a collective identity. Claims for individual and communal identities and the sociopolitical origin of a community in history are based on the definition of borders and boundaries between "us" and "them." After all, borders and boundaries *make* the collective identity of social groups and communities possible and have a symbolic role in marking and defining the boundaries of the "we" group. Borders and boundaries—and processes of bordering, de-bordering, and re-bordering—are central to any understanding of the social and shape perception of the world. They can even be considered more important than identity, as they establish the basic, essential forms of categorization and classification that identities adopt to differentiate the self from the other.[11]

In the received narrative, however, borders are abstract and imposed; they are exogenous. Instead, modern nations were built from the political center outwards and imposed upon marginal groups or peripheral regions in a process of cultural and institutional assimilation and integration. In this view, national identity is the expression of a cultural unity and a national consciousness constructed within the political framework of a centralized state. The paradigmatic experience is France. The corollary idea is that peasants become national citizens only when they abandon their identity as peasants: a local sense of place and a local identity centered on the village or valley must be superseded and replaced by a sense of belonging to a more extended territory or nation.

But, as Van Gennep correctly understood, nationhood is the extension to the entire valley, the immense plain, the steppe, or the great city like Paris or Vienna, of the real or symbolic love felt for the corner of land that belongs to the commune. National identity means replacing the love of local territory with the love of national territory. State formation and nation building were two-way processes and have been at work since at least the seventeenth century. States did not simply impose their values and boundaries on local society. Rather, local society was a motive force in the formation and consolidation of nationhood and the territorial state. Political boundaries appeared in the borderland as the outcome of national political events—as a function of the different strengths, interests, and ultimately histories of France and Spain. But the shape and significance of the boundary line was first constructed out of local social relations in the borderland. For example, the boundaries of the village jurisdiction ceded to France in the 1660 division of the Cerdanya valley (in the eastern Pyrenees, between the two countries) were not specified, nor were they undisputed among village communities. The historical appearance of territory (the territorialization of sovereignty) was matched and shaped by a territorialization of the village communities, and it was the dialectic of local and national interests that produced the boundaries of national territory.

In the same way, national identity—the Frenchman or Spaniard—appeared on the periphery before it was built by the center. It appeared not as a result of state intentions, but rather arose from the local process of adopting and appropriating the national without abandoning local interests, a local sense of place, or a local identity. At once opposing and using the state for its own ends, local society brought the nation into the village. In the French-Spanish borderland, it was this sense of difference (between us and them) that was so critical in defining an identity. Imagining oneself a member of a community or a nation meant perceiving a significant difference between oneself and the other across the boundaries. The proximity of the other across the French-Spanish boundary structured the appearance of national identity long before local society was assimilated to a dominant center.[12]

Being-at-Home in the World and the Collapse: Turnbull and De Martino

Home is a place where the subject, in an ideal situation, should feel safe and secure, protected in and by symbolic and physical borders—this is what "being at home" means: a state of mind created in the subject by a negotiation between place, identity, and experience. This implies that the disruption of a solid notion of place and identity make subjects feel *Unheimlich*. It is the loss of that balance between "involvement and detachment" (Elias), which is a precondition of effective thought and practice (Thomassen 227). In this sense, to have a home means to have real, human, and existential commitment.

The powerful and controversial ideas by the social and cultural anthropologist Colin Turnbull (*The Forest People*; *The Mountain People*), which social theorist Arpad Szakolczai has invited to rediscovery in social science and critical theory, fit and reinforce this point ("Citizenship" 64). In his work with the Mbuti Pygmies of the tropical rain forest, Turnbull saw how human life might have been before the invention of settlement, and realized that for the Pygmies, a separation between home and the world does not exist. Consequently, they feel at home anywhere in their world—a few miles in diameter in the forest in which they dwell. As Szacolczai tells us, Turnbull demonstrated that "the experience of being at home in the world is the condition of possibility of any decent human life" ("Citizenship" 64). Conversely, in his other classic work concerning the Ik—living in the mountainous region in between Kenya, Uganda, and Sudan and following precisely a moment of forced settlement and the decomposition of the fiber of social life—Turnbull captured the profound significance of the experience of a settlement that was not, as an evolutionary reading of history would argue, the consequence of the "agricultural revolution," but rather an excruciating and harrowing experience: the collapse of the identity of home and world, a "trauma" that "would only be eased with the rise of the first genuine city culture" ("Citizenship" 64). As archeologists have demonstrated, settling down in houses (approximately 8500 to 7900 BC) must have meant profound changes in the way humans viewed each other, their surroundings, and their world. It was a phenomenon that fundamentally transformed human social organization and perhaps the human psychological paradigm (Banning 5; Wilson 4; Watkins).

The Italian anthropologist and ethnographer Ernesto De Martino (1908–65), perhaps one the most interesting and little-known social scientists, reached a similar conclusion on the importance of homeland space in his research in southern Italy in the 1950s. In his *La fine del mondo* (*The end of the world*) De Martino recalls that in the 1950s, driving in Calabria (the southern tip of peninsular Italy), he asked a peasant for directions. As the explanation was not clear, De Martino asked the old shepherd to get into his automobile and show him the way. Then he observed the old man's behavior:

> His [initial] diffidence was slowly changing into anxiety because now, from the window he was constantly looking out of, he had lost sight of the bell tower of Marcellinara, the point of reference for his extremely narrow domestic space. As the bell tower had disappeared, the poor old man felt completely bewildered; and

> it was hard work to take him as far as the right junction and find out what we needed to know. Then we took him back, hastily, as we had agreed: and all the time he has his head out of the window, gazing into the horizon to see if Marcellinara's bell tower had reappeared; until, when he finally saw it, his face relaxed and his old heart was calmed, as if he had reconquered a lost *patria.* (De Martino 480–81)

The old peasant felt lost without his cultural "patria."[13] This, in the understanding of De Martino, is the place and space of life, memories, and projects. It is a domesticated background, shaped by the lives, thoughts, and actions of previous generations. It is a physical, concrete space, as well as a symbolic place that delimits the world. As a specific cultural space, it demarks the presence of human beings in the world. Indeed, emotional attachment to a place generates strong feelings of identity and belonging, which link people to their past, even to a civilizational tradition, as manifest in shared historical memories rooted and embedded in a space. Once this link between social actor and the cultural *patria* (*habitus*) is broken; once the axis (the tower bell) giving meaning and providing the unit of measure to the world disappears—then the "end of the world" and "existential" anxiety, or "the crisis of presence," erupts and human beings lose their ability to stay and to be in the world. Without this background, no cognitive effort can begin, and no operation or project can be actualized in the present. In this sense, *patria culturale* refers to a profound dimension of belonging that does not coincide with the conscious content of macro-identity as promoted by aggressive nationalism. In fact, because of its nature as the implicit background of daily life, *patria culturale* is profoundly different from fundamentalist, exclusivist, essentialist ideologies and it can be defined in opposition to ideology.

Home and Politics

Even if home represents the ultimate background on which political allegiance can be built, it is only the broad, social, "existential," or "experiential" basis. The question of how a proper political allegiance can be built on this basis is another matter and it involves the transference of broader allegiance, or a sense of home, to a political entity. The old peasant in De Martino's car felt that his presence in the world, his being-in-the-world, had come into crisis. He had crossed the threshold and the boundary of risk. He had lost his symbolic world maintenance, his existential references—he was exposed to nothingness. It is the experience of feeling lost that Max Weber termed "disenchantment." Feeling lost is the human condition that generates disenchantment with the world and the destruction of the political, in the sense that politics is polis, which is a physical place as well as a society: a means for orienting ourselves in the world. The opposite of feeling lost is feeling at home—the feeling that arises when humans live within the horizon where things and the world of things are where they should be and can be taken for granted.

Home in this broad sense, therefore, bridges the experiential everyday with the concept of the political. In fact, home was implied in the early conception of the political, though the broader meaning of home was obscured by the equation/conflation of home with the *oikos* (family, property, house). In the footsteps of Hannah Arendt (*The Human Condition*), Giorgio Agamben (*Homo Sacer*) has argued that simple natural life was excluded from the sphere of the polis and remained confined—as to the sphere of the oikos in the classical Greek city-state. Contrary to Arendt, however, Agamben does not maintain that the Greek city-state was thereby immune to bio-political rationality: reproductive life (*zoê*) was included in the political form of life (*bios*) in the mode of exclusion. In effect, the very act of exclusion constitutes the negative foundation of the political life of the polis. In fact, the relation between oikos and polis was not diametric opposition. To the contrary, for the classical Greeks, it was self-evident that an oikos was a part of the polis. Life of the Greek oikos, particularly in Athens during the democratic period, was controlled and regulated by magistrates with a number of laws and ordinances. In classical political theory, this regulatory tendency is even more obvious: in Plato's and Aristotle's works on politics, even the tiniest details of everyday life are controlled and regulated by legislators and magistrates. Finally, it is contestable whether the art of household (*oikonomia*) and the art of politics (*techne politike*) were such different arts, as has been claimed in modern political theory. Even Aristotle—perhaps the first to propose a clear-cut distinction between the authority of the statesman (*politikon*) and that of the head of an estate (*oikonomikon*)—uses oikos vocabulary extensively in his reflections of the political administration of the polis.[14]

Nonetheless, as Arpad Szakolczai has argued, the links between home and politics became invisible in the modern age. Modernity, the language of law and human rights created an antidote to the violence and absurdity of authoritarian and totalitarian states, without resolving the problem of how to incorporate and institutionalize everyday background practices into the modern economy, civil society, and the administrative external sphere of politics ("Citizenship" 66). This link has become visible when the sense of home and the need to defend the symbolic, geographic and existential boundaries is under attack—which happens particularly in terms of war and revolution. Warfare is perhaps the most important source for the creation of feeling of belonging and political allegiance, as distinct from social allegiance (based on clan and family) or religious allegiance (a congregation, a church, a sect) ("Citizenship" 65; see also Weber). In the republican tradition, from Greece to Machiavelli and beyond, the duty to take up arms was considered central to the *polis*. After all, war, as Alessandro Pizzorno has written, "is a great producer of devotion" (54). War comes as the ultimate threat to an individual's home and to the homes of everyone else in the community. Thus, a common threat triggers the emergence of the political interest in communal defense, which in turn helps to solidify a sense of belonging and of political allegiance.

In this sense, and taking a cue from Van Gennep, one might even argue that nations and nationalisms are a liminal creation.[15] They are made not only made from the geographical margins and from below, they are also made and re-made in-the-between in a temporal sense, in a time of political and existential crisis, and especially in times of war and revolution. It is not coincidental that nationalism has assumed a paramount importance in historical moments dominated by war and revolution, such as the decade after World War I (when national allegiances eroded class-based, social, and socialist allegiances, opening the way for forms of radical authoritarian nationalism and eventually fascisms and totalitarianism), or the after the French Revolution, the event that gave rise and political content to the double ideas of sovereignty (sovereignty of the individual over his/her conscience and sovereignty of the nation-state engendered by a "contract" between atomized and free individuals). Revolution led to political modernity and to the concept of nationalism in the first place.

Conclusion

This paper has argued that dominant political theory and social science analysis of nations and nationalism are blind to the crucial question of background experiences, or the latent and hidden experiential and anthropological practices that take for granted the reference point of human life, the experience of home. To have a home or share an experience of home is the solid and basic necessary basis for human life (for any human life) to have a meaning.

Nations and nationalism must be understood as the translation of the need to have a home—or to share the experience of home—into a larger political entity, a participation in a broader cosmic entity, and the creation of political allegiance under conditions of existential uncertainty. Intellectuals and observers do not usually understand that nationalism has been such a powerful phenomenon precisely because it is based on the endless revaluation and symbolization of the nation-state as home, which cannot be simply overcome with the cosmopolitan paradigm of taking the world as home.

Historical experiences show that the anthropological need to share a home can crystallize in political revolution and war and become the master narrative of nationalism that blossoms into a fully developed, violent, and exclusionary doctrine. However, this process of abstraction is by no means unidirectional, and highly elaborated nationalism can open to a healthier sense of the nation as home. After all, although nationalism has not often proved to be great at creating multiethnic coalitions, specific egalitarian redistributive politics have historically been correlated with national projects. In short, the nation can be based on recognition and familiarity—an important term for all its banality. The nation in this sense can exclude abstraction, alienation, and violence aggressively pitched against the other/the enemies. Boundaries and borders between "homes" can re-unify common things between individuals and communities. Or, to put differently, there are not common things to share without boundaries and borders.

Membership in a cosmopolitan world produces a weak form of identity and an ideological-legalistic construct, which cannot serve as the basis of commonalities, shared identities, and meaningful political communities—all of which are necessary to address the tearing of the world. A meaningful, stable political allegiance must engage peoples' energies and values by drawing forth the existential dimension of human beings and their experience of home as expressed in cultural and anthropological practices rooted in localizing processes.

Notes

1. I understand the word "liberal" not in the narrow US sense of "liberal versus conservative" but as generally denoting those committed to the Enlightenment, which in the US context would include both liberals and conservatives, or at least most of them.

2. See also Held; Ohmae; Sassen; Nodia.

3. See also Beck, "The Cosmopolitan Condition"; "Beyond Class"; "Varieties."

4. Gellner, *Nations*; Anderson's *Imagined Communities* was first published in 1983 and then in 1991 in a revised version.

5. See also Shils; Van Den Berghe.

6. See Thomassen, 222-27; Szakolczai, "The Spirit"; "Citizenenship"; O'Connor; Forlenza and Luccarelli.

7. Schutz's concern with the taken for granted was taken up by Peter Berger and Thomas Luckmann.

8. See Lévy Bruhl; Turnbull, *The Forest People*.

9. I owe this "rediscovery" to Bjørn Thomassen.

10. Van Gennep, *Traité*; see also Llobera.

11. Rumford, 106; Baarth; Cohen, Abner; Paasi; Newman and Paasi.

12. See Sahlins; see also Cohen, Anthony.

13. The Italian term *patria* has no accurate translation. *Patria* remains the common term for "homeland," "fatherland," "motherland" in many languages, based on the Greek πατρίδα ("native /ancestral land"). The Italian *patria*, however, is more similar to the Latin/Roman *patria*, and refers to the *res publica*, the political constitution, the laws, and the resulting way of life (and thus also culture). *Patria* does not coincide with a specific territory. Romans had the term *natio* to define the place of birth and cultural/ethnic/linguistic features connoted to such a territory.

14. See Ojakangas; Nagle.

15. See Van Gennep, *The Rites*; Thomassen.

Works Cited

Agamben, Giorgio. *Homo Sacer. Il potere sovrano e la nuda vita (Homo sacer I)*. Einaudi, 1999.

Anderson, Benedict. *Imagined Communities: Reflections on the Origin and Spread of Nationalism*. Verso, 1991.

Appadurai, Arjun. *Modernity at Large: Cultural Dimensions of Globalization*. U of Minnesota P, 1996.

Arendt, Hannah. *The Human Condition*. U of Chicago P, 1958.

Austin, John L. *How to Do Things with Words: The William James Lectures Delivered at Harvard University*, edited by J. O. Urmson and M. Sbisà, Harvard UP, 1975.

Banning, Edward B. "Housing Neolithic Farmers." *Near Eastern Archaeology*, vol. 66, no. 1, 2003, pp. 4–21.

Baarth, Fredrik, editor. *Ethnic Groups and Boundaries: The Social Organization of Cultural Difference*. Allen and Unwin, 1969.

Bateson, Gregory. *Steps to an Ecology of Mind: Collected Essays in Anthropology, Psychiatry, Evolution and Epistemology*. U of Chicago P, 1972.

Beck, Ulrich. "Beyond Class and Nation: Reframing Social Inequalities in a Globalized World." *British Journal of Sociology*, vol. 58, no. 4, 2007, pp. 680–705.

———. "The Cosmopolitan Condition: Why Methodological Nationalism Fails." *Theory, Culture & Society*, vol. 24, nos. 7–8, 2007, pp. 286–91.

———. "The Cosmopolitan Society and Its Enemies." *Theory, Culture & Society*, vol. 19, nos. 1–2, 2002, pp. 17–44.

———. "Varieties of Second Modernity and the Cosmopolitan Vision." *Theory, Culture & Society*, vol. 33, nos. 7–8, pp. 257–70.

Bell, Duncan S. A. "Mythscapes: Memory, Mythology, and National Identity." *British Journal of Sociology*, vol. 54, no. 1, 2003, pp. 63–81.

Berger, Peter L., and Luckmann, Thomas. *The Social Construction of Reality. A Treatise in the Sociology of Knowledge*. Anchor Books, 1966.

Clingerman, Forest. "Homecoming and the Half Remembered: Environmental Amnesia, the Uncanny, and the Path Home." *Resisting the Place of Belonging Uncanny Homecoming in Religion, Narrative, and the Arts*, edited by Daniel Boscaljon, Ashgate, 2013, pp. 38–45.

Cohen, Abner. *The Symbolic Construction of Community*. Routledge, 1985.

Cohen, Anthony C. *Symbolizing Boundaries: Identity and Diversity in British Cultures*. Manchester UP, 1986.

De Martino, Ernesto. *La fine del mondo. Contributo all'analisi delle apocalissi culturali*. Einaudi, 1977.

Donohoe Janet. "The Place of Home." *Environmental Philosophy*, vol. 8, no. 1, 2011, pp. 25–40.

Eliade, Mircea. *Solilocvii*. Editura Nu, 1991.

Elias Norbert. *Engagement und Distanzierung: Arbeiten zur Wissenssoziologie*. Suhrkamp, 1983.

Forlenza, Rosario, and Mark Luccarelli. "The Failure of Global Cosmopolitanism: Re-Symbolization of the Nation and the Longing for Home." 2017. Unpublished paper.

Foucault, Michel. *Archaeology of Knowledge*. 1969. Translated by. A. M. Sheridan Smith. Routledge, 2002.

———. "What Is an Author?" *Language, Counter-Memory, Practice: Selected Essays and Interviews by Michel Foucault*, edited by D. B. Bouchard, translated by D. F. Bouchard and S. Simon, Cornell UP, 1980, pp. 113–39.

Geertz, Clifford. "The Integrative Revolution: Primordial Sentiments and Civil Politics in the New State." *Old Societies and New States: The Quest for Modernity in Asia and Africa*. The Free Press, 1963, pp. 105–57.

Gellner Ernest. *Nations and Nationalism*. Cornell UP, 1983.

———. *Thought and Change*. Weidenfeld and Nicholson, 1964.

Goffman, Erving. *Frame Analysis: An Essay on the Organization of Experience*. Harvard UP, 1974.

Heidegger, Martin. "Building Dwelling Thinking." *Poetry, Language, Thought*, translated by A. Hofstadter, Harper Colophon, 1971, pp. 141–60.

———. *On Time and Being.* 1927. Translated by J. Stambaugh, U of Chicago P, 2002.

Held, David. "The Decline of the Nation State." *New Times: The Changing Face of Politics in the 1990s*, edited by Stuart Hall and Martin Jacques, Lawrence and Wishart, 1990, pp. 191–204.

Hobsbawm, Eric J. N*ations and Nationalism Since 1780: Programme, Myth, Reality.* Cambridge UP, 1990.

Husserl, Edmund. *The Crisis of European Sciences and Transcendental Phenomenology: An Introduction to Phenomenological Philosophy.* 1936. Translated by D. Carr, Northwestern UP, 1970.

Jacobson, Kirsten. "The Experience of Home and the Space of Citizenship." *The Southern Journal of Philosophy*, vol. 48, no. 3, 2010, pp. 219–45.

Kedourie, Elie. *Nationalism.* The Humanities Press, 1961.

Lévy-Bruhl, Lucian. *The Notebooks on Primitive Mentality.* Harper, 1975.

Llobera, Josep R. "Anthropological Approaches to the Study of Nationalism in Europe: The Work of Van Gennep and Mauss." *The Anthropology of Europe: Identities and Boundaries in Conflict*, edited by Victoria A. Goddard, Josep R. Llobera, and Cris Shore, Berg, 1994, pp. 93–111.

Nagle, Brendan. *The Household as the Foundation of Aristotle's Polis.* Cambridge UP, 2006.

Nodia, Ghia. "The End of the Post-National Illusion." *Journal of Democracy*, vol. 28, no. 2, 2017, pp. 5–19.

Ohmae, Kenichi. *The End of the Nation State: The Rise of Regional Economies.* Simon and Schuster, 1995.

Ojakangas, Mika. *On the Greek Origins of Biopolitics: A Reinterpretation of the History of Biopower.* Routldedge, 2016.

O'Connor, Paul. *Home: The Foundations of Belonging.* Routledge, 2017.

Paasi, Anssi. *Territory, Boundaries and Consciousness.* John Wiley, 1996.

Pizzorno, Alessandro. "Politics Unbound." *Changing Boundaries of the Political*, edited by Charles S. Maier, Cambridge UP, 1987, pp. 27–62.

Newman, David, and Paasi, Anssi. "Fences and Neighbours in the Post-modern World: Boundary Narratives in Political Geography." *Progress in Human Geography*, vol. 22, no. 2, 1998, pp. 186–207.

Rumford, Chris. "Introduction: Theorizing Borders," *European Journal of Social Theory*, vol. 9, no. 2, 2006, pp. 155–69.

Sahlins, Peter. *Boundaries: The Making of France and Spain in the Pyrenees.* U of California P, 1989.

Sassen, Saskia. *De-Nationalization.* Princeton UP, 2002.

Searle, John. *Intentionality: An Essay in the Philosophy of Mind.* Cambridge UP, 1983.

Schütz, Alfred. *The Phenomenology of the Social World.* 1932. Translated by G. Walsh and Frederick Lehnert, Northwestern UP, 1967.

Shils, Edward "Primordial, Personal, Sacred and Civil Ties: Some Particular Observations on the Relationships of Sociological Research and Theory." *British Journal of Sociology*, vol. 8, no. 2, 1957, pp. 13–45.

Smith, Anthony D. *The Cultural Foundations of Nations: Hierarchy, Covenant, and Republic*. Blackwell, 2008.

———. *Ethnic Revival*. Cambridge UP, 1981.

———. *Theories of Nationalism*. Duckworth, 1983.

———. *The Ethnic Origin of Nations*. Blackwell, 1986.

———. *National Identity*. Penguin, 1991.

———. *Nationalism and Modernism*. Routledge, 1998.

———. *Myths and Memories of the Nation*. Oxford UP, 1999.

Szakolczai, Arpad. "Citizenship and Home: Political Allegiance and Its Background." *International Political Anthropology*, vol. 1, no. 1, 2008, pp. 57–75.

———. *Reflexive Historical Sociology*. Routledge, 2000.

———. "The Spirit of the Nation State: Nation, Nationalism and Inner-worldly Eschatology in the Work of Eric Voegelin." *International Political Anthropology*, vol. 1, no. 2, 2008, 193–210.

Thomassen, Bjørn. *Liminality and the Modern: Living through the In-between*. Ashgate, 2014.

Turnbull, Colin M. *The Forest People*. Simon and Schuster, 1968.

———. *The Mountain People*. Jonhatan Cape, 1973.

Van Gennep, Arnold. *The Rites of Passage: A Classical Study of Cultural Celebrations*. 1909. Translated by M. B. Vizedom and G. L. Caffee, U of Chicago P, 1960.

———. *Traité comparatif des nationalités*. Payot, 1921.

Van den Berghe, Pierre. *The Ethnic Phenomenon*. Elsevier, 1981.

Voegelin, Eric. "Equivalences of Experience and Symbolization in History (1970)." *The Collected Works*, vol. 12, *Published Essays, 1966–1985*, edited by E. Sandoz, Louisiana State UP, 1990, pp. 115–33.

Watkins, Trevor. "The Origins of House and Home?" *World Archaeology*, vol. 21, no. 3, 1990, pp. 336–47.

Weber, Max. *Economy and Society: An Outline of Interpretative Sociology*. 1922. Edited by. G. Roth and C. Wittich, U of California P, 1978.

Wilson, Peter J. *The Domestication of the Human Species*. Yale UP, 1988.

Wittgenstein, Ludwig. *Philosophical Investigations*. 1953. Translated by G. E. M. Anscombe, Blackwell, 2001.

Contributors

Stefano Adamo received his PhD from Siena University in 2007. He is an assistant professor of Italian history and culture at the University of Banja Luka in Bosnia and Herzegovina. His main research interest is in the way in which economic ideas are disseminated in cultural products such as movies, dramas, novels, and other narrative forms. His studies on historical periods such as the Elizabethan and Jacobean eras or Republican Italy have been sponsored by various research institutions in Italy and the United States and have appeared in peer-reviewed journals of modern history and literary studies alike. He is presently working on a book on the response of Italian writers to the global financial crisis, covering the years 2008 to 2014.

Bruce Barnhart is associate professor of American literature at the University of Oslo, Norway, and codirector of the project Literature, Rights, and Imagined Communities. His research interests include African American literature, twentieth-century American literature, critical theory, and the connections between music and literature. In his book *Jazz and the Time of the Novel* Barnhart investigates the connections between the temporality of different aesthetic forms and the dependence of traditional forms of property rights on the temporality of expectation and exclusion. Barnhart has published work on the Harlem Renaissance, the temporality of the novel, jazz, and the early civil rights figure James Weldon Johnson. He is currently at work on a book entitled *Trading on Racial Futures*, an examination of the ways in which American novels and economic practices construct different versions of a usable future.

Werner Bigell works as an associate professor of English at the University of Tromsø, Norway. In the past, he worked at universities in Germany, Cuba, Kyrgyzstan, and Palestine (West Bank). His doctoral dissertation examines the concept of nature in the American writer Edward Abbey. He is interested in cultural differences in the use and perception of nature and has published articles on landscape and anti-landscape, eco-museums, German allotment gardens, and the concept of beauty. Currently he works on the question of what role intercultural communication can play in English teacher education.

Steven Colatrella teaches international political theory at the University of Padua and is associate adjunct professor of government and sociology at the University of Maryland University College. His main research interests are global governance, democracy, and the relationship between social classes and institutional change. He was an early observer of globalization, writing about it in his senior thesis at Bard College in 1982. In 2011, he foresaw the coming crisis of legitimacy of the organizations of global governance, arguing that the governments and classes associated with that project were weaker than appeared due to their narrow social bases. He has published several articles on that issue and the resulting risk of great power conflict. He is currently at work on a book titled *The Good Life: Politics and Economics for the Post-Global Era*.

Rosario Forlenza is a fellow at the Remarque Institute, New York University, and a fellow at Potsdam University's Center for Citizenship, Social Pluralism, and Religious Diversity. He is a historian of modern Europe and twentieth-century Italy whose main fields of expertise are political anthropology, politics and religion, authoritarianism and revolution, nationalism and the politics of memory, democracy and democratization, and the Cold War. He has previously worked at the University of Cambridge, Princeton University, Columbia University, and the University of Padova, and he has held visiting fellowships at the University of Oslo and at the Australian Catholic University in Melbourne. He publishes in journals across history and the social sciences. Recent books include *Italian Modernities: Competing Narratives of Nationhood* (coauthored with Bjørn Thomassen) and *On the Edge of Democracy: Italy 1943–1948*.

Mark Luccarelli is associate professor of American studies at the University of Oslo. His fields include American politics, political theory, urban and regional planning, literature, and art, with particular interests in nationalism and democracy, sustainability and national development, and the relation of nature and culture. Luccarelli has published *Lewis Mumford and the Ecological Region: The Politics of Planning* (1995) and *The Eclipse of Urbanism and* *the Greening of Public Space: The Search for a Commons in the United States* (2016); he is coeditor with P. G. Røe of *Green Oslo: Visions, Planning and Discourse* (2012) and coeditor with Sigurd Bergmann of *Spaces in-between: Cultural and Political Perspectives on Environmental Discourse* (2015).

Venla Oikkonen received her PhD from the University of Helsinki in 2010. She is currently an academy research fellow at Tampere University, Finland. She works at the intersection of feminist science studies and feminist cultural studies. Her research interests include evolutionary theory, population genetics, and vaccine controversies as well as theoretical questions related to affect and intersectionality. Oikkonen is the author of two monographs: *Gender, Sexuality and Reproduction in Evolutionary Narratives* (2013) and *Population Genetics and Belonging* (2017), as well as a number of research articles in journals such as *Social Studies of Science*, *Signs*, *Feminist Theory*, *Journal of American Studies*, *Science as Culture*, and *Modern Fiction Studies*. In 2015, she received the Catharine Stimpson Prize for Outstanding Feminist Scholarship.

Sergio Sabbatini receieved his candidatus philologiae at the University of Oslo in 2001. He is a lecturer in Italian language and literature at the University of Oslo, Norway, with a background from the University of Bologna, Italy. His main research interest focuses on contemporary Italian writers and LBGTQ+ studies. He has published articles on contemporary Italian literature and LBGTQ themes and on writers like Pier Vittorio Tondelli, Silvia Ballestra, and Sibilla Aleramo.

Ole Sneltvedt received his MA from the University of Oslo in 2014. He is a doctoral research fellow in the literature, area studies, and European languages department at the University of Oslo. He wrote his master's thesis in American studies, investigating links between American populism and republicanism. His main research interest concerns the connection between political theory and political action and the history of ideas and their materialization. He is currently part of the project Discourses of the Nation and the National, where he is writing his doctoral dissertation on the connection between patriotism, built environment, cultural landscape, and technology.

Index

www.ingramcontent.com/pod-product-compliance
Lightning Source LLC
LaVergne TN
LVHW050153080826
844660LV00002B/193

* 9 7 8 1 4 3 8 4 7 7 7 3 2 *